2010 SUPPLEMENT
CASES AND MATERIALS

Intellectual Property
Trademark, Copyright and Patent Law

SECOND EDITION

by

ROCHELLE COOPER DREYFUS
Pauline Newman Professor of Law
Co–Director, Engelberg Center on Innovation Law & Policy
New York University School of Law

ROBERTA ROSENTHAL KWALL
Raymond P. Niro Professor of Intellectual Property Law
DePaul University College of Law

KATHERINE J. STRANDBURG
Professor of Law
Co–Director, Engelberg Center on Innovation Law & Policy
New York University School of Law

DIANE LEENHEER ZIMMERMAN
Samuel Tilden Professor of Law Emerita
New York University School of Law

FOUNDATION PRESS
2010

THOMSON REUTERS

© 2006, 2007 FOUNDATION PRESS
© 2009 THOMSON REUTERS/FOUNDATION PRESS
© 2010 By THOMSON REUTERS/FOUNDATION PRESS
       1 New York Plaza, 34th Floor
       New York, NY 10004
       Phone Toll Free 1–877–888–1330
       Fax 646–424–5201
       foundation–press.com
Printed in the United States of America

ISBN 978–1–59941–801–8

Mat #40956018

TABLE OF CONTENTS

TABLE OF CASES

Principal cases are in bold type. Non-principal cases are in roman type. References are to pages.

viii

ASSIGNMENT 3—INFRINGEMENT AND CONTRIBUTORY INFRINGEMENT

INSERT ON PAGE 100 AFTER *TWO PESOS*:

KP Permanent Make-Up, Inc. v. Lasting Impression I, Inc.

Supreme Court of the United States, 2004.
543 U.S. 111.

■ JUSTICE SOUTER delivered the opinion of the Court.

The question here is whether a party raising the statutory affirmative defense of fair use to a claim of trademark infringement, 15 U.S.C. § 1115(b)(4), has a burden to negate any likelihood that the practice complained of will confuse consumers about the origin of the goods or services affected. We hold it does not.

I

Each party to this case sells permanent makeup, a mixture of pigment and liquid for injection under the skin to camouflage injuries and modify nature's dispensations, and each has used some version of the term "micro color" (as one word or two, singular or plural) in marketing and selling its product. Petitioner KP Permanent Make-Up, Inc., claims to have used the single-word version since 1990 or 1991 on advertising flyers and since 1991 on pigment bottles. Respondents Lasting Impression I, Inc., and its licensee, MCN International, Inc. (Lasting, for simplicity), deny that KP began using the term that early, but we accept KP's allegation as true for present purposes; the District and Appeals Courts took it to be so, and the disputed facts do not matter to our resolution of the issue. In 1992, Lasting applied to the United States Patent and Trademark Office (PTO) under 15 U.S.C. § 1051 for registration of a trademark consisting of the words "Micro Colors" in white letters separated by a green bar within a black square. The PTO registered the mark to Lasting in 1993, and in 1999 the registration became incontestable. § 1065.

It was also in 1999 that KP produced a 10-page advertising brochure using "microcolor" in a large, stylized typeface, provoking Lasting to

1

demand that KP stop using the term. Instead, KP sued Lasting in the Central District of California, seeking, on more than one ground, a declaratory judgment that its language infringed no such exclusive right as Lasting claimed.[a] Lasting counterclaimed, alleging, among other things, that KP had infringed Lasting's "Micro Colors" trademark.

KP sought summary judgment on the infringement counterclaim, based on the statutory affirmative defense of fair use, 15 U.S.C. § 1115(b)(4). After finding that Lasting had conceded that KP used the term only to describe its goods and not as a mark, the District Court held that KP was acting fairly and in good faith because undisputed facts showed that KP had employed the term "microcolor" continuously from a time before Lasting adopted the two-word, plural variant as a mark. Without inquiring whether the practice was likely to cause confusion, the court concluded that KP had made out its affirmative defense under § 1115(b)(4) and entered summary judgment for KP on Lasting's infringement claim. See SA CV 00-276-GLT (EEx), (May 16, 2001), pp. 8-9, App. to Cert. 29a-30a.

On appeal, 328 F.3d 1061 (2003), the Court of Appeals for the Ninth Circuit thought it was error for the District Court to have addressed the fair use defense without delving into the matter of possible confusion on the part of consumers about the origin of KP's goods. The reviewing court took the view that no use could be recognized as fair where any consumer confusion was probable, and although the court did not pointedly address the burden of proof, it appears to have placed it on KP to show absence of consumer confusion. Id., at 1072 ("Therefore, KP can only benefit from the fair use defense if there is no likelihood of confusion between KP's use of the term 'micro color' and Lasting's mark"). Since it found there were disputed material facts relevant under the Circuit's eight-factor test for assessing the likelihood of confusion, it reversed the summary judgment and remanded the case.

---

[a] We summarize the proceedings in this litigation only as they are relevant to the question before us. The District Court's findings as to the generic or descriptive nature of the term "micro color" and any secondary meaning that term has acquired by any of the parties, see SA CV 00-276-GLT (EEx) (CD Cal. May 16, 2001), pp. 3-5, 5-8, are not before us. Nor are the Court of Appeals's holdings on these issues. See 328 F.3d 1061, 1068-1071 (C.A.9 2003). Nor do we address the Court of Appeals's discussion of "nominative fair use." Id., at 1071-1072.

We granted KP's petition for certiorari, 540 U.S. 1099, 124 S.Ct. 981, 157 L.Ed.2d 811 (2004), to address a disagreement among the Courts of Appeals on the significance of likely confusion for a fair use defense to a trademark infringement claim, and the obligation of a party defending on that ground to show that its use is unlikely to cause consumer confusion. We now vacate the judgment of the Court of Appeals.

II
A.

The Trademark Act of 1946, known for its principal proponent as the Lanham Act, 60 Stat. 427, as amended, 15 U.S.C. § 1051 et seq., provides the user of a trade or service mark with the opportunity to register it with the PTO, §§ 1051, 1053. If the registrant then satisfies further conditions including continuous use for five consecutive years, "the right ... to use such registered mark in commerce" to designate the origin of the goods specified in the registration "shall be incontestable" outside certain listed exceptions. § 1065.

The holder of a registered mark (incontestable or not) has a civil action against anyone employing an imitation of it in commerce when "such use is likely to cause confusion, or to cause mistake, or to deceive." § 1114(1). This plaintiff's burden has to be kept in mind when reading the relevant portion of the further provision for an affirmative defense of fair use, available to a party whose "use of the name, term, or device charged to be an infringement is a use, otherwise than as a mark, ... of a term or device which is descriptive of and used fairly and in good faith only to describe the goods or services of such party, or their geographic origin ...." § 1115(b)(4). Two points are evident. Section 1115(b) places a burden of proving likelihood of confusion (that is, infringement) on the party charging infringement even when relying on an incontestable registration. And Congress said nothing about likelihood of confusion in setting out the elements of the fair use defense in § 1115(b)(4).

Starting from these textual fixed points, it takes a long stretch to claim that a defense of fair use entails any burden to negate confusion. It is just not plausible that Congress would have used the descriptive phrase "likely to cause confusion, or to cause mistake, or to deceive" in § 1114 to describe the requirement that a markholder show likelihood of consumer

3

confusion, but would have relied on the phrase "used fairly" in § 1115(b)(4) in a fit of terse drafting meant to place a defendant under a burden to negate confusion. "'[W]here Congress includes particular language in one section of a statute but omits it in another section of the same Act, it is generally presumed that Congress acts intentionally and purposely in the disparate inclusion or exclusion.'" *Russello v. United States*, 464 U.S. 16, 23, 104 S.Ct. 296, 78 L.Ed.2d 17 (1983) (quoting *United States v. Wong Kim Bo*, 472 F.2d 720, 722 (C.A.5 1972)) (alteration in original).

Nor do we find much force in Lasting's suggestion that "used fairly" in § 1115(b)(4) is an oblique incorporation of a likelihood-of-confusion test developed in the common law of unfair competition. Lasting is certainly correct that some unfair competition cases would stress that use of a term by another in conducting its trade went too far in sowing confusion, and would either enjoin the use or order the defendant to include a disclaimer. But the common law of unfair competition also tolerated some degree of confusion from a descriptive use of words contained in another person's trademark. See, e.g., *William R. Warner & Co. v. Eli Lilly & Co.*, 265 U.S. 526, 528, 44 S.Ct. 615, 68 L.Ed. 1161 (1924) (as to plaintiff's trademark claim, "[t]he use of a similar name by another to truthfully describe his own product does not constitute a legal or moral wrong, even if its effect be to cause the public to mistake the origin or ownership of the product"); *Canal Co. v. Clark*, 13 Wall. 311, 327, 20 L.Ed. 581 (1872) ("Purchasers may be mistaken, but they are not deceived by false representations, and equity will not enjoin against telling the truth"). While these cases are consistent with taking account of the likelihood of consumer confusion as one consideration in deciding whether a use is fair, see Part II-B, infra, they do not stand for the proposition that an assessment of confusion alone may be dispositive. Certainly one cannot get out of them any defense burden to negate it entirely.

Finally, a look at the typical course of litigation in an infringement action points up the incoherence of placing a burden to show nonconfusion on a defendant. If a plaintiff succeeds in making out a prima facie case of trademark infringement, including the element of likelihood of consumer confusion, the defendant may offer rebutting evidence to undercut the force of the plaintiff's evidence on this (or any) element, or raise an affirmative defense to bar relief even if the prima facie case is sound, or do both. But it would make no sense to give the defendant a defense of showing affirmatively that the plaintiff cannot succeed in proving some element (like confusion); all the defendant needs to do is to leave the factfinder unpersuaded that the plaintiff has carried its own burden on that point. Put another way, it is only when a plaintiff has shown likely confusion by a preponderance of the evidence that a defendant could have any need of an affirmative defense, but under Lasting's theory the defense would be foreclosed in such a case. "[I]t defies logic to argue that a defense may not be asserted in the only situation where it even becomes relevant." *Shakespeare Co. v. Silstar Corp.*, 110 F.3d, at 243. Nor would it make sense to provide an affirmative defense of no confusion plus good faith, when merely rebutting the plaintiff's case on confusion would entitle the defendant to judgment, good faith or not.

B.

Since the burden of proving likelihood of confusion rests with the plaintiff, and the fair use defendant has no free-standing need to show confusion unlikely, it follows (contrary to the Court of Appeals's view) that some possibility of consumer confusion must be compatible with fair use, and so it is. The common law's tolerance of a certain degree of confusion on the part of consumers followed from the very fact that in cases like this one an originally descriptive term was selected to be used as a mark, not to mention the undesirability of allowing anyone to obtain a complete monopoly on use of a descriptive term simply by grabbing it first. This right to describe is the reason that descriptive terms qualify for registration as trademarks only after taking on secondary meaning as "distinctive of the applicant's goods," 15 U.S.C. § 1052(f), with the registrant getting an exclusive right not in the original, descriptive sense, but only in the secondary one associated with the markholder's goods.

While we thus recognize that mere risk of confusion will not rule out fair use, we think it would be improvident to go further in this case, for deciding anything more would take us beyond the Ninth Circuit's consideration of the subject. It suffices to realize that our holding that fair use can occur along with some degree of confusion does not foreclose the relevance of the extent of any likely consumer confusion in assessing whether a defendant's use is objectively fair. Two Courts of Appeals have found it relevant to consider such scope, and commentators and amici here

5

have urged us to say that the degree of likely consumer confusion bears not only on the fairness of using a term, but even on the further question whether an originally descriptive term has become so identified as a mark that a defendant's use of it cannot realistically be called descriptive.

III

In sum, a plaintiff claiming infringement of an incontestable mark must show likelihood of consumer confusion as part of the prima facie case, 15 U.S.C. § 1115(b), while the defendant has no independent burden to negate the likelihood of any confusion in raising the affirmative defense that a term is used descriptively, not as a mark, fairly, and in good faith, § 1115(b)(4).

Because we read the Court of Appeals as requiring KP to shoulder a burden on the issue of confusion, we vacate the judgment and remand the case for further proceedings consistent with this opinion.
It is so ordered.

INSERT ON PAGE 101 IN LIEU OF *MOSELEY*:

Tiffany Inc. v. eBay, Inc.
United States Court for the Southern District of New York, 2008.
576 F.Supp.2d 463.

■ RICHARD J. SULLIVAN, DISTRICT JUDGE.

Tiffany, the famous jeweler with the coveted blue boxes, brings this action against eBay, the prominent online marketplace, for the sale of counterfeit Tiffany silver jewelry on its website. Specifically, Tiffany alleges that hundreds of thousands of counterfeit silver jewelry items were offered for sale on eBay's website from 2003 to 2006. Tiffany seeks to hold eBay liable for direct and contributory trademark infringement, unfair competition, false advertising, and direct and contributory trademark dilution, on the grounds that eBay facilitated and allowed these counterfeit items to be sold on its website.

Tiffany acknowledges that individual sellers, rather than eBay, are responsible for listing and selling counterfeit Tiffany items. Nevertheless, Tiffany argues that eBay was on notice that a problem existed and accordingly, that eBay had the obligation to investigate and control the illegal activities of these sellers-specifically, by preemptively refusing to post any listing offering five or more Tiffany items and by immediately suspending sellers upon learning of Tiffany's belief that the seller had engaged in potentially infringing activity. In response, eBay contends that it is Tiffany's burden, not eBay's, to monitor the eBay website for counterfeits and to bring counterfeits to eBay's attention. eBay claims that in practice, when potentially infringing listings were reported to eBay, eBay immediately removed the offending listings. It is clear that Tiffany and eBay alike have an interest in eliminating counterfeit Tiffany merchandise from eBay-Tiffany to protect its famous brand name, and eBay to preserve the reputation of its website as a safe place to do business. Accordingly, the heart of this dispute is not whether counterfeit Tiffany jewelry should flourish on eBay, but rather, who should bear the burden of policing Tiffany's valuable trademarks in Internet commerce.

Having held a bench trial in this action, the Court issues the following Findings of Fact and Conclusions of Law. Specifically, after carefully considering the evidence introduced at trial, the arguments of counsel, and the law pertaining to this matter, the Court concludes that Tiffany has failed to carry its burden with respect to each claim alleged in the complaint. First, the Court finds that eBay's use of Tiffany's trademarks in its advertising, on its homepage, and in sponsored links purchased through Yahoo! and Google, is a protected, nominative fair use of the marks.

Second, the Court finds that eBay is not liable for contributory trademark infringement. In determining whether eBay is liable, the standard is not whether eBay could reasonably anticipate possible infringement, but rather whether eBay continued to supply its services to sellers when it knew or had reason to know of infringement by those sellers. *See Inwood Labs., Inc. v. Ives Labs., Inc.,* 456 U.S. 844, 854 (1982). Indeed, the Supreme Court has specifically disavowed the reasonable anticipation standard as a "watered down" and incorrect standard. Here, when Tiffany put eBay on notice of specific items that Tiffany believed to be infringing, eBay immediately removed those listings. eBay refused, however, to monitor its website and preemptively remove listings of Tiffany jewelry before the listings became public. The law does not impose liability for contributory trademark infringement on eBay for its refusal to take such preemptive steps in light of eBay's "reasonable anticipation" or generalized knowledge that counterfeit goods

7

might be sold on its website. Quite simply, the law demands more specific knowledge as to which items are infringing and which seller is listing those items before requiring eBay to take action.

The result of the application of this legal standard is that Tiffany must ultimately bear the burden of protecting its trademark. Policymakers may yet decide that the law as it stands is inadequate to protect rights owners in light of the increasing scope of Internet commerce and the concomitant rise in potential trademark infringement. Nevertheless, under the law as it currently stands, it does not matter whether eBay or Tiffany could more efficiently bear the burden of policing the eBay website for Tiffany counterfeits-an open question left unresolved by this trial. Instead, the issue is whether eBay continued to provide its website to sellers when eBay knew or had reason to know that those sellers were using the website to traffic in counterfeit Tiffany jewelry. The Court finds that when eBay possessed the requisite knowledge, it took appropriate steps to remove listings and suspend service. Under these circumstances, the Court declines to impose liability for contributory trademark infringement.

Third, the Court finds that Tiffany has failed to meet its burden in proving its claims for unfair competition. Fourth, in regard to Tiffany's claim for false advertising, the Court concludes that eBay's use of the Tiffany trademarks in advertising is a protected, nominative fair use of the marks. Finally, the Court finds that Tiffany has failed to prove that eBay's use of the TIFFANY Marks is likely to cause dilution.

FINDINGS OF FACT
The Parties
Tiffany and Its Business
Tiffany's Famous Marks

Over its 170-year history, Tiffany has achieved great renown as a purveyor of high quality and luxury goods under the TIFFANY Marks, including jewelry, watches, and home items such as china, crystal, and clocks. The TIFFANY Marks are indisputably famous, and are a valuable asset owned by Tiffany. The protection of the quality and integrity of the brand and the trademarks is critical to Tiffany's success as a retailer of luxury goods.

eBay and Its Business
eBay's Listings, Buyers, and Sellers

eBay is a well-known online marketplace, located at www.ebay.com that allows eBay sellers to sell goods directly to eBay buyers. The listings are created and posted by third-party users, who register with eBay and agree to abide by a User Agreement. While users often go by descriptive user names instead of their real names, users are required to supply identifying information to eBay when registering. Sellers can also use multiple user names.

To conduct a transaction on eBay, registered sellers choose the appropriate category for their listed item, including, for example, Jewelry and Watches, Toys and Hobbies, Collectibles, or Health and Beauty. Sellers then create a listing for the item that they wish to sell. A listing can include either a single item or several items. In addition, sellers can post multiple listings at any given time, including multiple listings for the same type of item or one listing with multiple quantities of the same item.

While eBay is perhaps best known for auction-style listings, sellers can also choose to sell their goods through fixed price or "Buy It Now" listings. Sellers are responsible for setting the parameters and conditions of the sale, including the minimum acceptable bid, the Buy It Now price (if applicable), and the duration of the listing. Sellers are also responsible for the content of the listings, including the titles and descriptions of the items.

Potential buyers can view listings on eBay in several ways. Buyers can click on keywords on the eBay home page, which bring them to pages of listings for products including those keywords. Buyers can also browse through eBay categories or use keywords to search through listing titles and descriptions. To bid on items, buyers, like sellers, must register with eBay.

eBay's role is to connect buyers and sellers and to enable transactions, which are carried out directly between eBay members. When a buyer purchases an item, the buyer and seller contact each other to arrange for payment and shipment of the goods. While eBay provides the venue for the sale and support for the transaction, it does not itself sell the items. Indeed, items sold on eBay are never in eBay's physical possession. eBay generally does not know whether or when an item is delivered to the buyer. eBay has become very successful: more than six million new listings are posted on eBay daily, and at any given time, some 100 million listings appear on the website.

eBay's Business Model and Support to Sellers

eBay's business model is based on two components: first, the creation of listings, and second, the successful completion of sales between the seller and the buyer. For each posted listing, sellers pay an initial insertion fee, ranging from $0.20 to $4.80 depending on the starting price. If the item is successfully sold, sellers pay a final value fee based upon the final price for the item. Final value fees range from 5.25% to 10% of the final price of the item. I n addition, sellers who opt for various additional features to differentiate their listings, such as a border or bold-faced type, are charged additional fees.

In this way, eBay's revenue is based on sellers using eBay to list their products and successfully completing sales through eBay. Gary Briggs, eBay's Chief Marketing Officer, testified that in 2006, approximately 33% of eBay North America's income was derived from listing fees and approximately 45% from final value fees. eBay also profits from fees charged by PayPal, an eBay company, to process the transaction. PayPal charges the eBay seller a fee ranging from 1.9% to 2.9% of the sale price, plus $0.30.

Because eBay's revenue and profit growth is dependent, in significant part, on the completion of sales between eBay sellers and eBay buyers, eBay works closely with sellers to foster the increase of their sales on eBay, including the sales of Tiffany jewelry. As Briggs testified, eBay "want[s] to have [its] sellers understand what buyers are interested in, and [it] feels that [it is] very much in the business of trying to help [its] sellers succeed."

This assistance includes seminars and workshops to educate sellers on growing their business.

eBay's Control Over Sales Made On Its Website

eBay is an electronic marketplace, not a retailer. Thus, eBay itself never takes physical possession of the goods sold through its website; instead, it facilitates a transaction between two independent parties. Nevertheless, eBay exercises some limited control over those who trade on its website by requiring all users to register with eBay and sign eBay's User Agreement. The User Agreement requires users to refrain from violating any laws, third party rights, including intellectual property rights, and eBay policies. If a user violates the terms or conditions of the User Agreement, eBay may take disciplinary action against the seller, including removing the seller's listings, issuing a warning, and/or suspending the user.

In addition to exercising some control over users, eBay also restricts the types of items which can be listed on its website. For example, eBay maintains a list of prohibited items, *e.g.*, drugs, firearms, and alcohol, for which it routinely screens in order to prevent such items from being offered for sale on eBay. [The court then describes eBay's extensive anti-fraud measures.]

The Sale of Tiffany Goods on eBay
eBay's Brand Management and Attempts to Develop Jewelry Sales

At all times pertinent to this litigation, eBay management teams were responsible for overseeing the growth of products sold on eBay within each formal product category, such as Jewelry & Watches. eBay provided its sellers with "the most effective keywords," and highlighted the words that provided the best return on investments. eBay identified "Tiffany" as one of the top-searched keywords and provided it to top sellers during these calls. eBay encouraged its sellers to view the eBay Pulse webpage, which tracked buyer trends, "hot picks," "top searches," and "most watched items." In September 2006, eBay told users that the terms "Tiffany" and "Tiffany & Co." were top search terms.

eBay Advertised Tiffany Goods

Prior to 2003, eBay actively advertised the availability of Tiffany merchandise on its website. Additionally, as with many other brand names, eBay purchased sponsored link advertisements on Yahoo! and Google advertising the availability of Tiffany items on eBay. After Tiffany complained to eBay in May 2003, eBay advised Tiffany that it had

11

ceased purchasing those links. Nevertheless, eBay continued to use a third party, Commission Junction, to run what was known as the "affiliate program." Through that program, sellers who registered as "affiliates" contracted with Commission Junction and then bought sponsored links on Google.

[In the next part of the opinion, the court describes eBay's extensive efforts, costing over $20 million a year, to rid its site of counterfeit goods and the ways in which it cooperated with trademark holders in identifying counterfeiters and stopping their activities.]

CONCLUSIONS OF LAW

[In the first two parts of this section, the court describes the claims for trademark infringement and finds, as described above, that eBay is not liable.]

3. Trademark Dilution under Federal and Common Law

Tiffany [next] alleges that eBay's activities constitute trademark dilution under the Lanham Act, 15 U.S.C. § 1125(c), as well as under New York General Business Law § 360-*l*. Specifically, Tiffany argues that eBay is liable for dilution by blurring because eBay uses the Tiffany name to advertise and sell products that eBay knows to be counterfeit, thus resulting in the " 'diminution of the capacity of [Plaintiff's] mark [ ] to serve as a unique identifier of its products and services.'" Tiffany also alleges that eBay is liable for dilution by tarnishment because eBay's use of the TIFFANY Marks harms Tiffany's reputation. Tiffany submits that by linking Tiffany's marks to products of shoddy quality, "the public will associate, and continue to associate, the lack of quality or lack of prestige in the goods sold on eBay with genuine Tiffany goods." The Court concludes that Tiffany has failed to prove that eBay is liable for trademark dilution and that even assuming *arguendo* that eBay could be liable for dilution, eBay's use of the TIFFANY Marks is a protected, nominative fair use.

a. Legal Standard

The legal theory of dilution is grounded in the notion that a trademark can lose its "ability ... to clearly and unmistakably distinguish one source through unauthorized use." Anti-dilution statutes protect against the "gradual whittling away of a firm's distinctive trade-mark or name. Trademark dilution is a broader, and more subtle, principle than classic trademark infringement.[a]

As a preliminary matter, the Court must consider which federal anti-dilution statute applies to this case. When Tiffany filed its Amended Complaint on July 14, 2004, it did so under the Federal Trademark Dilution Act ("FTDA"), 15 U.S.C. § 1125(c) (2004). After the Amended Complaint had been filed, Congress enacted the Trademark Dilution Revision Act of 2006 ("TDRA"), which entitles the owner of a famous, distinctive mark to an injunction against the user of a mark that is "likely to cause dilution" of the famous mark. 15 U.S.C. § 1125(c)(1). Congress thus overruled the Supreme Court's holding in *Moseley v. V Secret Catalogue, Inc.*, 537 U.S. 418, 433 (2003), that the FTDA requires a showing of "actual dilution," and reasserted the less stringent "likelihood of dilution" standard to dilution cases.[b]

The Second Circuit has held that the TDRA applies retroactively to a claim filed before the TDRA went into effect to the extent that the plaintiff seeks injunctive relief.

The TDRA provides that:

---

[a] One of the key distinctions between trademark infringement and trademark dilution is that the anti-dilution statutes provide more expansive protection than trademark infringement claims. In a classic trademark infringement claim, the owner of a mark may bar another from using a mark in a manner that creates a likelihood of consumer confusion as to the source of goods. See 15 U.S.C. § 1125(a). Thus, "as a general proposition, under traditional trademark law, a mark is enforceable within the area of commerce in which the mark has been established. However, its establishment in one segment of commerce generally does not prevent others from using the same or a similar mark in a different, non-competing area" because "ordinarily, little confusion will result when the junior use is in an area of commerce that is outside the senior owner's area." By contrast, federal anti-dilution law permits the owner of a qualified, famous mark to enjoin junior uses throughout commerce, regardless of the absence of competition or confusion. See15 U.S.C. § 1125(c)(1). Specifically, this means that trademark dilution can be found even when the defendant's goods are in a wholly different area of commerce than plaintiff's goods, and thus do not cause any likelihood of confusion.
[b] In addition, the TDRA required that the defendant show "use in commerce," rather than the FTDA's "commercial use of the mark in commerce." See *Louis Vuitton Malletier v. Dooney & Bourke, Inc.*, 454 F.3d 108, 118 (2d Cir.2006).

Subject to the principles of equity, the owner of a famous mark that is distinctive, inherently or through acquired distinctiveness, shall be entitled to an injunction against another person who, at any time after the owner's mark has become famous, commences use of a mark or trade name in commerce that is likely to cause dilution by blurring or dilution by tarnishment of the famous mark, regardless of the presence or absence of actual or likely confusion, of competition, or of actual economic injury.

15 U.S.C. § 1125(c)(1). Under the TDRA, therefore, to establish a violation of the Act, a plaintiff must show that: (1) its mark is famous; (2) the defendant is making use of the mark in commerce; (3) the defendant's use began after the mark became famous; and (4) the defendant's use is likely to cause dilution by tarnishment or dilution by blurring.

b. Analysis

The Court concludes that the first and third elements of trademark dilution have been met. With respect to the first, it is abundantly clear that the TIFFANY Marks at issue in this litigation are famous; indeed, eBay has not disputed the point. *See also* 4 McCarthy § 24:87 ("Clearly, nationally famous marks like ... TIFFANY ... have the strong, distinctive quality of fame which is deserving of protection from dilution.") (citing *Tiffany & Co. v. Boston Club, Inc.*, 231 F.Supp. 836, 842-43 (D.Mass.1964)). With respect to the third element, it is clear from the record and undisputed by the parties that eBay began its use of the mark well after Tiffany's marks became famous.

Nevertheless, even assuming *arguendo* that Tiffany can establish the third element of trademark dilution-eBay's use of the TIFFANY Marks in commerce-the Court finds that Tiffany has failed to show that eBay used the marks in a way that was likely to cause either dilution by blurring or dilution by tarnishment. Moreover, the Court further finds that eBay's use of the TIFFANY Marks on its website and through its purchase of sponsored links was protected by the statutory defense of nominative fair use.

i. Dilution by Blurring

Dilution by blurring is defined in the TDRA as an "association arising from the similarity between a mark or trade name and a famous mark that

14

impairs the distinctiveness of the famous mark." 15 U.S.C. § 1125(c)(2)(B). Blurring occurs "where the defendant uses or modifies the plaintiff's trademark to identify the defendant's goods and services, raising the possibility that the mark will lose its ability to serve as a unique identifier of the plaintiff's product." *Deere & Co. v. MTD Products, Inc.,* 41 F.3d 39, 43 (2d Cir.1994) (emphasis omitted).

Trademark dilution claims usually arise where a defendant has used the plaintiff's trademark to directly identify a different product of the defendant. Thus, dilution may occur "where the defendant uses or modifies the plaintiff's trademark to identify the defendant's goods and services." Such use of the plaintiff's trademark may "dilute" or weaken the ability of the famous mark to "clearly identify and distinguish only one source." 4 McCarthy § 24:67. For example, hypothetical examples of dilution by blurring might include Dupont shoes, Buick aspirin, Kodak pianos, or Bulova gowns. *See Mead Data Cent., Inc. v. Toyota Motor Sales, U.S.A., Inc.,* 875 F.2d 1026, 1031 (2d Cir.1989). Indeed, the "primary application of the Act is to cases involving widely different goods (*i.e.,* Kodak pianos and Kodak film)." *I.P. Lund Trading ApS v. Kohler Co.,* 163 F.3d 27, 49 (1st Cir.1998). As the First Circuit noted, "[n]o one would confuse Kodak pianos with Kodak film, but the use of the name on the piano could dilute its effectiveness as a mark for the film." *Id.*

In this case, Tiffany has failed to demonstrate that eBay's promotional efforts were likely to dilute the identification of the TIFFANY Marks with the Tiffany brand. While eBay has certainly used the plaintiff's trademark to describe products available on the eBay website, eBay has *not* used the Tiffany mark to identify *its own* goods and services. To the contrary, eBay never used the TIFFANY Marks in an effort to create an association with its own product, but instead, used the marks directly to advertise and identify the availability of authentic Tiffany merchandise on the eBay website.

Moreover, although Tiffany may have viable trademark dilution claims against individual sellers who listed counterfeit Tiffany merchandise on eBay, *see General Motors Corp. v. Autovation Technologies Inc.,* 317 F.Supp.2d 756, 763 (E.D.Mich.2004) (use of counterfeit trademarks on automotive parts "would likely cause blurring of the source of the goods" and thus satisfies the final element of trademark dilution) (internal quotations omitted), those claims could hardly be extended to eBay, which, as noted above, consistently removed such listings upon notice that Tiffany had a good faith belief that the listings might be infringing.

Under these circumstances, Tiffany has not established dilution by blurring in eBay's use of the TIFFANY Marks.

ii. Dilution by Tarnishment

Dilution by tarnishment reflects an "association arising from the similarity between a mark or a trade name and a famous mark that harms the reputation of the famous mark." 15 U.S.C. § 1125(c). A trademark may be tarnished when it is "linked to products of shoddy quality, or is portrayed in an unwholesome or unsavory context," with the result that "the public will associate the lack of quality or lack of prestige in the defendant's goods with the plaintiff's unrelated goods." *Deere & Co.,* 41 F.3d at 43. The mark may also be tarnished if it loses its ability to serve as a "wholesome identifier" of plaintiff's product. *Id; see also GTFM, Inc. v. Solid Clothing, Inc.,* 215 F.Supp.2d 273, 301 (S.D.N.Y.2002) (explaining that tarnishment is likely when a lower quality product is marketed with a substantially similar mark to that of a higher quality product of the same type); *Toys R Us, Inc. v. Feinberg,* 26 F.Supp.2d 639, 644 (S.D.N.Y.1998), *rev'd on other grounds,* 201 F.3d 432 (2d Cir.1999) (noting that tarnishment can result from a mark's association with an inferior product, not just an offensive product). Indeed, "the *sine qua non* of tarnishment is a finding that the plaintiff's mark will suffer negative associations through defendant's use."

Nevertheless, just as the dilution by blurring claim fails because eBay has never used the TIFFANY Marks to refer to eBay's own product, the dilution by tarnishment claim also fails. Indeed, while eBay has used the Tiffany trademarks in promotional efforts and in advertising, the Tiffany trademarks have always been associated with products that individual third party sellers have characterized as Tiffany items. Any identification of a different product was the result of third-party eBay-users offering for sale counterfeit Tiffany items. The evidence established that when eBay obtained knowledge of listings offering such items, it removed them. Indeed, having concluded that when eBay has knowledge or a reason to know of infringement on its website, it takes appropriate steps to discontinue supplying its website to the infringer, it would defy logic to

16

nevertheless conclude that eBay is tarnishing Tiffany's mark. Under these circumstances, Tiffany has failed to demonstrate dilution by tarnishment in eBay's use of the TIFFANY Marks.

iii. Defenses to Dilution

Even assuming *arguendo* that Tiffany had established the elements of its dilution claim, the TDRA excludes several forms of trademark use from dilution claims. These exclusions include "[a]ny fair use, including a nominative or descriptive fair use, or facilitation of such fair use, of a famous mark by another person other than as a designation of source for the person's own goods or services, including use in connection with advertising or promotion that permits consumers to compare goods or services." 15 U.S.C. § 1125(c)(3)(A)(i). In *Playboy Enters., Inc. v. Welles,* 279 F.3d 796 (9th Cir.2002), the Ninth Circuit addressed the nominative fair use exception to the antidilution statute, and held that "[u]ses that do not create an improper association between a mark and a new product but merely identify the trademark holder's products should be excepted from the reach of the anti-dilution statute. Such uses cause no harm." 279 F.3d at 806; *see also Toni & Guy (USA) Ltd. v. Nature's Therapy, Inc.,* No. 03 CV 2420(RMB), 2006 U.S. Dist. LEXIS 25291, at *40, 2006 WL 1153354, at *6 (S.D.N.Y. May 1, 2006) (declining to impose liability for trademark dilution where defendant's use of plaintiff's mark was comparative advertisement and posed no risk of diluting selling power of the competitor's mark, but instead allowed consumers to compare relative merit s of competing products).

Under the same principle, the Court holds that eBay's use of the TIFFANY Marks falls into the anti-dilution statute's nominative fair use exception. First, as described earlier in this decision, eBay's promotional use of the TIFFANY Marks is protected, nominative fair use. Second, eBay's use of the TIFFANY Marks does not designate the source for eBay's goods; instead, it simply indicates that products bearing the TIFFANY Mark are available through eBay. Finally, while eBay's use of the TIFFANY Marks is not in connection with comparative advertising, it is in connection with advertising of the availability of products through the eBay website, and thus allows consumers to compare prices and the availability of specific Tiffany designs. Accordingly, the Court finds that even if Tiffany had made out a viable claim for trademark dilution, it would be barred by the nominative fair use exception recognized in the anti-dilution statute.

4. Contributory Dilution

In addition to alleging that eBay has engaged in direct trademark dilution, Tiffany also urges the Court to find that eBay has contributorily diluted its trademark. "The one court to recognize the contributory dilution cause of action defined the claim as encouraging others to dilute." *Lockheed Martin,* 194 F.3d at 986 (citing *Kegan v. Apple Computer Inc.,* 42 U.S.P.Q.2D (BNA) 1053, 1062 (N.D.Ill.1996)). Contributory dilution has not been recognized in the Second Circuit Court of Appeals. Indeed, even the one district court in this circuit that mentioned the doctrine acknowledged that it is somewhat "novel." *Steinway, Inc. v. Ashley,* No. 01 Civ. 9703(GEL), 2002 U.S. Dist. LEXIS 1372, at *7, 2002 WL 122929, at *2 (S.D.N.Y. Jan. 29, 2002) (denying motion to dismiss on contributory infringement claim).

However, even assuming *arguendo* that a contributory dilution claim exists, it would fail for the reasons set forth above with respect to Tiffany's contributory infringement claims.

Having found that Tiffany has not carried its burden with respect to contributory trademark infringement, the Court likewise concludes that Tiffany's contributory dilution claim must fail. Put simply, Tiffany has failed to demonstrate that eBay knowingly encouraged others to dilute Tiffany's trademarks. Rather, to the extent that eBay may have possessed general knowledge of infringement and dilution by sellers on its website, eBay did not possess knowledge or a reason to know of specific instances of trademark infringement or dilution as required under the law. *See Inwood,* 456 U.S. at 854, 102 S.Ct. 2182. Moreover, in those instances in which the filing of a NOCI provided eBay with a reason to know of possible infringement or dilution, it is clear that eBay took immediate and affirmative steps to remove the challenged listings from its website. Thus, it cannot be argued that eBay was "contributorily responsible for any harm done as a result of the deceit" by third party sellers. *Id.*

* * * * * *

In sum, the Court concludes that Tiffany has failed to meet its burden in proving its claims. The Court makes no finding as to whether Tiffany might prevail were it to sue individual eBay sellers on any of these legal theories, or as to whether criminal prosecutions might be initiated against

18

individual sellers. Nevertheless, given Tiffany's choice to sue eBay, rather than individual sellers, and this Court's conclusion that eBay does not continue to supply its services to those whom it knows or has reason to know are infringing Tiffany's trademarks, Tiffany's claims against eBay must fail.

CONCLUSION

The rapid development of the Internet and websites like eBay have created new ways for sellers and buyers to connect to each other and to expand their businesses beyond geographical limits. These new markets have also, however, given counterfeiters new opportunities to expand their reach. The Court is not unsympathetic to Tiffany and other rights owners who have invested enormous resources in developing their brands, only to see them illicitly and efficiently exploited by others on the Internet. Nevertheless, the law is clear: it is the trademark owner's burden to police its mark, and companies like eBay cannot be held liable for trademark infringement based solely on their generalized knowledge that trademark infringement might be occurring on their websites.

INSERT THE FOLLOWING ON PAGE 108:

(3) Infringement on the Internet
(a) The use in commerce requirement

Rescuecom Corp. v. Google, Inc.
United States Court of Appeals, Second Circuit (2009).
562 F.3d 123.

■ LEVAL, CIRCUIT JUDGE:

Appeal by Plaintiff Rescuecom Corp. from a judgment dismissing its action against Google, Inc., under Rule 12(b)(6) for failure to state a claim upon which relief may be granted. Rescuecom's Complaint alleges that Google is liable under §§ 32 and 43 of the Lanham Act, 15 U.S.C. §§ 1114 & 1125, for infringement, false designation of origin, and dilution of Rescuecom's eponymous trademark. The district court believed the dismissal of the action was compelled by our holding in *1-800 Contacts, Inc. v. WhenU.Com, Inc.*, 414 F.3d 400 (2d Cir.2005) ("*1-800*"), because, according to the district court's understanding of that opinion, Rescuecom failed to allege that Google's use of its mark was a "use in commerce" within the meaning of § 45 of the Lanham Act, 15 U.S.C. § 1127. We believe this misunderstood the holding of *1-800*. While we express no view as to whether Rescuecom can prove a Lanham Act violation, an actionable claim is adequately alleged in its pleadings. Accordingly, we vacate the judgment dismissing the action and remand for further proceedings.

BACKGROUND

Rescuecom is a national computer service franchising company that offers on-site computer services and sales. Rescuecom conducts a substantial amount of business over the Internet and receives between 17,000 to 30,000 visitors to its website each month. It also advertises over the Internet, using many web-based services, including those offered by Google. Since 1998, "Rescuecom" has been a registered federal trademark, and there is no dispute as to its validity.

Google operates a popular Internet search engine, which users access by visiting www.google.com. Using Google's website, a person searching for the website of a particular entity in trade (or simply for information about it) can enter that entity's name or trademark into Google's search engine and launch a search. Google's proprietary system responds to such a search request in two ways. First, Google provides a list of links to websites, ordered in what Google deems to be of descending relevance to the user's search terms based on its proprietary algorithms. Google's search engine assists the public not only in obtaining information about a provider, but also in purchasing products and services. If a prospective purchaser, looking for goods or services of a particular provider, enters the provider's trademark as a search term on Google's website and clicks to activate a search, within seconds, the Google search engine will provide on the searcher's computer screen a link to the webpage maintained by that provider (as well as a host of other links to sites that Google's program determines to be relevant to the search term entered). By clicking on the link of the provider, the searcher will be directed to the provider's website, where the searcher can obtain information supplied by the provider about its products and services and can perhaps also make purchases from the provider by placing orders.

The second way Google responds to a search request is by showing context-based advertising. When a searcher uses Google's search engine by submitting a search term, Google may place advertisements on the user's screen. Google will do so if an advertiser, having determined that its ad is likely to be of interest to a searcher who enters the particular term, has purchased from Google the placement of its ad on the screen of the searcher who entered that search term. What Google places on the searcher's screen is more than simply an advertisement. It is also a link to the advertiser's website, so that in response to such an ad, if the searcher clicks on the link, he will open the advertiser's website, which offers not only additional information about the advertiser, but also perhaps the option to purchase the goods and services of the advertiser over the Internet. Google uses at least two programs to offer such context-based links: AdWords and Keyword Suggestion Tool.

AdWords is Google's program through which advertisers purchase terms (or keywords). When entered as a search term, the keyword triggers the appearance of the advertiser's ad and link. An advertiser's purchase of a particular term causes the advertiser's ad and link to be displayed on the user's screen whenever a searcher launches a Google search based on the purchased search term. Advertisers pay Google based on the number of times Internet users "click" on the advertisement, so as to link to the advertiser's website.

In addition to AdWords, Google also employs Keyword Suggestion Tool, a program that recommends keywords to advertisers to be purchased. The program is designed to improve the effectiveness of advertising by helping advertisers identify keywords related to their area of commerce, resulting in the placement of their ads before users who are likely to be responsive to it.

Once an advertiser buys a particular keyword, Google links the keyword to that advertiser's advertisement. The advertisements consist of a combination of content and a link to the advertiser's webpage. Google displays these advertisements on the search result page either in the right margin or in a horizontal band immediately above the column of relevance-based search results. These advertisements are generally associated with a label, which says "sponsored link." Rescuecom alleges, however, that a user might easily be misled to believe that the advertisements which appear on the screen are in fact part of the relevance-based search result and that the appearance of a competitor's ad

21

and link in response to a searcher's search for Rescuecom is likely to cause trademark confusion as to affiliation, origin, sponsorship, or approval of service. This can occur, according to the Complaint, because Google fails to label the ads in a manner which would clearly identify them as purchased ads rather than search results. The Complaint alleges that when the sponsored links appear in a horizontal bar at the top of the search results, they may appear to the searcher to be the first, and therefore the most relevant, entries responding to the search, as opposed to paid advertisements.

Google's objective in its AdWords and Keyword Suggestion Tool programs is to sell keywords to advertisers. Rescuecom alleges that Google makes 97% of its revenue from selling advertisements through its AdWords program. Google therefore has an economic incentive to increase the number of advertisements and links that appear for every term entered into its search engine.

Many of Rescuecom's competitors advertise on the Internet. Through its Keyword Suggestion Tool, Google has recommended the Rescuecom trademark to Rescuecom's competitors as a search term to be purchased. Rescuecom's competitors, some responding to Google's recommendation, have purchased Rescuecom's trademark as a keyword in Google's AdWords program, so that whenever a user launches a search for the term "Rescuecom," seeking to be connected to Rescuecom's website, the competitors' advertisement and link will appear on the searcher's screen. This practice allegedly allows Rescuecom's competitors to deceive and divert users searching for Rescuecom's website. According to Rescuecom's allegations, when a Google user launches a search for the term "Rescuecom" because the searcher wishes to purchase Rescuecom's services, links to websites of its competitors will appear on the searcher's screen in a manner likely to cause the searcher to believe mistakenly that a competitor's advertisement (and website link) is sponsored by, endorsed by, approved by, or affiliated with Rescuecom.

The District Court granted Google's 12(b)(6) motion and dismissed Rescuecom's claims. The court believed that our *1-800* decision compels the conclusion that Google's allegedly infringing activity does not involve use of Rescuecom's mark in commerce, which is an essential element of an action under the Lanham Act. The district court explained its decision saying that even if Google employed Rescuecom's mark in a manner likely

essential element of action under Lanham Act = "use in commerce"

22

to cause confusion or deceive searchers into believing that competitors are affiliated with Rescuecom and its mark, so that they believe the services of Rescuecom's competitors are those of Rescuecom, Google's actions are not a "use in commerce" under the Lanham Act because the competitor's → OC advertisements triggered by Google's programs did not exhibit Rescuecom's trademark. The court rejected the argument that Google "used" Rescuecom's mark in recommending and selling it as a keyword to trigger competitor's advertisements because the court read *1-800* to compel the conclusion that this was an internal use and therefore cannot be a "use in commerce" under the Lanham Act.

DISCUSSION

I. Google's Use of Rescuecom's Mark Was a "Use in Commerce"

Our court ruled in *1-800* that a complaint fails to state a claim under the Lanham Act unless it alleges that the defendant has made "use in = Holding in commerce" of the plaintiff's trademark as the term "use in commerce" is 1-800 defined in 15 U.S.C. § 1127. The district court believed that this case was on all fours with *1-800*, and that its dismissal was required for the same reasons as given in *1-800*. We believe the cases are materially different. The allegations of Rescuecom's complaint adequately plead a use in commerce.

In *1-800*, the plaintiff alleged that the defendant infringed the plaintiff's trademark through its proprietary software, which the defendant freely distributed to computer users who would download and install the program on their computer. The program provided contextually relevant advertising to the user by generating pop-up advertisements to the user depending on the website or search term the user entered in his browser. For example, if a user typed "eye care" into his browser, the defendant's program would randomly display a pop-up advertisement of a company engaged in the field of eye care. Similarly, if the searcher launched a search for a particular company engaged in eye care, the defendant's program would display the pop-up ad of a company associated with eye care. The pop-up ad appeared in a separate browser window from the 1-800 website the user accessed, and the defendant's brand was displayed in the window frame surrounding the ad, so that there was no confusion as to the nature of the pop-up as an advertisement, nor as to the fact that the defendant, not the trademark owner, was responsible for displaying the ad,

23

in response to the particular term searched.

Sections 32 and 43 of the Act, 15 U.S.C. §§ 1114 & 1125, impose liability for unpermitted "use in commerce" of another's mark which is "likely to cause confusion, or to cause mistake, or to deceive,"§ 1114, "as to the affiliation ... or as to the origin, sponsorship or approval of his or her goods [or] services ... by another person."§ 1125(a)(1)(A). The *1-800* opinion looked to the definition of the term "use in commerce" provided in § 45 of the Act, 15 U.S.C. § 1127. That definition provides in part that "a mark shall be deemed to be in use in commerce ... (2) on services when it is used or displayed in the sale or advertising of services and the services are rendered in commerce." 15 U.S.C. § 1127. Our court found that the plaintiff failed to show that the defendant made a "use in commerce" of the plaintiff's mark, within that definition.

At the outset, we note two significant aspects of our holding in *1-800*, which distinguish it from the present case. A key element of our court's decision in *1-800* was that under the plaintiff's allegations, the defendant did not use, reproduce, or display the plaintiff's mark *at all*. The search term that was alleged to trigger the pop-up ad was the plaintiff's *website address*. *1-800* noted, notwithstanding the similarities between the website address and the mark, that the website address was not used or claimed by the plaintiff as a trademark. Thus, the transactions alleged to be infringing were not transactions involving use of the plaintiff's trademark. *Id.* at 408-09.[a] *1-800* suggested in dictum that is highly relevant to our case that had the defendant used the plaintiff's *trademark* as the trigger to pop-up an advertisement, such conduct might, depending on other elements, have been actionable.

---

[a] We did not imply in *1-800* that a website can never be a trademark. In fact, the opposite is true. *See* Trademark Manual of Examining Procedures § 1209.03(m) (5th ed. 2007) ("A mark comprised of an Internet domain name is registrable as a trademark or service mark only if it functions as an identifier of the source of goods or services."); *see also Two Pesos, Inc. v. Taco Cabana, Inc.,* 505 U.S. 763, 768, 112 S.Ct. 2753, 120 L.Ed.2d 615 (1992) (Section 43(a) of the Lanham Act protects unregistered trademarks as long as the mark could qualify for registration under the Lanham Act.); *Thompson Med. Co., Inc. v. Pfizer Inc.,* 753 F.2d 208, 215-216 (2d Cir.1985) (same). The question whether the plaintiff's website address was an unregistered trademark was never properly before the *1-800* court because the plaintiff did not claim that it used its website address as a trademark.

24

[handwritten margin notes:]
2 distinctions b/t 1-800 & this case:
(1) * in 1-800, P's WEBSITE was the trigger, not their trademark

1-800 → dicta

Second, as an alternate basis for its decision, *1-800* explained why the defendant's program, which might randomly trigger pop-up advertisements upon a searcher's input of the plaintiff's website address, did not constitute a "use in commerce," as defined in § 1127. In explaining why the plaintiff's mark was not "used or displayed in the sale or advertising of services,"*1-800* pointed out that, under the defendant's program, advertisers could not request or purchase keywords to trigger their ads.

The present case contrasts starkly with those important aspects of the *1-800* decision. First, in contrast to *1-800,* where we emphasized that the defendant made no use whatsoever of the plaintiff's trademark, here what Google is recommending and selling to its advertisers is Rescuecom's trademark. Second, in contrast with the facts of *1-800* where the defendant did not "use or display," much less sell, trademarks as search terms to its advertisers, here Google displays, offers, and sells Rescuecom's mark to Google's advertising customers when selling its advertising services. In addition, Google encourages the purchase of Rescuecom's mark through its Keyword Suggestion Tool. Google's utilization of Rescuecom's mark fits literally within the terms specified by 15 U.S.C. § 1127. According to the Complaint, Google uses and sells Rescuecom's mark "in the sale ... of [Google's advertising] services ... rendered in commerce."§ 1127.

Google, supported by amici, argues that *1-800* suggests that the inclusion of a trademark in an internal computer directory cannot constitute trademark use. Several district court decisions in this Circuit appear to have reached this conclusion. *See e.g., S & L Vitamins, Inc. v. Australian Gold, Inc.,* 521 F.Supp.2d 188, 199-202 (E.D.N.Y.2007) (holding that use of a trademark in metadata did not constitute trademark use within the meaning of the Lanham Act because the use "is strictly internal and not communicated to the public"); *Merck & Co., Inc. v. Mediplan Health Consulting, Inc.,* 425 F.Supp.2d 402, 415 (S.D.N.Y.2006) (holding that the internal use of a keyword to trigger advertisements did not qualify as trademark use). This over-reads the *1-800* decision. First, regardless of whether Google's use of Rescuecom's mark in its internal search algorithm could constitute an actionable trademark use, Google's recommendation and sale of Rescuecom's mark to its advertising customers are not internal uses. Furthermore, *1-800* did not imply that use of a trademark in a software program's internal directory precludes a finding of trademark use. Rather, influenced by the fact that

25

the defendant was not using the plaintiff's trademark at all, much less using it as the basis of a commercial transaction, the court asserted that the particular use before it did not constitute a use in commerce. We did not imply in *1-800* that an alleged infringer's use of a trademark in an internal software program insulates the alleged infringer from a charge of infringement, no matter how likely the use is to cause confusion in the marketplace. If we were to adopt Google and its amici's argument, the operators of search engines would be free to use trademarks in ways designed to deceive and cause consumer confusion. This is surely neither within the intention nor the letter of the Lanham Act.

Needless to say, a defendant must do more than use another's mark in commerce to violate the Lanham Act. The gist of a Lanham Act violation is an unauthorized use, which "is likely to cause confusion, or to cause mistake, or to deceive as to the affiliation, ... or as to the origin, sponsorship, or approval of ... goods [or] services." *See* 15 U.S.C. § 1125(a). We have no idea whether Rescuecom can prove that Google's use of Rescuecom's trademark in its AdWords program causes likelihood of confusion or mistake. Rescuecom has alleged that it does, in that would-be purchasers (or explorers) of its services who search for its website on Google are misleadingly directed to the ads and websites of its competitors in a manner which leads them to believe mistakenly that these ads or websites are sponsored by, or affiliated with Rescuecom. This is particularly so, Rescuecom alleges, when the advertiser's link appears in a horizontal band at the top of the list of search results in a manner which makes it appear to be the most relevant search result and not an advertisement. Whether Google's actual practice is in fact benign or confusing is not for us to judge at this time. We consider at the 12(b)(6) stage only what is alleged in the Complaint.

REMANDED   The judgment of the district court is vacated and the case is remanded for further proceedings.

(b) The UDRP and § 43(d)

INSERT THE FOLLOWING AS NOTE 1h ON PAGE 124:

h. *Likelihood of confusion and fair use.* The *Welles* case involves nominative fair use which occurs when the defendant is using the plaintiff's mark to describe the plaintiff rather than the defendant's own product. In contrast, *KP Permanent Make-Up* involves the classic fair use situation in which the defendant is using the plaintiff's mark to describe the defendant's goods. Although not specifically discussed in *KP Permanent Make-Up*, a defendant must prove the following in order to prevail on a fair use defense: (1) it used the subject matter in question in a non-trademark capacity; (2) the matter is descriptive of the defendant's goods or services; and (3) the defendant used the material 'fairly and in good faith" only for the purpose of describing its goods or services.[1] This defense also is discussed in Note 5 of Assignment 4.

In the *KP Permanent Make-Up* decision, the Court left open the possibility that courts can consider likelihood of confusion as relevant to the issue of the fairness of a particular usage, although it did not specify how much confusion will result in eliminating the fair use defense in any given situation. On remand in *KP Permanent Make-Up*, the district court granted summary judgment in favor of KP, the alleged infringer, in part on the ground that its use was fair and no discussion of likelihood of confusion was necessary. The Ninth Circuit reversed, holding that on the record before the court, there existed some genuine issues of material fact regarding likelihood of confusion and that "the degree of customer confusion remains a factor in evaluating fair use."[2]

SUBSTITUTE THE FOLLOWING FOR NOTE 6 ON PAGE 128:

6. *Dilution: § 43(c)*. As noted in the Introduction, dilution is intended to cover activities that impair the value of the mark *outside* the context of consumer confusion as to source or origin. Because these claims are not confined to situations where consumers may be misled, the right to enjoin dilution can have a much greater impact on communication, including in commercial dealings, than claims under §§ 1114 and 43(a). Perhaps for that reason, legislatures and courts have shown considerable reluctance to embrace this right of action. About half the states did not offer protection against dilution at the time the federal statute was first enacted. And once the original version of the federal statute became law, many courts

---

[1] See *Diana Packman v. Chicago Tribune Co.*, 267 F.3d 628 (7th Cir. 2001) (holding that the Chicago Tribune's use of the phrase "the joy of six" on merchandise in connection with the Bulls' sixth NBA championship constitutes fair use of the plaintiff's mark).
[2] See *KP Permanent Make-Up, Inc. v. Lasting Impression I, Inc.*, 408 F.3d 596, 609 (9th Cir. 2005).

interpreted it as imposing high standards on plaintiffs, thus avoiding results that they saw as reducing social welfare.[3]

Moseley v. V Secret Catalogue, Inc., 537 U.S. 418, 433 (2003), the case cited by the eBay Court is a good example of the skepticism with which dilution claims were originally greeted. In that case, the Supreme Court insisted that the plaintiff prove actual dilution and actual economic harm, thus erecting an almost insurmountable obstacle to winning a case. Ironically, even if the plaintiff did win, the damage must, by definition, have already been done.

Especially surprising was the *Moseley* Court's suggestion that federal law may only cover "blurring." In states that had previously enacted dilution protection, the claim was regarded as encompassing two components, blurring and tarnishment. Tarnishment had always been thought relatively easy to understand as an association that brings the mark into disrepute. The quintessential example was *Dallas Cowboys Cheerleaders, Inc. v. Pussycat Cinema, Ltd.*,[4] where the movie's protagonist, Debbie, "dons a uniform strikingly similar to that worn by the Dallas Cowboy Cheerleaders and for approximately twelve minutes of film footage engages in various sex acts while clad or partially clad in the uniform."[5] Since there are many people who might object to watching this sort of activity, it is obvious why the Cowboys would think that reputational interests were at stake. In contrast, the concept of blurring has always been strongly contested. Because many words have multiple meanings, people are well versed in resolving ambiguities. Families, for example, have ways of determining which "David" is meant when both father and son share that name. Thus, it is hard to believe that Dupont or Buick or Kodak would be less effective as signals for particular chemicals, cars, or cameras just because the terms also appear in conjunction with shoes, aspirin, or pianos. Indeed, consumers arguably become better acquainted with a mark if they encounter it more often and have to think through its meaning carefully.

The new statute, which was enacted in 2007, removed all three limitations imposed by the *Moseley* decision. Section 43(c)(1) uses the words "likely to cause dilution by blurring or tarnishment" (both concepts

---

[3] Clarisa Long, *Dilution*, 106 COLUM. L. REV. 1029 (2006).

[4] 604 F.2d 200 (2d Cir.1979).

[5] Id. at 202-03 (footnote omitted).

are also defined, § 43(c)(2)(B) & (C)). Further, § 43(c)(1) explicitly states that the right applies "regardless of the presence or absence of . . . actual economic injury."

The new statute also eliminates other obstacles that lower courts had erected. Thus, at the time of *Moseley*, some lower courts had limited the ambit of dilution to marks that were inherently distinctive, leaving marks with a descriptive dimension free for use in the absence of confusion.[6] In contrast, the new statute makes clear that the right applies to marks that are "distinctive, inherently or through acquired distinctiveness." Furthermore, the earlier statute required the offending use to be a "commercial use in commerce," leading some lower courts to erect a stringent test of commercial use.[7] Section 43(c)(1) now refers to "use of a mark or trade name in commerce"—a formulation that appears to encompass a wider range of uses.

Still, the new statute contains several important limitations. Most crucially, the mark must be famous. As defined by § 43(c)(2), this means the mark must be "recognized by the general consuming public of the United States as a designation of source of the goods or services of the owner." This provision contrasts sharply with some older case law, which had held that fame in a localized market, or among a specialized group of consumers, was sufficient. An example is *Times Mirror Magazines, Inc. v. Las Vegas Sports News*,[8] where the court held that the mark, "The Sporting News" for a weekly publication on sports was famous enough:

> We are persuaded that a mark not famous to the general public is nevertheless entitled to protection from dilution where both the plaintiff and defendant are operating in the same or related markets,

---

[6] See, e.g., *TCPIP Holding Co., Inc. v. Haar Communications, Inc.*, 244 F.3d 88 (2d Cir. 2001); *I.P. Lund Trading ApS v. Kohler Co*, 163 F.3d 27, 50 (1st Cir. 1998). See generally Anne E. Kennedy, *From Delusion to Dilutions: Proposals to Improve Problematic Aspects of the Federal Trademark Dilution Act*, 9 N.Y.U. J. LEGIS. & PUB. POL'Y 399 (2005-2006).

[7] See, e.g., *Mattel, Inc. v. MCA Records, Inc.*, 296 F.3d 894 (9th Cir. 2002), which concerned Aqua's song "Barbie." The song was on an album that was sold commercially. Nonetheless, Judge Kozinski held that the trademark "Barbie" was not used commercially within the meaning of the statute because it was not in a proposal for a commercial transaction.

[8] 212 F.3d 157, 54 U.S.P.Q.2d 1577 (3d Cir. 2000), cert. denied, 121 S. Ct. 760 (2001).

so long as the plaintiff's mark possesses a high degree of fame in its niche market.

The new definition of famousness should, as a dissent in *Times Mirror* had suggested, cabin the reach of § 43(c) claims.

The new statute includes at least two other important safeguards. Although trade dress can also be the basis of a dilution claim, the plaintiff bears the burden of proving that the trade dress is not functional, § 43(c)(4)(A). Furthermore, the statute now contains a well-developed list of exceptions, designed to protect communication. Under § 43(c)(3)(A), fair use, including nominative or descriptive fair use, is permissible in connection with advertising, parodying, or commenting. Subsection (B) covers all forms of news reporting and subsection (C) covers "any noncommercial use."

The new language in the defenses to dilution has yet to be interpreted. One interesting question is whether the explicitness of this language will have an impact on the construction of the defenses to ordinary infringement, where these concepts are not so carefully spelled out, *see, e.g.,* § 1115(b)(4).

INSERT AS NEW NOTE 7a ON PAGE 130:

7a. *The Fraudulent Online Identity Sanctions Act.* Registrar Databases would become meaningless if the information contained by them was intentionally false. If every website address that allegedly adversely affects the value of a trademark was registered by John Doe, living at 123 Fake Street, proceedings to obtain proper ownership would be made even more difficult for trademark owners. In order to discourage this type of behavior, Congress passed the Fraudulent Online Identity Sanctions Act as part of the Intellectual Property Protection and Courts Amendments Act of 2004.[9] The Act creates a presumption that a trademark violation was willful if the alleged violator provided false information when registering a website address which was used in connection with the infringement.[10] As is discussed in Assignment 5, a finding of willfulness further enhances the amount and scope of remedies

---

[9] PL 108-482 (HR 3632).
[10] § 504(c)(3)(A) (2005).

available to a successful plaintiff. The Act makes similar amendments to other sections where such a presumption of willfulness would change the remedies available for the violation.[11]

ADD AT THE END OF NOTE 13 ON PAGE 138:

The *eBay* case represents a new chapter in the use of contributory infringement claims. The court says in many places in its opinion that Tiffany could have brought successful actions against the actual sellers for infringement and dilution. Why did it fail to do so? One reason is that it would be difficult to find and sue each and every seller. In contrast, eBay is a "chokehold"—a point at which counterfeiting could arguably be stemmed in a single suit for contributory liability.

Why then was the court so unsympathetic to Tiffany's claim? *eBay*, which also has a strong interest in making sure that customers are satisfied, was already spending more than $20 million a year to remove counterfeit merchandise from its site. Had Tiffany won, certainly other trademark holders would have quickly followed in its footsteps. As a result of many successful suits, online auctions might have turned out to be an unviable business model. Could part of Tiffany's plan have been to put eBay out of business? Note that the reason it is so difficult to spot counterfeiters is that there are also legitimate sellers of Tiffany goods on the eBay site—these are vendors who sell used genuine goods, presumably at a price that is below the price at which Tiffany sells new goods. The contributory infringement claim in this case should therefore be considered as similar to claims you will see later against contributory copyright infringers—as attempts to end new business models that reduce the rewards that existing right holders can reap.

---

[11] § 1117(e).

ASSIGNMENT 5—REMEDIES

See also the Insert to Assignment 3 supra regarding the Fraudulent Online Identity Sanctions Act.

INSERT THE FOLLOWING AT THE END OF THE TOP PARAGRAPH ON PAGE 210:

In 2006, legislation was passed that amended this statute by criminalizing the trafficking in counterfeit labels and packaging and allowing courts to order the destruction of these items and the machines used for their manufacture.

INSERT THE FOLLOWING AT THE END OF THE FIRST PARAGRAPH OF NOTE 9 ON PAGE 211:

In *SKF USA Inc. v. International Trade Commission*,[1] the court held that although differences other than physical ones can be considered in establishing trademark infringement involving gray market goods, the plaintiff must show that "all or substantially all of its sales are accompanied by the asserted material difference in order to show that its goods are materially different." The court reasoned that "[i]f less than all or substantially all of a trademark owner's products possess the material difference, then the trademark owner has placed into the stream of commerce a substantial quantity of goods that are or may be the same or similar to those of the importer, and then there is no material difference."[2]

---

[1] 423 F.3d 1307 (Fed. Cir. 2005), cert. denied, 126 S. Ct. 2968 (2006).
[2] Id. at 1315.

ASSIGNMENT 6—COPYRIGHT PROTECTION: INTRODUCTION

ADD THE FOLLOWING TO THE END OF THE LAST PARAGRAPH OF SECTION 1A. ON PAGE 215:

For many years, several lower courts treated the requirement that registration be made as a prerequisite for filing an infringement action to be jurisdictional in nature. In 2010, however, the United States Supreme Court concluded that the requirement was instead a claims-processing rule, simply establishing an element of a cause of action for infringement. *Reed Elsevier, Inc. v. Muchnick*, 130 S. Ct. 1237, 1248-49 (2010).

SUBSTITUTE THE FOLLOWING FOR FOOTNOTE 11 ON PAGE 215:

As of August 1, 2009, the filing fee was increased to $50.00 for a paper registration while remaining $35.00 for one filed electronically.

AMENDMENT TO PAGE 218 RE BERNE SIGNATORIES:

Today, about 164 countries are members of Berne.

ASSIGNMENT 7—THE REQUIREMENTS OF ORIGINALITY AND AUTHORSHIP

REPLACE *HEARN V. MEYER*, PAGES 248-255, WITH THE FOLLOWING:

Schrock v. Learning Curve International

United States Court of Appeals, 7th Circuit, 2009
586 F.3d 513

I. Background

HIT is the owner of the copyright in the "Thomas & Friends" properties, and Learning Curve is a producer and distributor of children's toys. HIT and Learning Curve entered into a licensing agreement granting Learning Curve a license to create and market toys based on HIT's characters. HIT and Learning Curve maintain (through an affidavit of HIT's vice-president of licensing) that HIT retained all intellectual-property rights in the works produced under the license. The licensing agreement, however, is not in the record.

In 1999 Learning Curve retained Daniel Schrock to take product photographs of its toys, including those based on HIT's characters, for use in promotional materials. On numerous occasions during the next four years, Schrock photographed several lines of Learning Curve's toys, including many of the "Thomas & Friends" toy trains, related figures, and train-set accessories. Schrock invoiced Learning Curve for this work, and some of the invoices included "usage restrictions" purporting to limit Learning Curve's use of his photographs to two years. Learning Curve paid the invoices in full--in total more than $400,000.

Learning Curve stopped using Schrock's photography services in mid-2003 but continued to use some of his photos in its printed advertising, on packaging, and on the internet. In 2004 Schrock registered his photos for copyright protection and sued HIT and Learning Curve for infringement; he also alleged several state-law claims. HIT and Learning Curve moved for summary judgment, arguing primarily that Schrock's photos were derivative works and not sufficiently original to claim copyright

34

protection, and that neither HIT nor Learning Curve ever authorized Schrock to copyright the photos. They argued in the alternative that Schrock granted them an unlimited oral license to use the photos.

The district court granted summary judgment for the defendants. The judge began by noting the long tradition of recognizing copyright protection in photographs but said he would nonetheless "eschew" the question whether Schrock's photographs were sufficiently original to copyright. The judge focused instead on whether the photos were derivative works under the Copyright Act and concluded that they were. Then, following language in *Gracen,* the judge held that Learning Curve's permission to make the photos was not enough to trigger Schrock's copyright in them; the judge said Schrock must also have Learning Curve's permission to copyright the photos. Schrock did not have that permission, so the judge concluded that Schrock had no copyright in the photos and dismissed his claim for copyright infringement. Schrock appealed.

II. Discussion

Schrock argues that the district judge mistakenly classified his photos as derivative works and misread or misapplied *Gracen.* He contends that his photos are not derivative works, and even if they are, his copyright is valid and enforceable because he had permission from Learning Curve to photograph the underlying copyrighted works and his photos contained sufficient incremental original expression to qualify for copyright. HIT and Learning Curve defend the district court's determination that the photos are derivative works and argue that the court properly read *Gracen* to require permission to copyright as well as permission to make the derivative works. Alternatively, they maintain that Schrock's photographs contain insufficient originality to be copyrightable and that copyright protection is barred under the *scènes à faire* or merger doctrines. Finally, the defendants ask us to affirm on the independent ground that Schrock orally granted them an unlimited license to use his works.

As a general matter, a plaintiff asserting copyright infringement must prove: "(1) ownership of a valid copyright, and (2) copying of constituent elements of the work that are original." *Feist Publ'ns, Inc. v. Rural Tel. Serv. Co.,* 499 U.S. 340, 361, 111 S.Ct. 1282, 113 L.Ed.2d 358 (1991). There is no dispute here about copying; Learning Curve used Schrock's photos in its promotional materials. The focus instead is on the validity of Schrock's asserted copyright in the photos. The Copyright Act provides that "[c]opyright protection subsists . . . in original works of authorship fixed in any tangible medium of expression . . . from which they can be perceived, reproduced, or otherwise communicated, either directly or with the aid of a machine or device." 17 U.S.C. § 102(a). In this circuit, copyrightability is an issue of law for the court. *Gaiman v. McFarlane,* 360 F.3d 644, 648-49 (7th Cir. 2004).

Much of the briefing on appeal--and most of the district court's analysis--concerned the classification of the photos as derivative works. A "derivative work" is:

> [A] work based upon one or more preexisting works, such as a translation, musical arrangement, dramatization, fictionalization, motion picture version, sound recording, art reproduction, abridgment, condensation, or any other form in which a work may be recast, transformed, or adapted. A work consisting of editorial revisions, annotations, elaborations, or other modifications which, as a whole, represent an original work of authorship, is a "derivative work".

17 U.S.C. § 101. The Copyright Act specifically grants the author of a derivative work copyright protection in the incremental original expression he contributes as long as the derivative work does not infringe the underlying work. *See id.* § 103(a), (b); *see also Pickett v. Prince,* 207 F.3d 402, 405 (7th Cir. 2000); *Lee v. A.R.T. Co.,* 125 F.3d 580, 582 (7th Cir. 1997). The copyright in a derivative work, however, "extends only to the material contributed by the author of such work, as distinguished from the preexisting material employed in the work." 17 U.S.C. § 103(b).

A. Photographs as Derivative Works

Whether photographs of a copyrighted work are derivative works is the subject of deep disagreement among courts and commentators alike. *See* 1 MELVILLE B. NIMMER & DAVID NIMMER, NIMMER ON COPYRIGHT § 3.03[C][1], at 3-20.3 (Aug.2009). The district court held that Schrock's photos came within the definition of derivative works because they "recast, transformed, or adapted" the three-dimensional toys into a different, two-dimensional medium. For this conclusion the judge relied in part on language in *Gracen* and in the Ninth Circuit's decision in *Ets-Hokin v. Skyy Spirits, Inc.*, 225 F.3d 1068 (9th Cir. 2000), recognizing, however, that neither decision directly decided the matter. *Gracen* did not involve photographs at all, and although *Ets-Hokin* did, the Ninth Circuit ultimately sidestepped the derivative-works question and rested its decision on other grounds. *Id.* at 1081.

The judge also cited other decisions in this circuit that appear to support the conclusion that photographs are derivative works, but these, too (and again, as the judge properly acknowledged), did not directly address the question. *Ty, Inc. v. Publications International Ltd.*, 292 F.3d 512, 519 (7th Cir. 2002), involved unauthorized "Beanie Babies" collector's guides that incorporated photographs of the popular beanbag plush toys into the text. We said there that "photographs of Beanie Babies are derivative works from the copyrighted Beanie Babies themselves," but this statement was based entirely on the parties' concession that the photographs were derivative works. *Id. Saturday Evening Post Co. v. Rumbleseat Press, Inc.*, 816 F.2d 1191 (7th Cir. 1987), made a passing remark suggesting that photographs of Norman Rockwell illustrations were derivative works, but that was not an issue in the case, *id.* at 1201; the issue instead was whether certain terms in a licensing agreement (specifically, no-contest and arbitration clauses) were enforceable, *id.* at 1193.

We need not resolve the issue definitively here. The classification of Schrock's photos as derivative works does not affect the applicable legal standard for determining copyrightability, although as we have noted, it does determine the scope of copyright protection. Accordingly, we will assume without deciding that each of Schrock's photos qualifies as a derivative work within the meaning of the Copyright Act.

B. Originality and Derivative Works

As a constitutional and statutory matter, "[t]he *sine qua non* of copyright is originality." *Feist Publ'ns, Inc.*, 499 U.S. at 345, 111 S.Ct. 1282; *see* 17 U.S.C. § 102. Originality in this context "means only that the work was independently created by the author ... and that it possesses at least some minimal degree of creativity." *Feist Publ'ns, Inc.*, 499 U.S. at 345, 111 S.Ct. 1282. The Supreme Court emphasized in *Feist* that "the requisite level of creativity is extremely low; even a slight amount will

37

suffice." *Id.* The Court also explained that "[o]riginality does not signify novelty; a work may be original even though it closely resembles other works." *Id.* What is required is "independent creation plus a modicum of creativity." *Id.* at 346, 111 S.Ct. 1282.

Federal courts have historically applied a generous standard of originality in evaluating photographic works for copyright protection. *See, e.g., Ets-Hokin,* 225 F.3d at 1073-77; *SHL Imaging, Inc. v. Artisan House, Inc.,* 117 F. Supp. 2d 301, 305 (S.D.N.Y. 2000). In some cases, the original expression may be found in the staging and creation of the scene depicted in the photograph. *See, e.g., Mannion v. Coors Brewing Co.,* 377 F. Supp. 2d 444, 452 (S.D.N.Y. 2005). But in many cases, the photographer does not invent the scene or create the subject matter depicted in it. Rather, the original expression he contributes lies in the *rendition* of the subject matter--that is, the effect created by the combination of his choices of perspective, angle, lighting, shading, focus, lens, and so on. *See id.; Rogers v. Koons,* 960 F.2d 301, 307 (2d Cir. 1992) ("Elements of originality in a photograph may include posing the subjects, lighting, angle, selection of film and camera, evoking the desired expression, and almost any other variant involved."). Most photographs contain at least some originality in their rendition, *see Mannion,* 377 F. Supp. 2d at 452 ("Unless a photograph replicates another work with total or near-total fidelity, it will be at least somewhat original in the rendition."), except perhaps for a very limited class of photographs that can be characterized as "slavish copies" of an underlying work, *Bridgeman Art Library, Ltd. v. Corel Corp.,* 25 F. Supp. 2d 421, 427 (S.D.N.Y. 1998) (finding no originality in transparencies of paintings where the goal was to reproduce those works exactly and thus to minimize or eliminate any individual expression).

Our review of Schrock's photographs convinces us that they do not fall into the narrow category of photographs that can be classified as "slavish copies," lacking any independently created expression. To be sure, the photographs are accurate depictions of the three-dimensional "Thomas & Friends" toys, but Schrock's artistic and technical choices combine to create a two-dimensional image that is subtly but nonetheless sufficiently his own. This is confirmed by Schrock's deposition testimony describing his creative process in depicting the toys. Schrock explained how he used various camera and lighting techniques to make the toys look more "life like," "personable," and "friendly." He explained how he tried to give the toys "a little bit of dimension" and that it was his goal to make the toys "a little bit better than what they look like when you actually see them on the shelf." The original expression in the representative sample is not particularly great (it was not meant to be), but it is enough under the applicable standard to warrant the limited copyright protection accorded derivative works under § 103(b).

The defendants' argument is that it is not enough that Schrock's photographs might pass the ordinary test for originality; they claim that as derivative works, the photos are subject to a higher standard of originality. A leading copyright commentator disagrees. The Nimmer treatise maintains that the quantum of originality required for copyright in a derivative work is the same as that required for copyright in any other work. *See* 1 NIMMER ON COPYRIGHT § 3.01, at 3-2, § 3.03[A], at 3-7. More particularly, Nimmer says the relevant standard is whether a derivative work contains a "nontrivial" variation from the preexisting work "sufficient to render the derivative work distinguishable from [the] prior work in any meaningful manner." *Id.* § 3.03[A], at 3-10. The caselaw generally follows this formulation. *See, e.g., Eden Toys, Inc. v. Florelee Undergarment Co.,* 697 F.2d 27, 34-35 (2d Cir. 1982) (holding that numerous minor changes in an illustration of Paddington Bear were sufficiently nontrivial because they combined to give Paddington a "different, cleaner 'look' "); *Millworth Converting Corp. v. Slifka,* 276 F.2d 443, 445 (2d Cir. 1960) (holding that embroidered reproduction of a public-domain embroidery of Peter Pan was sufficiently distinguishable because the latter gave a "three-dimensional look" to the former embroidery).

Learning Curve and HIT argue that our decision in *Gracen* established a more demanding standard of originality for derivative works. *Gracen* involved an artistic competition in which artists were invited to submit paintings of the character Dorothy from the Metro-Goldwyn-Mayer ("MGM") movie *The Wizard of Oz.* Participating artists were given a still photograph of Dorothy from the film as an exemplar, and the paintings were solicited and submitted with the understanding that the best painting would be chosen for a series of collector's plates. *Gracen,* 698 F.2d at 301. Plaintiff Gracen prevailed in the competition, but she refused to sign the contract allowing her painting to be used in the collector's plates. The competition sponsor commissioned another artist to create a similar plate, and Gracen sued the sponsor, MGM, and the artist for copyright infringement. We held that Gracen could not maintain her infringement suit because her painting, a derivative work, was not "substantially different from the underlying work to be copyrightable." *Id.* at 305.

Gracen drew this language from an influential Second Circuit decision, *L. Batlin & Son, Inc. v. Snyder,* 536 F.2d 486 (2d Cir. 1976). Read in context, however, the cited language from *L. Batlin* did not suggest that a heightened standard of originality applies to derivative works. To the contrary, the Second Circuit said only that to be copyrightable a work must " 'contain some substantial, not merely trivial originality.' " *Id.* at 490 (quoting *Chamberlin v. Uris Sales Corp.,* 150 F.2d 512, 513 (2d Cir. 1945)). The court explained that for derivative works, as for any other work, "[t]he test of originality is concededly one with a low threshold in that all that is needed is that the author contributed something more than a merely trivial variation, something recognizably his own." *Id.* (internal quotation marks and ellipsis omitted).

The concern expressed in *Gracen* was that a derivative work could be so similar in appearance to the underlying work that in a subsequent infringement suit brought by a derivative author, it would be difficult to separate the original elements of expression in the derivative and underlying works in order to determine whether one derivative work infringed another. The opinion offered the example of artists A and B who both painted their versions of the Mona Lisa, a painting in the public domain. *See Gracen,* 698 F.2d at 304. "[I]f the difference between the original and A's reproduction is slight, the difference between A's and B's reproductions will also be slight, so that if B had access to A's reproductions the trier of fact will be hard-pressed to decide whether B was copying A or copying the Mona Lisa itself." *Id.*

No doubt this concern is valid. But nothing in the Copyright Act suggests that derivative works are subject to a more exacting originality requirement than other works of authorship. Indeed, we have explained since *Gracen* that "the only 'originality' required for [a] new work to by copyrightable . . . is enough expressive variation from public-domain or other existing works to enable the new work to be readily distinguished from its predecessors." *Bucklew,* 329 F.3d at 929. We emphasized in *Bucklew* that this standard does not require a "high degree of [incremental] originality." *Id.*

We think *Gracen* must be read in light of *L. Batlin,* on which it relied, and *Bucklew,* which followed it. And doing so reveals the following general principles: (1) the originality requirement for derivative works is not more demanding than the originality requirement for other works; and (2) the key inquiry is whether there is sufficient nontrivial expressive variation in the derivative work to make it distinguishable from the underlying work in some meaningful way. This focus on the presence of nontrivial "distinguishable variation" adequately captures the concerns articulated in *Gracen* without unduly narrowing the copyrightability of derivative works. It is worth repeating that the copyright in a derivative work is thin, extending only to the incremental original expression contributed by the author of the derivative work. *See* 17 U.S.C. § 103(b).

As applied to photographs, we have already explained that the original expression in a photograph generally subsists in its rendition of the subject matter. If the photographer's rendition of a copyrighted work varies enough from the underlying work to enable the photograph to be distinguished from the underlying work (aside from the obvious shift from three dimensions to two), then the photograph contains sufficient incremental originality to qualify for copyright. Schrock's photos of the "Thomas & Friends" toys are highly accurate product photos but contain minimally sufficient variation in angle, perspective, lighting, and dimension to be distinguishable from the underlying works; they are not "slavish copies." Accordingly, the photos qualify for the limited derivative-work copyright provided by § 103(b). *See SHL Imaging,* 117 F.Supp.2d at 311 (holding that copyright protection in product-accurate photographs was "thin"); *see also Rockford Map Publishers, Inc. v. Directory Serv. Co. of Colo., Inc.,* 768 F.2d 145, 148 (7th Cir. 1985) ("Perhaps the smaller the effort the smaller the contribution; if so, the copyright simply bestows fewer rights."). However narrow that copyright might be, it at least protects against the kind of outright copying that occurred here.

***

Accordingly, for all the foregoing reasons, we REVERSE the judgment of the district court and REMAND for further proceedings consistent with this opinion.

REPLACE FIRST TWO PARAGRAPHS OF NOTE 2 ON PAGE 256 WITH THE FOLLOWING:

2. *The essence of "authorship": originality and creativity.* In order to receive protection, the 1976 Act states that a work must be an "original work of authorship." From what you have read, do you believe there is a difference between originality and a "work of authorship"? Does the work of authorship requirement mandate that the creator be human (as opposed to a computer program) and that she infuse some of her own personality into the work? Since it now seems not to be enough that a work be original in the sense of not being copied from another source, how would you define the degree of creative authorship necessary for copyright protection?

Sometimes courts invoke a higher originality standard for derivative works. As noted in the Schrock case, Judge Posner, in deciding an infringement claim involving plate designs based on stills from the movie "The Wizard of Oz," stated that a derivative work, to be copyrightable, should contain "sufficiently gross" differences from the underlying work; otherwise, he cautioned, copyright might well inhibit others from making derivative works based on the same original.[1] The court in *Schrock* also refers to a Second Circuit opinion that has similarly been interpreted by some as requiring significant independent contribution by the author of the derivative work to render it eligible for its own independent copyright. At one point, the Second Circuit speaks of a need for "some substantial variation, not merely a trivial variation such as might occur in the translation to a different medium,"[2] and then goes on to discuss the need to demonstrate "true artistic skill" in order to copyright a reproduction.[3] Should the originality requirement be higher for derivative works? As you can see, *Schrock* rejects this idea, essentially indicating that Judge Posner (and those who understand *Batlin* as requiring a higher level of originality) are wrong. Does the *Schrock* opinion go further, however? When the court writes that all that is necessary to satisfy the requirement of originality in a derivative work is "enough expressive variation from public-domain or other existing works to enable the new work to be readily distinguished from its predecessors," is the court readopting the

---

[1] *Gracen v. Bradford Exch.*, 698 F.2d 300, 305 (7th Cir. 1983).
[2] *L. Batlin & Son v. Snyder*, 536 F.2d 486, 491 (2d Cir. 1976).
[3] Id.

standard discussed earlier in the Assignment in the *Alfred Bell* case? If so, is *Schock* consistent or inconsistent with *Feist*?

INSERT IN PLACE OF FOURTH PARAGRAPH OF NOTE 4 (BEGINNING WITH "SIGNIFICANTLY, THERE IS ...") ON PAGE 259:

Significantly, there is also a reciprocity provision: protection is available to non-EU nationals only if their country offers comparable protection.[4] This provision intensified efforts to pass similar legislation in the United States. Although bills have been introduced, significant opposition has resulted in no legislation being enacted. The opponents have several concerns. First, they are skeptical that legislation is needed. *Feist*, after all, is now over a decade old, and the database industry has not crumbled. Nor has it succumbed to European competition. In fact, the European Commission studied the impact of its database directive in 2005 and concluded that "the new instrument has had no proven impact on the production of databases."[5] Second, U.S. opponents are worried about the anticompetitive effects of exclusive rights in so-called sole source databases—material that cannot feasibly be collected by a second-comer (the database in *Feist* and a database comprising material from Dead Sea Scrolls are two examples). Third, they believe the rollover provision has the potential for creating perpetual protection.[6]

INSERT IN PLACE OF THE LAST SENTENCE OF NOTE 4 ON PAGE 260:

Examples of recent cases applying misappropriation theory to protect collections of data are *Associated Press v. All Headline News Corp.*[7] and *Barclays Capital, Inc. v. Theflyonthewall.com.*[8] In the first case, the

---

[4] Council Directive 96/9/EC of 11 March 1996, on the Legal Protection of Databases, 1996 O.J. (L 77) 20, recital 56.

[5] Commission of the European Communities, *DG Internal Market and Services Working Paper: First Evaluation of Directive 96/9/EC on the Legal Protection of Databases*, at 5 (Dec. 12, 2005), available at http://ec.europa.eu/internal_market/copyright/docs/databases/evaluation_report_en.pdf.

[6] See, e.g., Jonathan Band & Makoto Kono, *The Database Protection Debate in the 106h Congress*, 62 OHIO ST. L.J. 869 (2001); J.H. Reichman & Pamela Samuelson, *Intellectual Property Rights in Data?*, 50 VAND. L. REV. 51 (1997).

[7] 608 F. Supp. 2d 454 (S.D.N.Y. 2009).

[8] No. 06 Civ. 4908, 2010 WL 1005160 (S.D.N.Y. Mar. 18, 2010).

district court allowed the plaintiffs to proceed on a misappropriation cause of action against a defendant whose online news service did none of its own reporting, but relied instead on the contents of news reports its staff culled from the Internet. In the second, the court found for the plaintiff on misappropriation grounds where the defendants reported the recommendations of investment analysts, in some cases before the companies for which the analysts worked had disseminated the recommendations to their own clients. The use of misappropriation theory in both these cases is limited to information that can be characterized as "hot news." Is the use of state tort law to achieve what copyright will not permit appropriate? What are the first amendment implications of laws that restrict the dissemination of publicly known factual information? Assignment 13 discussing preemption and misappropriation bears on these issues.

INSERT AFTER THE FIRST PARAGRAPH OF NOTE 5 ON PAGE 260:

What is meant by "sufficiently permanent or stable" to qualify as a fixed work has become more complicated in the era of digital communication. Questions have been raised about whether transient capture of digital material in the random access memory of a computer constitutes fixation, and also whether the display of video games with their continually changing audiovisual displays should be viewed fixed. In both cases, the current consensus is that fixation exists,[9] although the conclusion has drawn scholarly dissent.[10] Recently, however, the Second

---

[9] With regard to content in the computer's random access memory, see § 117, referring to such content as a "copy," a term that seems to presuppose the existence of fixation. See also *MAI Systems Corp. v. Peak Computer, Inc.*, 991 F.2d 511 (9th Cir. 1993). With regard to game displays with changing imagery, see *Williams Electronics, Inc. v. Arctic Intern., Inc.*, 685 F.2d 870 (3d Cir. 1982).

[10] See, e.g., Russ VerSteeg, *Copyright in the Twenty-First Century: Jurimetric Copyright: Future Shock for the Visual Arts*, 13 CARDOZO ARTS & ENT. L.J. 125, 132 (1994) (arguing that recognizing information temporarily stored in computer RAM as fixed could be used to extend copyright to transitory works of visual art); Jessica Litman, *Copyright in the Twenty-First Century: The Exclusive Right to Read*, 13 CARDOZO ARTS & ENT. L.J. 29, 40 (1994) (criticizing the claim that copying RAM was fixation on the ground that such a ruling would render any viewing or reading of works in digital form actionable copying); James Boyle, *Intellectual Property Policy Online: A Young Person's Guide*, 10 HARV. J.L. & TECH. 47, 83-95 (1996). Cf. Pamela Samuelson, *The U.S. Digital Agenda at WIPO*, 37 VA. J. INT'L L. 369, 383-93 (1997) (critical discussion of attempt by

Circuit concluded that where sequences of television programming remained in a cable company's buffer for a little over a second before being overwritten, the material was indeed capable of being perceived, but for too transient a period to be considered "fixed."[11]

INSERT THE FOLLOWING ON PAGE 261 AT THE END OF NOTE 5 BEFORE "SEE ALSO ASSIGNMENT 13":

These provisions have been the subject of a few decisions, in which courts have concluded that the Copyright Clause does not forbid Congress from extending copyright-like protection to works of authorship that are not fixed by relying instead on the Commerce Clause.[12] Just recently, the Second Circuit held that the criminal liability provision was not authorized by the Copyright Clause because it does not allocate property rights in expression or share other defining characteristics of copyright law.[13] The court held, however, that the provision was validly enacted pursuant to the Commerce Clause.[14] The Second Circuit, however, limited its opinion to the criminal provisions, expressing no view on the validity of § 1101 (the civil liability section). The question of whether Congress can rely on the Commerce Clause to protect material that does not satisfy the

---

U.S. to get a provision adopted in a WIPO treaty that would treat temporary digital copies as reproductions).

[11] *Cartoon Network LP v. CSC Holdings, Inc.*, 536 F.3d 121, 127-30 (2d Cir. 2008), cert. denied sub nom. *Cable News Network, Inc. v. CSC Holdings, Inc.*, 129 S. Ct. 2890 (2009).

[12] See, e.g., *United States v. Moghadam*, 175 F.3d 1269 (11th Cir. 1999), *cert. denied*, 529 U.S. 1036 (2000) (concluding that § 2319A was properly enacted pursuant to the Commerce Clause); *Kiss Catalog, Ltd. v. Passport International Prod., Inc.*, 405 F. Supp. 2d 1169 (D.C. Cal. 2005) (concluding that § 1101 was properly enacted pursuant to the Commerce Clause).

[13] *United States v. Martignon*, 492 F.3d 140, 151 (2d Cir. 2007).

[14] The weight of scholarly authority appears to be in accord with the district court decision, which held that the provision was invalid under the Copyright Clause, since it granted rights to performers that were unlimited in time and, also, invalid under the Commerce Clause given the provision's conflict with the duration limitation imposed by the Copyright Clause. See, e.g., Richard B. Graves III, *Globalization, Treaty Powers, and the Limits of the Intellectual Property Clause*, 50 J. COPYRIGHT SOC'Y U.S.A. 199, 218 n.119 (2003) (citing several articles supporting the general principle that Congress cannot bypass the restrictions in the Copyright Clause by legislating pursuant to another clause).

requirements of the Copyright and Patent Clause of the Constitution has long been debated and remains unresolved.[15]

---

[15] For the argument that Congress cannot use the Commerce Clause to create intellectual property rights that are inconsistent with Art. I, Sec. 8, cl. 8, see Malla Pollack, *Unconstitutional Incontestability? The Intersection of the Intellectual Property and Commerce Clauses of the Constitution: Beyond a Critique of* Shakespeare Co. V. Silstar Corp., 18 SEATTLE U. L. REV. 259 (1995); for a contrary view, see Thomas B. Nachbar, *Intellectual Property and Constitutional Norms,* 104 COLUM. L. REV. 272 (2004). For another interesting discussion of the issue, see Paul J. Heald & Suzanna Sherry, *Implied Limits on the Legislative Power: The Intellectual Property Clause as an Absolute Constraint on Congress,* 2000 U. ILL. L. REV. 1119, 1192 n.515 (2000).

ASSIGNMENT 9—THE RECIPIENTS OF COPYRIGHT'S INCENTIVES

ADD TO END OF NOTE FOLLOWING *TASINI* OPINION ON PAGE 341:

The dispute continues. In 2007, the Court of Appeals for the Second Circuit held that the district court lacked jurisdiction under § 411(a) of the Copyright Act to approve a settlement of a class action brought by affected freelancers because the vast majority of claims in the case involved unregistered works. The statute makes registration a prerequisite for filing an infringement action. *In re Literary Works in Electronic Databases Copyright Litigation*, 509 F.3d 116 (2d Cir. 2007), rev'd sub nom. *Reed Elsevier, Inc. v. Muchnick*, 130 S. Ct. 1237, 1248-49 (2010). As noted in Assignment 6, the Supreme Court reversed, concluding instead that registration was part of the cause of action for infringement, not a jurisdictional requirement, and the case was remanded to the court below.

ASSIGNMENT 10—SCOPE OF COPYRIGHT HOLDER'S RIGHTS: INFRINGEMENT

ADD THE FOLLOWING TO THE END OF NOTE 6 ON PAGE 407:

In a recent ruling by the Second Circuit, the result in MAI Systems was distinguished, and possibly called into doubt. Cablevision, a cable systems operator, began in 2006 offering its subscribers remote storage capability. The subscriber could select programs to be recorded in somewhat the same way they could be on a home digital video recorder, but on equipment resident with the company. The recorded shows could then be called up by the subscriber for viewing at a later time.[1] One step in making the recordings for viewers was to create buffer copies, in short segments, of the entire program, each brief segment overriding and erasing the next. The duration of each part of the total was approximately a tenth of a second, but was of sufficient duration to enable the making of the persistent copy that was stored and made available to the individual subscriber. The Court held that these successive buffer copies were of insufficient duration to constitute a "fixation" of the work.

---

[1] *Cartoon Network LP v. CSC Holdings, Inc.*, 536 F.3d 121 (2d Cir. 2008), cert. denied sub nom. *Cable News Network, Inc. v. CSC Holdings, Inc.*, 129 S. Ct. 2890 (2009).

ASSIGNMENT 11—PUBLIC ACCESS CONSIDERATIONS AND THE FAIR USE DOCTRINE

ADD THE FOLLOWING CASE TO THE *SONY* OPINION ON PAGE 429:

Metro-Goldwyn-Mayer Studios, Inc., v. Grokster, Ltd.
Supreme Court of the United States, 2005.
545 U.S. 913.

■ JUSTICE SOUTER delivered the opinion of the Court.

The question is under what circumstances the distributor of a product capable of both lawful and unlawful use is liable for acts of copyright infringement by third parties using the product. We hold that one who distributes a device with the object of promoting its use to infringe copyright, as shown by clear expression or other affirmative steps taken to foster infringement, is liable for the resulting acts of infringement by third parties.

I
A.

Respondents, Grokster, Ltd., and StreamCast Networks, Inc., defendants in the trial court, distribute free software products that allow computer users to share electronic files through peer-to-peer networks, so called because users' computers communicate directly with each other, not through central servers. The advantage of peer-to-peer networks over information networks of other types shows up in their substantial and growing popularity. Because they need no central computer server to mediate the exchange of information or files among users, the high-bandwidth communications capacity for a server may be dispensed with, and the need for costly server storage space is eliminated. Since copies of a file (particularly a popular one) are available on many users' computers, file requests and retrievals may be faster than on other types of networks, and since file exchanges do not travel through a server, communications can take place between any computers that remain connected to the

49

network without risk that a glitch in the server will disable the network in its entirety. Given these benefits in security, cost, and efficiency, peer-to-peer networks are employed to store and distribute electronic files by universities, government agencies, corporations, and libraries, among others.

Other users of peer-to-peer networks include individual recipients of Grokster's and StreamCast's software, and although the networks that they enjoy through using the software can be used to share any type of digital file, they have prominently employed those networks in sharing copyrighted music and video files without authorization. A group of copyright holders (MGM for short, but including motion picture studios, recording companies, songwriters, and music publishers) sued Grokster and StreamCast for their users' copyright infringements, alleging that they knowingly and intentionally distributed their software to enable users to reproduce and distribute the copyrighted works in violation of the Copyright Act, 17 U.S.C. § 101 *et seq.* (2000 ed. and Supp. II). MGM sought damages and an injunction.

Discovery during the litigation revealed the way the software worked, the business aims of each defendant company, and the predilections of the users. Grokster's eponymous software employs what is known as FastTrack technology, a protocol developed by others and licensed to Grokster. StreamCast distributes a very similar product except that its software, called Morpheus, relies on what is known as Gnutella technology. A user who downloads and installs either software possesses the protocol to send requests for files directly to the computers of others using software compatible with FastTrack or Gnutella. On the FastTrack network opened by the Grokster software, the user's request goes to a computer given an indexing capacity by the software and designated a supernode, or to some other computer with comparable power and capacity to collect temporary indexes of the files available on the computers of users connected to it. The supernode (or indexing computer) searches its own index and may communicate the search request to other supernodes. If the file is found, the supernode discloses its location to the computer requesting it, and the requesting user can download the file directly from the computer located. The copied file is placed in a designated sharing folder on the requesting user's computer, where it is available for other users to download in turn, along with any other file in that folder.

In the Gnutella network made available by Morpheus, the process is mostly the same, except that in some versions of the Gnutella protocol there are no supernodes. In these versions, peer computers using the protocol communicate directly with each other. When a user enters a search request into the Morpheus software, it sends the request to computers connected with it, which in turn pass the request along to other connected peers. The search results are communicated to the requesting computer, and the user can download desired files directly from peers' computers. As this description indicates, Grokster and StreamCast use no servers to intercept the content of the search requests or to mediate the file transfers conducted by users of the software, there being no central point through which the substance of the communications passes in either direction.

Although Grokster and StreamCast do not therefore know when particular files are copied, a few searches using their software would show what is available on the networks the software reaches. MGM commissioned a statistician to conduct a systematic search, and his study showed that nearly 90% of the files available for download on the FastTrack system were copyrighted works. Grokster and StreamCast dispute this figure, raising methodological problems and arguing that free copying even of copyrighted works may be authorized by the rightholders. They also argue that potential noninfringing uses of their software are significant in kind, even if infrequent in practice.

MGM's evidence gives reason to think that the vast majority of users' downloads are acts of infringement, and because well over 100 million copies of the software in question are known to have been downloaded, and billions of files are shared across the FastTrack and Gnutella networks each month, the probable scope of copyright infringement is staggering.

Grokster and StreamCast concede the infringement in most downloads, and it is uncontested that they are aware that users employ their software primarily to download copyrighted files, even if the decentralized FastTrack and Gnutella networks fail to reveal which files are being copied, and when. From time to time, moreover, the companies have learned about their users' infringement directly, as from users who have sent e-mail to each company with questions about playing copyrighted movies they had downloaded, to whom the companies have responded with guidance. And MGM notified the companies of 8 million copyrighted files that could be obtained using their software.

Grokster and StreamCast are not, however, merely passive recipients of information about infringing use. The record is replete with evidence that from the moment Grokster and StreamCast began to distribute their free software, each one clearly voiced the objective that recipients use it to download copyrighted works, and each took active steps to encourage infringement.

After the notorious file-sharing service, Napster, was sued by copyright holders for facilitation of copyright infringement, *A & M Records, Inc.* v. *Napster, Inc.,* 114 F. Supp. 2d 896 (ND Cal. 2000), aff'd in part, rev'd in part, 239 F.3d 1004 (CA9 2001), StreamCast gave away a software program of a kind known as OpenNap, designed as compatible with the Napster program and open to Napster users for downloading files from other Napster and OpenNap users' computers.

StreamCast monitored both the number of users downloading its OpenNap program and the number of music files they downloaded. It also used the resulting OpenNap network to distribute copies of the Morpheus software and to encourage users to adopt it. Internal company documents indicate that StreamCast hoped to attract large numbers of former Napster users if that company was shut down by court order or otherwise, and that StreamCast planned to be the next Napster. A kit developed by StreamCast to be delivered to advertisers, for example, contained press articles about StreamCast's potential to capture former Napster users, and it introduced itself to some potential advertisers as a company "which is similar to what Napster was." It broadcast banner advertisements to users of other Napster-compatible software, urging them to adopt its OpenNap.

The evidence that Grokster sought to capture the market of former Napster users is sparser but revealing, for Grokster launched its own OpenNap system called Swaptor and inserted digital codes into its Web site so that computer users using Web search engines to look for "Napster" or "free filesharing" would be directed to the Grokster Web site, where they could download the Grokster software. And Grokster's name is an apparent derivative of Napster.

StreamCast's executives monitored the number of songs by certain commercial artists available on their networks, and an internal communication indicates they aimed to have a larger number of copyrighted songs available on their networks than other file-sharing networks. The point, of course, would be to attract users of a mind to infringe, just as it would be with their promotional materials developed showing copyrighted songs as examples of the kinds of files available through Morpheus.

In addition to this evidence of express promotion, marketing, and intent to promote further, the business models employed by Grokster and StreamCast confirm that their principal object was use of their software to download copyrighted works. Grokster and StreamCast receive no revenue from users, who obtain the software itself for nothing. Instead, both companies generate income by selling advertising space, and they stream the advertising to Grokster and Morpheus users while they are employing the programs. As the number of users of each program increases, advertising opportunities become worth more.

Finally, there is no evidence that either company made an effort to filter copyrighted material from users' downloads or otherwise impedes the sharing of copyrighted files. Although Grokster appears to have sent e-mails warning users about infringing content when it received threatening notice from the copyright holders, it never blocked anyone from continuing to use its software to share copyrighted files. StreamCast not only rejected another company's offer of help to monitor infringement, but blocked the Internet Protocol addresses of entities it believed were trying to engage in such monitoring on its networks.

B.

After discovery, the parties on each side of the case cross-moved for summary judgment. The District Court limited its consideration to the asserted liability of Grokster and StreamCast for distributing the current versions of their software, leaving aside whether either was liable "for damages arising from *past* versions of their software, or from other past activities." 259 F. Supp. 2d 1029, 1033 (CD Cal. 2003). The District Court held that those who used the Grokster and Morpheus software to download copyrighted media files directly infringed MGM's copyrights, a conclusion not contested on appeal, but the court nonetheless granted summary judgment in favor of Grokster and StreamCast as to any liability arising from distribution of the then current versions of their software. Distributing that software gave rise to no liability in the court's view, because its use did not provide the distributors with actual knowledge of specific acts of infringement.

The Court of Appeals affirmed. 380 F.3d 1154 (CA9 2004). In the court's analysis, a defendant was liable as a contributory infringer when it had knowledge of direct infringement and materially contributed to the infringement. But the court read *Sony Corp. of America* v. *Universal City Studios, Inc.*, 464 U.S. 417, 78 L. Ed. 2d 574, 104 S. Ct. 774 (1984), as holding that distribution of a commercial product capable of substantial noninfringing uses could not give rise to contributory liability for infringement unless the distributor had actual knowledge of specific instances of infringement and failed to act on that knowledge. The fact that the software was capable of substantial noninfringing uses in the Ninth Circuit's view meant that Grokster and StreamCast were not liable, because they had no such actual knowledge, owing to the decentralized architecture of their software. The court also held that Grokster and StreamCast did not materially contribute to their users' infringement because it was the users themselves who searched for, retrieved, and stored the infringing files, with no involvement by the defendants beyond providing the software in the first place.

The Ninth Circuit also considered whether Grokster and StreamCast could be liable under a theory of vicarious infringement. The court held against liability because the defendants did not monitor or control the use of the software, had no agreed-upon right or current ability to supervise its use, and had no independent duty to police infringement. We granted certiorari.

II
A.

MGM and many of the *amici* fault the Court of Appeals's holding for upsetting a sound balance between the respective values of supporting creative pursuits through copyright protection and promoting innovation in new communication technologies by limiting the incidence of liability for copyright infringement. The more artistic protection is favored, the more technological innovation may be discouraged; the administration of copyright law is an exercise in managing the trade-off.

The tension between the two values is the subject of this case, with its claim that digital distribution of copyrighted material threatens copyright holders as never before, because every copy is identical to the original, copying is easy, and many people (especially the young) use file-sharing software to download copyrighted works. This very breadth of the software's use may well draw the public directly into the debate over copyright policy, and the indications are that the ease of copying songs or movies using software like Grokster's and Napster's is fostering disdain for copyright protection. As the case has been presented to us, these fears are said to be offset by the different concern that imposing liability, not only on infringers but on distributors of software based on its potential for unlawful use, could limit further development of beneficial technologies.

The argument for imposing indirect liability in this case is, however, a powerful one, given the number of infringing downloads that occur every day using StreamCast's and Grokster's software. When a widely shared service or product is used to commit infringement, it may be impossible to enforce rights in the protected work effectively against all direct infringers, the only practical alternative being to go against the distributor of the copying device for secondary liability on a theory of contributory or vicarious infringement. *See In re Aimster Copyright Litigation*, 334 F.3d 643, 645-646 (CA7 2003).

One infringes contributorily by intentionally inducing or encouraging direct infringement, and infringes vicariously by profiting from direct infringement while declining to exercise a right to stop or limit it.[a] Although "the Copyright Act does not expressly render anyone liable for infringement committed by another," these doctrines of secondary liability emerged from common law principles and are well established in the law.

B.

Despite the currency of these principles of secondary liability, this Court has dealt with secondary copyright infringement in only one recent

---

[a] Because we resolve the case based on an inducement theory, there is no need to analyze separately MGM's vicarious liability theory.

case, and because MGM has tailored its principal claim to our opinion there, a look at our earlier holding is in order. In *Sony Corp.* v. *Universal City Studios, supra,* this Court addressed a claim that secondary liability for infringement can arise from the very distribution of a commercial product.

There, the product, novel at the time, was what we know today as the videocassette recorder or VCR. [W]ith no evidence of stated or indicated intent to promote infringing uses, the only conceivable basis for imposing liability was on a theory of contributory infringement arising from its sale of VCRs to consumers with knowledge that some would use them to infringe. But because the VCR was "capable of commercially significant noninfringing uses," we held the manufacturer could not be faulted solely on the basis of its distribution.

In sum, where an article is "good for nothing else" but infringement, there is no legitimate public interest in its unlicensed availability, and there is no injustice in presuming or imputing an intent to infringe. Conversely, the doctrine absolves the equivocal conduct of selling an item with substantial lawful as well as unlawful uses, and limits liability to instances of more acute fault than the mere understanding that some of one's products will be misused. It leaves breathing room for innovation and a vigorous commerce.

The parties and many of the *amici* in this case think the key to resolving it is the *Sony* rule and, in particular, what it means for a product to be "capable of commercially significant noninfringing uses." *Sony Corp.* v. *Universal City Studios, supra,* at 442, 78 L. Ed. 2d 574, 104 S. Ct. 774. MGM advances the argument that granting summary judgment to Grokster and StreamCast as to their current activities gave too much weight to the value of innovative technology, and too little to the copyrights infringed by users of their software, given that 90% of works available on one of the networks was shown to be copyrighted. Assuming the remaining 10% to be its noninfringing use, MGM says this should not qualify as "substantial," and the Court should quantify Sony to the extent of holding that a product used "principally" for infringement does not qualify. Grokster and StreamCast reply by citing evidence that their software can be used to reproduce public domain works, and they point to copyright holders who actually encourage copying. Even if infringement is

56

the principal practice with their software today, they argue, the noninfringing uses are significant and will grow.

We agree with MGM that the Court of Appeals misapplied *Sony*, which it read as limiting secondary liability quite beyond the circumstances to which the case applied. *Sony* barred secondary liability based on presuming or imputing intent to cause infringement solely from the design or distribution of a product capable of substantial lawful use, which the distributor knows is in fact used for infringement. The Ninth Circuit has read *Sony*'s limitation to mean that whenever a product is capable of substantial lawful use, the producer can never be held contributorily liable for third parties' infringing use of it; it read the rule as being this broad, even when an actual purpose to cause infringing use is shown by evidence independent of design and distribution of the product, unless the distributors had "specific knowledge of infringement at a time at which they contributed to the infringement, and failed to act upon that information." 380 F.3d at 1162 (internal quotation marks and alterations omitted). Because the Circuit found the StreamCast and Grokster software capable of substantial lawful use, it concluded on the basis of its reading of *Sony* that neither company could be held liable, since there was no showing that their software, being without any central server, afforded them knowledge of specific unlawful uses.

This view of *Sony*, however, was error, converting the case from one about liability resting on imputed intent to one about liability on any theory. Because *Sony* did not displace other theories of secondary liability, and because we find below that it was error to grant summary judgment to the companies on MGM's inducement claim, we do not revisit *Sony* further, as MGM requests, to add a more quantified description of the point of balance between protection and commerce when liability rests solely on distribution with knowledge that unlawful use will occur. It is enough to note that the Ninth Circuit's judgment rested on an erroneous understanding of *Sony* and to leave further consideration of the *Sony* rule for a day when that may be required.

C.

[N]othing in *Sony* requires courts to ignore evidence of intent if there is such evidence, and the case was never meant to foreclose rules of fault-based liability derived from the common law. Thus, where evidence goes beyond a product's characteristics or the knowledge that it may be put to infringing uses, and shows statements or actions directed to promoting infringement, *Sony*'s staple-article rule will not preclude liability.

The classic case of direct evidence of unlawful purpose occurs when one induces commission of infringement by another, or "entices or persuades another" to infringe, Black's Law Dictionary 790 (8th ed. 2004), as by advertising. Thus at common law a copyright or patent defendant who "not only expected but invoked [infringing use] by advertisement" was liable for infringement "on principles recognized in every part of the law." *Kalem Co.* v. *Harper Brothers*, 222 U.S., at 62-63.

The rule on inducement of infringement as developed in the early cases is no different today. Evidence of "active steps . . . taken to encourage direct infringement," *Oak Industries, Inc.* v. *Zenith Electronics Corp.*, 697 F. Supp. 988, 992 (ND Ill. 1988), such as advertising an infringing use or instructing how to engage in an infringing use, show an affirmative intent that the product be used to infringe, and a showing that infringement was encouraged overcomes the law's reluctance to find liability when a defendant merely sells a commercial product suitable for some lawful use.

For the same reasons that *Sony* took the staple-article doctrine of patent law as a model for its copyright safe-harbor rule, the inducement rule, too, is a sensible one for copyright. We adopt it here, holding that one who distributes a device with the object of promoting its use to infringe copyright, as shown by clear expression or other affirmative steps taken to foster infringement, is liable for the resulting acts of infringement by third parties. We are, of course, mindful of the need to keep from trenching on regular commerce or discouraging the development of technologies with lawful and unlawful potential. Accordingly, just as *Sony* did not find intentional inducement despite the knowledge of the VCR manufacturer that its device could be used to infringe, mere knowledge of infringing potential or of actual infringing uses would not be enough here to subject a distributor to liability. Nor would ordinary acts incident to product distribution, such as offering customers technical support or product updates, support liability in themselves. The inducement rule, instead, premises liability on purposeful, culpable expression and conduct, and thus does nothing to compromise legitimate commerce or discourage innovation having a lawful promise.

III

A.

The only apparent question about treating MGM's evidence as sufficient to withstand summary judgment under the theory of inducement goes to the need on MGM's part to adduce evidence that StreamCast and Grokster communicated an inducing message to their software users.

Three features of this evidence of intent are particularly notable. First, Grokster and StreamCast's efforts to supply services to former Napster users, deprived of a mechanism to copy and distribute what were overwhelmingly infringing files, indicate a principal, if not exclusive, intent on the part of each to bring about infringement.

Second, this evidence of unlawful objective is given added significance by MGM's showing that neither company attempted to develop filtering tools or other mechanisms to diminish the infringing activity using their software. [W]e think this evidence underscores Grokster's and StreamCast's intentional facilitation of their users' infringement.

Third, there is a further complement to the direct evidence of unlawful objective. StreamCast and Grokster make money by selling advertising space, by directing ads to the screens of computers employing their software. As the record shows, the more the software is used, the more ads are sent out and the greater the advertising revenue becomes. Since the extent of the software's use determines the gain to the distributors, the commercial sense of their enterprise turns on high-volume use, which the record shows is infringing. This evidence alone would not justify an inference of unlawful intent, but viewed in the context of the entire record its import is clear.

The unlawful objective is unmistakable.

B.

In addition to intent to bring about infringement and distribution of a device suitable for infringing use, the inducement theory of course

59

requires evidence of actual infringement by recipients of the device, the software in this case. As the account of the facts indicates, there is evidence of infringement on a gigantic scale, and there is no serious issue of the adequacy of MGM's showing on this point in order to survive the companies' summary judgment requests.

* * *

In sum, this case is significantly different from *Sony* and reliance on that case to rule in favor of StreamCast and Grokster was error. *Sony* dealt with a claim of liability based solely on distributing a product with alternative lawful and unlawful uses, with knowledge that some users would follow the unlawful course.

MGM's evidence in this case most obviously addresses a different basis of liability for distributing a product open to alternative uses. If liability for inducing infringement is ultimately found, it will not be on the basis of presuming or imputing fault, but from inferring a patently illegal objective from statements and actions showing what that objective was.

There is substantial evidence in MGM's favor on all elements of inducement, and summary judgment in favor of Grokster and StreamCast was error. On remand, reconsideration of MGM's motion for summary judgment will be in order.

The judgment of the Court of Appeals is vacated, and the case is remanded for further proceedings consistent with this opinion.

It is so ordered.

■ JUSTICE GINSBURG, with whom THE CHIEF JUSTICE and JUSTICE KENNEDY join, concurring

I concur in the Court's decision, which vacates in full the judgment of the Court of Appeals for the Ninth Circuit, and write separately to clarify why I conclude that the Court of Appeals misperceived, and hence misapplied, our holding in *Sony Corp. of America* v. *Universal City Studios, Inc.,* 464 U.S. 417, 78 L. Ed. 2d 574, 104 S. Ct. 774 (1984).

"The staple article of commerce doctrine" applied to copyright, the [Sony] Court stated, "must strike a balance between a copyright holder's legitimate demand for effective—not merely symbolic—protection of the statutory monopoly, and the rights of others freely to engage in substantially unrelated areas of commerce." *Sony*, 464 U.S., at 442, 78 L. Ed. 2d 574, 104 S. Ct. 774. "Accordingly," the Court held, "the sale of copying equipment, like the sale of other articles of commerce, does not constitute contributory infringement if the product is widely used for legitimate, unobjectionable purposes. Indeed, it need merely be capable of substantial noninfringing uses." *Ibid.* Thus, to resolve the *Sony* case, the Court explained, it had to determine "whether the Betamax is capable of commercially significant noninfringing uses." *Ibid.*

There was no need in *Sony* to "give precise content to the question of how much [actual or potential] use is commercially significant." *Ibid.*[b] Further development was left for later days and cases.

The Ninth Circuit went astray when that court granted summary judgment to Grokster and StreamCast on the charge of contributory liability based on distribution of their software products. Although it acknowledged MGM's assertion that "the vast majority of the software use

---

[b] Justice Breyer finds in *Sony Corp. of America* v. *Universal City Studios, Inc.,* 464 U.S. 417, 78 L. Ed. 2d 574, 104 S. Ct. 774 (1984), a "clear" rule permitting contributory liability for copyright infringement based on distribution of a product only when the product "will be used *almost exclusively* to infringe copyrights." *Post*, at 9-10. But cf. *Sony*, 464 U.S., at 442, 78 L. Ed. 2d 574, 104 S. Ct. 774 (recognizing "copyright holder's legitimate demand for effective—not merely symbolic—protection"). *Sony*, as I read it, contains no clear, near-exclusivity test. Nor have Courts of Appeals unanimously recognized Justice Breyer's clear rule. Compare *A&M Records, Inc.* v. *Napster, Inc.*, 239 F.3d 1004, 1021 (CA9 2001) ("Evidence of actual knowledge of specific acts of infringement is required to hold a computer system operator liable for contributory copyright infringement."), with *In re Aimster Copyright Litigation*, 334 F.3d 643, 649-650 (CA7 2003) ("When a supplier is offering a product or service that has noninfringing as well as infringing uses, some estimate of the respective magnitudes of these uses is necessary for a finding of contributory infringement. . . . But the balancing of costs and benefits is necessary only in a case in which substantial noninfringing uses, present or prospective, are demonstrated."). See also *Matthew Bender & Co. v. West Publ. Co.*, 158 F.3d 693, 707 (CA2 1998) ("The Supreme Court applied [the *Sony*] test to prevent copyright holders from leveraging the copyrights in their original work to control distribution of . . . products that might be used incidentally for infringement, but that had substantial noninfringing uses . . . . The same rationale applies here [to products] that have substantial, predominant and noninfringing uses as tools for research and citation."). All Members of the Court agree, moreover, that "the Court of Appeals misapplied *Sony*," at least to the extent it read that decision to limit "secondary liability" to a hardly-ever category, "quite beyond the circumstances to which the case applied." *Ante*, at 16.

is for copyright infringement," the court concluded that Grokster's and StreamCast's proffered evidence met *Sony*'s requirement that "a product need only be *capable* of substantial noninfringing uses." 380 F.3d at 1162.

This case differs markedly from *Sony*. Here, there has been no finding of any fair use and little beyond anecdotal evidence of noninfringing uses.

In sum, when the record in this case was developed, there was evidence that Grokster's and StreamCast's products were, and had been for some time, overwhelmingly used to infringe, and that this infringement was the overwhelming source of revenue from the products. Fairly appraised, the evidence was insufficient to demonstrate, beyond genuine debate, a reasonable prospect that substantial or commercially significant noninfringing uses were likely to develop over time. On this record, the District Court should not have ruled dispositively on the contributory infringement charge by granting summary judgment to Grokster and StreamCast.

If, on remand, the case is not resolved on summary judgment in favor of MGM based on Grokster and StreamCast actively inducing infringement, the Court of Appeals, I would emphasize, should reconsider, on a fuller record, its interpretation of *Sony*'s product distribution holding.

■ JUSTICE BREYER, with whom JUSTICE STEVENS and JUSTICE O'CONNOR join, concurring.

I agree with the Court that the distributor of a dual-use technology may be liable for the infringing activities of third parties where he or she actively seeks to advance the infringement. I further agree that, in light of our holding today, we need not now "revisit" *Sony Corp. of America* v. *Universal City Studios, Inc.*, 464 U.S. 417, 78 L. Ed. 2d 574, 104 S. Ct. 774 (1984). Other Members of the Court, however, take up the *Sony* question: whether Grokster's product is "capable of 'substantial' or 'commercially significant' noninfringing uses." (GINSBURG, J., concurring) (quoting *Sony, supra*, at 442, 78 L. Ed. 2d 574, 104 S. Ct. 774). And they answer that question by stating that the Court of Appeals was wrong when it granted summary judgment on the issue in Grokster's favor. I write to explain why I disagree with them on this matter.

I

The Court's opinion in *Sony* and the record evidence (as described and analyzed in the many briefs before us) together convince me that the Court of Appeals' conclusion has adequate legal support.

[T]he evidence now before us shows that Grokster passes *Sony*'s test—that is, whether the company's product is capable of substantial or commercially significant noninfringing uses. *Id.*, at 442, 78 L. Ed. 2d 574, 104 S. Ct. 774.

II

The real question here, I believe, is not whether the record evidence satisfies *Sony*. As I have interpreted the standard set forth in that case, it does.

Instead, the real question is whether we should modify the *Sony* standard, as MGM requests, or interpret *Sony* more strictly, as I believe JUSTICE GINSBURG's approach would do in practice.

[T]o determine whether modification, or a strict interpretation, of *Sony* is needed, I would ask whether MGM has shown that *Sony* incorrectly balanced copyright and new-technology interests. In particular: (1) Has *Sony* (as I interpret it) worked to protect new technology? (2) If so, would modification or strict interpretation significantly weaken that protection? (3) If so, would new or necessary copyright-related benefits outweigh any such weakening?

A.

The first question is the easiest to answer. *Sony*'s rule, as I interpret it, has provided entrepreneurs with needed assurance that they will be shielded from copyright liability as they bring valuable new technologies to market.

Sony's rule is clear. That clarity allows those who develop new products that are capable of substantial noninfringing uses to know, *ex ante*, that distribution of their product will not yield massive monetary liability.

Sony's rule is strongly technology protecting. The rule deliberately makes it difficult for courts to find secondary liability where new technology is at issue. It establishes that the law will not impose copyright liability upon the distributors of dual-use technologies (who do not themselves engage in unauthorized copying) unless the product in question will be used *almost exclusively* to infringe copyrights (or unless they actively induce infringements as we today describe).

Sony's rule is forward looking. It does not confine its scope to a static snapshot of a product's current uses (thereby threatening technologies that have undeveloped future markets). Rather, as the VCR example makes clear, a product's market can evolve dramatically over time.

Given the nature of the *Sony* rule, it is not surprising that in the last 20 years, there have been relatively few contributory infringement suits—based on a product distribution theory—brought against technology providers (a small handful of federal appellate court cases and perhaps fewer than two dozen District Court cases in the last 20 years). I have found nothing in the briefs or the record that shows that *Sony* has failed to achieve its innovation-protecting objective.

B.

The second, more difficult, question is whether a modified *Sony* rule (or a strict interpretation) would significantly weaken the law's ability to protect new technology. JUSTICE GINSBURG's approach would require defendants to produce considerably more concrete evidence—more than was presented here—to earn *Sony*'s shelter. That heavier evidentiary demand, and especially the more dramatic (case-by-case balancing) modifications that MGM and the Government seek, would, I believe, undercut the protection that *Sony* now offers.

To require defendants to provide, for example, detailed evidence—say business plans, profitability estimates, projected technological modifications, and so forth—would doubtless make life easier for copyrightholder plaintiffs. But it would simultaneously increase the legal uncertainty that surrounds the creation or development of a new technology capable of being put to infringing uses.

C.

The third question—whether a positive copyright impact would outweigh any technology-related loss—I find the most difficult of the three. I do not doubt that a more intrusive *Sony* test would generally provide greater revenue security for copyright holders. But it is harder to conclude that the gains on the copyright swings would exceed the losses on the technology roundabouts.

Will an unmodified *Sony* lead to a significant diminution in the amount or quality of creative work produced? Since copyright's basic objective is creation and its revenue objectives but a means to that end, this is the underlying copyright question.

Unauthorized copying likely diminishes industry revenue, though it is not clear by how much. The extent to which related production has actually and resultingly declined remains uncertain, though there is good reason to believe that the decline, if any, is not substantial.

More importantly, copyright holders at least potentially have other tools available to reduce piracy and to abate whatever threat it poses to creative production. As today's opinion makes clear, a copyright holder may proceed against a technology provider where a provable specific intent to infringe (of the kind the Court describes) is present. Services like Grokster may well be liable under an inducement theory.

In addition, a copyright holder has always had the legal authority to bring a traditional infringement suit against one who wrongfully copies.

Further, copyright holders may develop new technological devices that will help curb unlawful infringement.

At the same time, advances in technology have discouraged unlawful copying by making *lawful* copying cheaper and easier to achieve. Consequently, many consumers initially attracted to the convenience and flexibility of services like Grokster are now migrating to lawful paid services (services with copying permission) where they can enjoy at little

65

cost even greater convenience and flexibility without engaging in unlawful swapping.

Finally, as *Sony* recognized, the legislative option remains available. Courts are less well suited than Congress to the task of "accommodating fully the varied permutations of competing interests that are inevitably implicated by such new technology." *Sony*, 464 U.S., at 431.

I do not know whether these developments and similar alternatives will prove sufficient, but I am reasonably certain that, given their existence, a strong demonstrated need for modifying *Sony* (or for interpreting *Sony*'s standard more strictly) has not yet been shown. That fact, along with the added risks that modification (or strict interpretation) would impose upon technological innovation, leads me to the conclusion that we should maintain *Sony*, reading its standard as I have read it. As so read, it requires affirmance of the Ninth Circuit's determination of the relevant aspects of the *Sony* question.

For these reasons, I disagree with JUSTICE GINSBURG, but I agree with the Court and join its opinion.

Editor's Note: On remand, the district court granted the plaintiffs summary judgment against StreamCast based on the inducement claim. Settlement agreements were reached with the other defendants. *Metro-Goldwyn-Mayer Studios, Inc. v. Grokster, Ltd.*[1]

---

[1] 454 F. Supp. 2d 966, 971 (C.D. Cal. 2006).

THE FOLLOWING CASE MAY BE ADDED IN LIEU OF, OR IN ADDITION TO, *A & M RECORDS, INC. v. NAPSTER, INC.* **ON PAGE 444:**

Perfect 10, Inc. v. Amazon.com, Inc.

United States Court of Appeals, Ninth Circuit, 2007.
508 F.3d 1146.

■ Ικυτα, Circuit Judge

In this appeal, we consider a copyright owner's efforts to stop an Internet search engine from facilitating access to infringing images. Perfect 10, Inc. sued Google, Inc., for infringing Perfect 10's copyrighted photographs of nude models, among other claims. The district court preliminarily enjoined Google from creating and publicly displaying thumbnail versions of Perfect 10's images, *Perfect 10 v. Google, Inc.,* 416 F. Supp. 2d 828 (C.D. Cal. 2006), but did not enjoin Google from linking to third-party websites that display infringing full-size versions of Perfect 10's images. Perfect 10 and Google both appeal the district court's order.

The district court handled this complex case in a particularly thoughtful and skillful manner. Nonetheless, the district court erred on certain issues, as we will further explain below. We affirm in part, reverse in part, and remand.

Background

Google's computers, along with millions of others, are connected to networks known collectively as the "Internet." "The Internet is a world-wide network of networks . . . all sharing a common communications technology." *Religious Tech. Ctr. v. Netcom On-Line Commc'n Servs., Inc.,* 923 F. Supp. 1231, 1238 n.1 (N.D. Cal. 1995). Computer owners can provide information stored on their computers to other users connected to the Internet through a medium called a webpage. A webpage consists of text interspersed with instructions written in Hypertext Markup Language ("HTML") that is stored in a computer. No images are stored on a webpage; rather, the HTML instructions on the webpage provide an address for where the images are stored, whether in the webpage publisher's computer or some other computer. In general, webpages are publicly available and can be accessed by computers connected to the Internet through the use of a web browser.

Google operates a search engine, a software program that automatically accesses thousands of websites (collections of webpages) and indexes them within a database stored on Google's computers. When a Google user accesses the Google website and types in a search query, Google's software searches its database for websites responsive to that search query. Google then sends relevant information from its index of websites to the user's computer. Google's search engines can provide results in the form of text, images, or videos.

The Google search engine that provides responses in the form of images is called "Google Image Search." In response to a search query, Google Image Search identifies text in its database responsive to the query and then communicates to users the images associated with the relevant text. Google's software cannot recognize and index the images themselves. Google Image Search provides search results as a webpage of small images called "thumbnails," which are stored in Google's servers. The thumbnail images are reduced, lower-resolution versions of full-sized images stored on third-party computers.

When a user clicks on a thumbnail image, the user's browser program interprets HTML instructions on Google's webpage. These HTML instructions direct the user's browser to cause a rectangular area (a "window") to appear on the user's computer screen. The window has two separate areas of information. The browser fills the top section of the screen with information from the Google webpage, including the thumbnail image and text. The HTML instructions also give the user's browser the address of the website publisher's computer that stores the full-size version of the thumbnail. By following the HTML instructions to access the third-party webpage, the user's browser connects to the website publisher's computer, downloads the full-size image, and makes the image appear at the bottom of the window on the user's screen. Google does not store the images that fill this lower part of the window and does not communicate the images to the user; Google simply provides HTML instructions directing a user's browser to access a third-party website. However, the top part of the window (containing the information from the Google webpage) appears to frame and comment on the bottom part of the window. Thus, the user's window appears to be filled with a single integrated presentation of the full-size image, but it is actually an image from a third-party website framed by information from Google's website. The process by which the webpage directs a user's browser to incorporate content from different computers into a single window is referred to as

68

"in-line linking." *Kelly v. Arriba Soft Corp.*, 336 F.3d 811, 816 (9th Cir. 2003). The term "framing" refers to the process by which information from one computer appears to frame and annotate the in-line linked content from another computer. *Perfect 10*, 416 F. Supp. 2d at 833-34.

Google also stores webpage content in its cache.[a] For each cached webpage, Google's cache contains the text of the webpage as it appeared at the time Google indexed the page, but does not store images from the webpage. *Id.* at 833. Google may provide a link to a cached webpage in response to a user's search query. However, Google's cache version of the webpage is not automatically updated when the webpage is revised by its owner. In other words, Google's cache copy could provide a user's browser with valid directions to an infringing image even though the updated webpage no longer includes that infringing image.

In addition to its search engine operations, Google generates revenue through a business program called "AdSense." Under this program, the owner of a website can register with Google to become an AdSense "partner." The website owner then places HTML instructions on its webpages that signal Google's server to place advertising on the webpages that is relevant to the webpages' content. Google's computer program selects the advertising automatically by means of an algorithm. AdSense participants agree to share the revenues that flow from such advertising with Google.

Perfect 10 markets and sells copyrighted images of nude models. Among other enterprises, it operates a subscription website on the Internet. Subscribers pay a monthly fee to view Perfect 10 images in a "members' area" of the site. Subscribers must use a password to log into the members' area. Google does not include these password-protected images from the members' area in Google's index or database. Perfect 10 has also licensed

---

[a] Generally, a "cache" is "a computer memory with very short access time used for storage of frequently or recently used instructions or data." *United States v. Ziegler*, 474 F.3d 1184, 1186 n.3 (9th Cir. 2007) (quoting MERRIAM-WEBSTER'S COLLEGIATE DICTIONARY 171 (11th ed. 2003)). There are two types of caches at issue in this case. A user's personal computer has an internal cache that saves copies of webpages and images that the user has recently viewed so that the user can more rapidly revisit these webpages and images. Google's computers also have a cache which serves a variety of purposes. Among other things, Google's cache saves copies of a large number of webpages so that Google's search engine can efficiently organize and index these webpages.

Fonestarz Media Limited to sell and distribute Perfect 10's reduced-size copyrighted images for download and use on cell phones.

Some website publishers republish Perfect 10's images on the Internet without authorization. Once this occurs, Google's search engine may automatically index the webpages containing these images and provide thumbnail versions of images in response to user inquiries. When a user clicks on the thumbnail image returned by Google's search engine, the user's browser accesses the third-party webpage and in-line links to the full-sized infringing image stored on the website publisher's computer. This image appears, in its original context, on the lower portion of the window on the user's computer screen framed by information from Google's webpage.

Procedural History. In May 2001, Perfect 10 began notifying Google that its thumbnail images and in-line linking to the full-size images infringed Perfect 10's copyright. Perfect 10 continued to send these notices through 2005.

Perfect 10 filed an action against Google that included copyright infringement claims. Perfect 10 sought a preliminary injunction to prevent Google from "copying, reproducing, distributing, publicly displaying, adapting or otherwise infringing, or contributing to the infringement" of Perfect 10's photographs; linking to websites that provide full-size infringing versions of Perfect 10's photographs; and infringing Perfect 10's username/password combinations."

Direct Infringement

The district court held that Perfect 10 was likely to prevail in its claim that Google violated Perfect 10's display right with respect to the infringing thumbnails. *Id.* at 844. However, the district court concluded that Perfect 10 was not likely to prevail on its claim that Google violated either Perfect 10's display or distribution right with respect to its full-size infringing images. *Id.* at 844-45.

A. Display Right.

We have not previously addressed the question when a computer displays a copyrighted work for purposes of *section 106(5).* The Copyright Act explains that "display" means "to show a copy of it, either directly or by means of a film, slide, television image, or any other device or process . . . ." 17 U.S.C. § 101.

A photographic image is a work that is "'fixed' in a tangible medium of expression," for purposes of the Copyright Act, when embodied (i.e., stored) in a computer's server (or hard disk, or other storage device). The image stored in the computer is the "copy" of the work for purposes of copyright law. The computer owner shows a copy "by means of a . . . device or process" when the owner uses the computer to fill the computer screen with the photographic image stored on that computer, or by communicating the stored image electronically to another person's computer. 17 U.S.C. § 101. In sum, based on the plain language of the statute, a person displays a photographic image by using a computer to fill a computer screen with a copy of the photographic image fixed in the computer's memory. There is no dispute that Google's computers store thumbnail versions of Perfect 10's copyrighted images and communicate copies of those thumbnails to Google's users. Therefore, Perfect 10 has made a prima facie case that Google's communication of its stored thumbnail images directly infringes Perfect 10's display right.

Google does not, however, display a copy of full-size infringing photographic images for purposes of the Copyright Act when Google frames in-line linked images that appear on a user's computer screen. Because Google's computers do not store the photographic images, Google does not have a copy of the images for purposes of the Copyright Act.

Instead of communicating a copy of the image, Google provides HTML instructions that direct a user's browser to a website publisher's computer that stores the full-size photographic image. Providing these HTML instructions is not equivalent to showing a copy. First, the HTML instructions are lines of text, not a photographic image. Second, HTML instructions do not themselves cause infringing images to appear on the user's computer screen. The HTML merely gives the address of the image to the user's browser. The browser then interacts with the computer that stores the infringing image. It is this interaction that causes an infringing image to appear on the user's computer screen. Google may facilitate the user's access to infringing images. However, such assistance raises only contributory liability issues.

Because Google's cache merely stores the text of webpages, our analysis of whether Google's search engine program potentially infringes Perfect 10's display and distribution rights is equally applicable to Google's cache. Perfect 10 is not likely to succeed in showing that a

71

cached webpage that in-line links to full-size infringing images violates such rights. For purposes of this analysis, it is irrelevant whether cache copies direct a user's browser to third-party images that are no longer available on the third party's website, because it is the website publisher's computer, rather than Google's computer, that stores and displays the infringing image.

Fair Use Defense. Because Perfect 10 has succeeded in showing it would prevail in its prima facie case that Google's thumbnail images infringe Perfect 10's display rights, the burden shifts to Google to show that it will likely succeed in establishing an affirmative defense. Google contends that its use of thumbnails is a fair use of the images and therefore does not constitute an infringement of Perfect 10's copyright. *See* 17 U.S.C. § 107.

In applying the fair use analysis in this case, we are guided by *Kelly v. Arriba Soft Corp.*, which considered substantially the same use of copyrighted photographic images as is at issue here. *See* 336 F.3d 811. In *Kelly*, a photographer brought a direct infringement claim against Arriba, the operator of an Internet search engine. The search engine provided thumbnail versions of the photographer's images in response to search queries. *Id.* at 815-16. We held that Arriba's use of thumbnail images was a fair use primarily based on the transformative nature of a search engine and its benefit to the public. *Id.* at 818-22. We also concluded that Arriba's use of the thumbnail images did not harm the photographer's market for his image. *Id.* at 821-22.

In this case, the district court determined that Google's use of thumbnails was not a fair use and distinguished *Kelly. Perfect 10,* 416 F. Supp. 2d at 845-51. We consider these distinctions in the context of the four-factor fair use analysis.

Purpose and character of the use. The central purpose of this inquiry is to determine whether and to what extent the new work is "transformative." *Campbell,* 510 U.S. at 579. A work is "transformative" when the new work does not "merely supersede the objects of the original creation" but rather "adds something new, with a further purpose or different character, altering the first with new expression, meaning, or message." *Id.* Conversely, if the new work "supersede[s] the use of the original," the use is likely not a fair use.

As noted in *Campbell*, a "transformative work" is one that alters the original work "with new expression, meaning, or message." *Campbell*, 510 U.S. at 579. "A use is considered transformative only where a defendant changes a plaintiff's copyrighted work or uses the plaintiff's copyrighted work in a different context such that the plaintiff's work is transformed into a new creation." *Wall Data*, 447 F.3d at 778.

Google's use of thumbnails is highly transformative. In *Kelly*, we concluded that Arriba's use of thumbnails was transformative because "Arriba's use of the images serve[d] a different function than Kelly's use-- improving access to information on the [I]nternet versus artistic expression." *Kelly*, 336 F.3d at 819. Although an image may have been created originally to serve an entertainment, aesthetic, or informative function, a search engine transforms the image into a pointer directing a user to a source of information. Just as a "parody has an obvious claim to transformative value" because "it can provide social benefit, by shedding light on an earlier work, and, in the process, creating a new one," *Campbell*, 510 U.S. at 579, a search engine provides social benefit by incorporating an original work into a new work, namely, an electronic reference tool. Indeed, a search engine may be more transformative than a parody because a search engine provides an entirely new use for the original work, while a parody typically has the same entertainment purpose as the original work.

The fact that Google incorporates the entire Perfect 10 image into the search engine results does not diminish the transformative nature of Google's use. As the district court correctly noted, *Perfect 10*, 416 F. Supp. 2d at 848-49, we determined in *Kelly* that even making an exact copy of a work may be transformative so long as the copy serves a different function than the original work, *Kelly*, 336 F.3d at 818-19. For example, the First Circuit has held that the republication of photos taken for a modeling portfolio in a newspaper was transformative because the photos served to inform, as well as entertain. *See Nez v. Caribbean Int'l News Corp.*, 235 F.3d 18, 22-23 (1st Cir. 2000). In contrast, duplicating a church's religious book for use by a different church was not transformative. *See Worldwide Church of God v. Phila. Church of God, Inc.*, 227 F.3d 1110, 1117 (9th Cir. 2000). Nor was a broadcaster's simple retransmission of a radio broadcast over telephone lines transformative, where the original radio shows were given no "new expression, meaning, or message." *Infinity Broad. Corp. v. Kirkwood*, 150 F.3d 104, 108 (2d

Cir. 1998). Here, Google uses Perfect 10's images in a new context to serve a different purpose.

The district court nevertheless determined that Google's use of thumbnail images was less transformative than Arriba's use of thumbnails in *Kelly* because Google's use of thumbnails superseded Perfect 10's right to sell its reduced-size images for use on cell phones. *See Perfect 10*, 416 F. Supp. 2d at 849. The district court stated that "mobile users can download and save the thumbnails displayed by Google Image Search onto their phones," and concluded "to the extent that users may choose to download free images to their phone rather than purchase [Perfect 10's] reduced-size images, Google's use supersedes [Perfect 10's]." *Id.*

Additionally, the district court determined that the commercial nature of Google's use weighed against its transformative nature. *Id.* Although *Kelly* held that the commercial use of the photographer's images by Arriba's search engine was less exploitative than typical commercial use, and thus weighed only slightly against a finding of fair use, *Kelly,* 336 F.3d at 818-20, the district court here distinguished *Kelly* on the ground that some website owners in the AdSense program had infringing Perfect 10 images on their websites, *Perfect 10,* 416 F. Supp. 2d at 846-47. The district court held that because Google's thumbnails "lead users to sites that directly benefit Google's bottom line," the AdSense program increased the commercial nature of Google's use of Perfect 10's images. *Id.* at 847.

In conducting our case-specific analysis of fair use in light of the purposes of copyright, *Campbell,* 510 U.S. at 581, we must weigh Google's superseding and commercial uses of thumbnail images against Google's significant transformative use, as well as the extent to which Google's search engine promotes the purposes of copyright and serves the interests of the public. Although the district court acknowledged the "truism that search engines such as Google Image Search provide great value to the public," *Perfect 10,* 416 F. Supp. 2d at 848-49, the district court did not expressly consider whether this value outweighed the significance of Google's superseding use or the commercial nature of Google's use. *Id.* at 849. The Supreme Court, however, has directed us to be mindful of the extent to which a use promotes the purposes of copyright and serves the interests of the public. *See Campbell,* 510 U.S. at 579; *Harper & Row,* 471 U.S. at 556-57; *Sony,* 464 U.S. at 431-32.

We note that the superseding use in this case is not significant at present: the district court did not find that any downloads for mobile phone use had taken place. *See Perfect 10,* 416 F. Supp. 2d at 849. Moreover, while Google's use of thumbnails to direct users to AdSense partners containing infringing content adds a commercial dimension that did not exist in *Kelly,* the district court did not determine that this commercial element was significant. *See id.* at 848-49. The district court stated that Google's AdSense programs as a whole contributed "$630 million, or 46% of total revenues" to Google's bottom line, but noted that this figure did not "break down the much smaller amount attributable to websites that contain infringing content." *Id.* at 847 & n.12 (internal quotation omitted).

We conclude that the significantly transformative nature of Google's search engine, particularly in light of its public benefit, outweighs Google's superseding and commercial uses of the thumbnails in this case. In reaching this conclusion, we note the importance of analyzing fair use flexibly in light of new circumstances. We are also mindful of the Supreme Court's direction that "the more transformative the new work, the less will be the significance of other factors, like commercialism, that may weigh against a finding of fair use." *Campbell,* 510 U.S. at 579.

Accordingly, we disagree with the district court's conclusion that because Google's use of the thumbnails could supersede Perfect 10's cell phone downloads use and because the use was more commercial than Arriba's, this fair use factor weighed slightly in favor of Perfect 10. *Perfect 10,* 416 F. Supp. 2d at 849. Instead, we conclude that the transformative nature of Google's use is more significant than any incidental superseding use or the minor commercial aspects of Google's search engine and website. Therefore, this factor weighs heavily in favor of Google.

The nature of the copyrighted work. With respect to the second factor, "the nature of the copyrighted work," 17 U.S.C. § 107(2), our decision in *Kelly* is directly on point. There we held that the photographer's images were "creative in nature" and thus "closer to the core of intended copyright protection than are more fact-based works." *Kelly,* 336 F.3d at 820 (internal quotation omitted). However, because the photos appeared on the Internet before Arriba used thumbnail versions in its search engine results, this factor weighed only slightly in favor of the photographer. *Id.*

Here, the district court found that Perfect 10's images were creative but also previously published. *Perfect 10,* 416 F. Supp. 2d at 850. Once Perfect 10 has exploited this commercially valuable right of first publication by putting its images on the Internet for paid subscribers, Perfect 10 is no longer entitled to the enhanced protection available for an unpublished work. Accordingly the district court did not err in holding that this factor weighed only slightly in favor of Perfect 10. *See Perfect 10,* 416 F. Supp. 2d at 849-50.

The amount and substantiality of the portion used. In *Kelly*, we held Arriba's use of the entire photographic image was reasonable in light of the purpose of a search engine. *Kelly*, 336 F.3d at 821. Specifically, we noted, "[i]t was necessary for Arriba to copy the entire image to allow users to recognize the image and decide whether to pursue more information about the image or the originating [website]. If Arriba only copied part of the image, it would be more difficult to identify it, thereby reducing the usefulness of the visual search engine." *Id.* Accordingly, we concluded that this factor did not weigh in favor of either party. *Id.* Because the same analysis applies to Google's use of Perfect 10's image, the district court did not err in finding that this factor favored neither party.

Effect of use on the market. In *Kelly*, we concluded that Arriba's use of the thumbnail images did not harm the market for the photographer's full-size images. *See Kelly,* 336 F.3d at 821-22. We reasoned that because thumbnails were not a substitute for the full-sized images, they did not harm the photographer's ability to sell or license his full-sized images. *Id.* The district court here followed *Kelly*'s reasoning, holding that Google's use of thumbnails did not hurt Perfect 10's market for full-size images. *See Perfect 10,* 416 F. Supp. 2d at 850-51.

Perfect 10 argues that the district court erred because the likelihood of market harm may be presumed if the intended use of an image is for commercial gain. However, this presumption does not arise when a work is transformative because market substitution is at least less certain, and market harm may not be so readily inferred. *Campbell,* 510 U.S. at 591. As previously discussed, Google's use of thumbnails for search engine purposes is highly transformative, and so market harm cannot be presumed.

Perfect 10 also has a market for reduced-size images, an issue not considered in *Kelly*. The district court held that "Google's use of thumbnails likely does harm the potential market for the downloading of [Perfect 10's] reduced-size images onto cell phones." *Perfect 10,* 416 F. Supp. 2d at 851 (emphasis omitted). The district court reasoned that persons who can obtain Perfect 10 images free of charge from Google are less likely to pay for a download, and the availability of Google's thumbnail images would harm Perfect 10's market for cell phone downloads. *Id.* As we discussed above, the district court did not make a finding that Google users have downloaded thumbnail images for cell phone use. This potential harm to Perfect 10's market remains hypothetical. We conclude that this factor favors neither party.

Having undertaken a case-specific analysis of all four factors, we now weigh these factors together in light of the purposes of copyright. *Campbell,* 510 U.S. at 578. In this case, Google has put Perfect 10's thumbnail images (along with millions of other thumbnail images) to a use fundamentally different than the use intended by Perfect 10. In doing so, Google has provided a significant benefit to the public. Weighing this significant transformative use against the unproven use of Google's thumbnails for cell phone downloads, and considering the other fair use factors, all in light of the purpose of copyright, we conclude that Google's use of Perfect 10's thumbnails is a fair use. Because the district court here found facts sufficient to evaluate each of the statutory factors ... [we] need not remand for further factfinding. *Harper & Row,* 471 U.S. at 560 (internal quotation omitted). We conclude that Google is likely to succeed in proving its fair use defense and, accordingly, we vacate the preliminary injunction regarding Google's use of thumbnail images.

Secondary Liability for Copyright Infringement

The district court ruled that Perfect 10 did not have a likelihood of proving success on the merits of either its contributory infringement or vicarious infringement claims with respect to the full-size images. *See Perfect 10,* 416 F. Supp. 2d at 856, 858. As a threshold matter, before we examine Perfect 10's claims that Google is secondarily liable, Perfect 10 must establish that there has been direct infringement by third parties. *See Napster,* 239 F.3d at 1013 n.2. [W]e must assess Perfect 10's arguments that Google is secondarily liable in light of the direct infringement that is undisputed by the parties: third-party websites' reproducing, displaying, and distributing unauthorized copies of Perfect 10's images on the Internet. *Id.* at 852.

A. Contributory Infringement

In order for Perfect 10 to show it will likely succeed in its contributory liability claim against Google, it must establish that Google's activities meet the definition of contributory liability recently enunciated in *Grokster*. [U]nder *Grokster*, an actor may be contributorily liable for intentionally encouraging direct infringement if the actor knowingly takes steps that are substantially certain to result in such direct infringement.

[W]e hold that a computer system operator can be held contributorily liable if it "has *actual* knowledge that *specific* infringing material is available using its system," *Napster,* 239 F.3d at 1022, and can "take simple measures to prevent further damage" to copyrighted works, *Netcom,* 907 F. Supp. at 1375, yet continues to provide access to infringing works.

Here, the district court held that even assuming Google had actual knowledge of infringing material available on its system, Google did not materially contribute to infringing conduct because it did not undertake any substantial promotional or advertising efforts to encourage visits to infringing websites, nor provide a significant revenue stream to the infringing websites. *Perfect 10,* 416 F. Supp. 2d at 854-56. This analysis is erroneous. There is no dispute that Google substantially assists websites to distribute their infringing copies to a worldwide market and assists a worldwide audience of users to access infringing materials. We cannot discount the effect of such a service on copyright owners, even though Google's assistance is available to all websites, not just infringing ones. Applying our test, Google could be held contributorily liable if it had knowledge that infringing Perfect 10 images were available using its search engine, could take simple measures to prevent further damage to Perfect 10's copyrighted works, and failed to take such steps.

The district court did not resolve the factual disputes over the adequacy of Perfect 10's notices to Google and Google's responses to these notices. Moreover, there are factual disputes over whether there are reasonable and feasible means for Google to refrain from providing access to infringing images. Therefore, we must remand this claim to the district court for further consideration whether Perfect 10 would likely succeed in establishing that Google was contributorily liable for in-line linking to full-size infringing images under the test enunciated today.

B. Vicarious Infringement

Perfect 10 also challenges the district court's conclusion that it is not likely to prevail on a theory of vicarious liability against Google. *Grokster* states that one "infringes vicariously by profiting from direct infringement while declining to exercise a right to stop or limit it." *Grokster,* 545 U.S. at 930.

We evaluate Perfect 10's arguments that Google is vicariously liable in light of the direct infringement that is undisputed by the parties, namely, the third-party websites' reproduction, display, and distribution of unauthorized copies of Perfect 10's images on the Internet. *Perfect 10,* 416 F. Supp. 2d at 852. In order to prevail at this preliminary injunction stage, Perfect 10 must demonstrate a likelihood of success in establishing that Google has the right and ability to stop or limit the infringing activities of third party websites. In addition, Perfect 10 must establish a likelihood of proving that Google derives a direct financial benefit from such activities. Perfect 10 has not met this burden.

Perfect 10 has not demonstrated a likelihood of showing that Google has the legal right to stop or limit the direct infringement of third-party websites. *See Grokster,* 545 U.S. at 930. Perfect 10 has not shown that Google has contracts with third-party websites that empower Google to stop or limit them from reproducing, displaying, and distributing infringing copies of Perfect 10's images on the Internet. Perfect 10 does point to Google's AdSense agreement, which states that Google reserves "the right to monitor and terminate partnerships with entities that violate others' copyright[s]." *Perfect 10,* 416 F. Supp. 2d at 858. However, Google's right to terminate an AdSense partnership does not give Google the right to stop direct infringement by third-party websites. An infringing third-party website can continue to reproduce, display, and distribute its infringing copies of Perfect 10 images after its participation in the AdSense program has ended.

Nor is Google similarly situated to Napster. Napster users infringed the plaintiffs' reproduction and distribution rights through their use of Napster's proprietary music-file sharing system. *Napster,* 239 F.3d at 1011-14. There, the infringing conduct was the use of Napster's "service to download and upload copyrighted music." *Id.* at 1014 (internal quotation omitted). Because Napster had a closed system requiring user registration, and could terminate its users' accounts and block their access to the Napster system, Napster had the right and ability to prevent its users from engaging in the infringing activity of uploading file names and downloading Napster users' music files through the Napster system. *Id.* at 1023-24. By contrast, Google cannot stop any of the third-party websites from reproducing, displaying, and distributing unauthorized copies of Perfect 10's images because that infringing conduct takes place on the third-party websites. Google cannot terminate those third-party websites or block their ability to "host and serve infringing full-size images" on the Internet. *Perfect 10,* 416 F. Supp. 2d at 831.

Moreover, the district court found that Google lacks the practical ability to police the third-party websites' infringing conduct. *Id.* at 857-58. Specifically, the court found that Google's supervisory power is limited because "Google's software lacks the ability to analyze every image on the [I]nternet, compare each image to all the other copyrighted images that exist in the world . . . and determine whether a certain image on the web infringes someone's copyright." *Id.* at 858. The district court also concluded that Perfect 10's suggestions regarding measures Google could implement to prevent its web crawler from indexing infringing websites and to block access to infringing images were not workable. *Id.* at 858 n.25. Rather, the suggestions suffered from both "imprecision and overbreadth." *Id.* We hold that these findings are not clearly erroneous. Without image-recognition technology, Google lacks the practical ability to police the infringing activities of third-party websites.

Because we conclude that Perfect 10 has not shown a likelihood of establishing Google's right and ability to stop or limit the directly infringing conduct of third-party websites, we agree with the district court's conclusion that Perfect 10 "has not established a likelihood of proving the [control] prong necessary for vicarious liability." *Perfect 10,* 416 F. Supp. 2d at 858.

We conclude that Google's fair use defense is likely to succeed at trial, and therefore we reverse the district court's determination that Google's thumbnail versions of Perfect 10's images likely constituted a direct infringement. The district court also erred in its secondary liability analysis because it failed to consider whether Google knew of infringing activities yet failed to take reasonable and feasible steps to refrain from providing access to infringing images. Therefore we must also reverse the district court's holding that Perfect 10 was unlikely to succeed on the merits of its secondary liability claim.

ADD THE FOLLOWING CASE TO ASSIGNMENT 11 FOLLOWING *SUNTRUST* AND BEFORE *ELCOM* ON PAGE 462:

Golan v. Holder

United States Court of Appeals, Tenth Circuit, June 21, 2010.
Nos. 09-1234, 09-1261, 2010 WL 2473217

■ BRISCOE, CHIEF JUDGE.

Plaintiffs brought this action challenging the constitutionality of Section 514 of the Uruguay Round Agreements Act ("URAA"), which granted copyright protection to various foreign works that were previously in the public domain in the United States. The district court granted plaintiffs' motion for summary judgment, concluding that Section 514 violates plaintiffs' freedom of expression under the First Amendment. Exercising jurisdiction pursuant to 28 U.S.C. § 1291, we reverse the judgment of the district court and conclude that Section 514 of the URAA is not violative of the First Amendment.

I. Statutory Background

In 1989, the United States joined the Berne Convention for the Protection of Literary and Artistic Works ("Berne Convention"). The Berne Convention requires each signatory to provide the same copyright protections to authors in other member countries that it provides to its own authors. Pursuant to Article 18, when a country joins the Convention, it must provide copyright protection to preexisting foreign works even when those works were previously in the public domain in that country. However, when the United States joined the Berne Convention, the implementing legislation did not extend copyrights to any foreign works that were already in the public domain in the United States.

In April 1994, the United States signed various trade agreements in the Uruguay Round General Agreement on Tariffs and Trade. Included in this round of agreements was the Agreement on Trade Related Aspects of Intellectual Property Rights (TRIPs). The TRIPs agreement required, in part, that its signatories comply with Article 18 of the Berne Convention, and thus, extend copyright protection to all works of foreign origin whose term of protection had not expired. Unlike the Berne Convention, the TRIPs agreement provided for dispute resolution before the World Trade

Organization. *See Patry on Copyright* at § 24:1.

In order to comply with these international agreements, Congress enacted the URAA. In particular, Section 514 of the URAA "restores" copyrights in foreign works that were formerly in the public domain in the United States for one of three specified reasons: failure to comply with formalities, lack of subject matter protection, or lack of national eligibility. *See* 17 U.S.C. § 104A(a), (h)(6)(C). Section 514 does not restore copyrights in foreign works that entered the public domain through the expiration of the term of protection. *See id.* § 104A(h)(6)(B).

Section 514 provides some protections for reliance parties such as plaintiffs who had exploited these works prior to their restoration. *See id.* § 104A(d)(2)-(4). In order to enforce a restored copyright against a reliance party, a foreign copyright owner must either file notice with the Copyright Office within twenty-four months of restoration, *id.* § 104A(d)(2)(A)(i), or serve actual notice on the reliance party, *id.* § 104A(d)(2)(B)(i). A reliance party is liable for infringing acts that occur after the end of a twelve month grace period, starting from notice of restoration, *id.* § 104A(d)(2)(A)(ii)(I), (d)(2)(B)(ii)(I). Reliance parties may sell or otherwise dispose of restored works during this grace period, *id.* § 109(a), but they cannot make additional copies during this time, *id.* § 104A(d)(2)(A)(ii)(III), (d)(2)(B)(ii)(III).

Section 514 provides further protections for reliance parties who, prior to restoration, created a derivative work that was based on a restored work. Under Section 514, "a reliance party may continue to exploit that derivative work for the duration of the restored copyright if the reliance party pays to the owner of the restored copyright reasonable compensation...." *Id.* § 104A(d)(3)(A). If the parties are unable to agree on reasonable compensation, a federal court will determine the amount of compensation. *See id.* § 104A(d)(3)(B).

II. Factual and Procedural Background

The factual background is not in dispute. Plaintiffs are orchestra conductors, educators, performers, publishers, film archivists, and motion picture distributors who have relied on artistic works in the public domain for their livelihoods. They perform, distribute, and sell public domain works. The late plaintiff Kapp created a derivative work--a sound recording based on several compositions by Dmitri Shostakovich. Section 514 of the URAA provided copyright protection to these foreign works, removing them from the public domain in the United States. As a result, plaintiffs are either prevented from using these works or are required to pay licensing fees to the copyright holders--fees that are often cost-prohibitive for plaintiffs.

Plaintiffs filed this action, challenging the constitutionality of the Copyright Term Extension Act, Pub. L. No 105-298, § 102(b), (d), 112 Stat. 2827, 2827-28 (1998), and Section 514 of the URAA, seeking declaratory and injunctive relief. Initially, the district court granted summary judgment to the government. On appeal, we concluded that plaintiffs' challenge to the Copyright Term Extension Act was foreclosed by the Supreme Court's decision in *Eldred v. Ashcroft,* 537 U.S. 186 (2003). *See Golan v. Gonzales,* 501 F.3d 1179, 1182 (10th Cir.2007) (*"Golan I "*). We also held that "[Section] 514 of the URAA ha[d] not exceeded the limitations inherent in the Copyright Clause" of the United States Constitution. *Id.* We recognized that "legislation promulgated pursuant to the Copyright Clause must still comport with other express limitations of the Constitution," *id.* at 1187, and concluded that plaintiffs had "shown sufficient free expression interests in works removed from the public domain to require First Amendment scrutiny of [Section] 514," *id.* at 1182. We then remanded the case to the district court to "assess whether [Section] 514 is content-based or content-neutral," *id.* at 1196, and to apply the appropriate level of constitutional scrutiny.

On remand, . . . [t]he government and plaintiffs agreed that Section 514 is a content-neutral regulation of speech, and thus should be subject to intermediate scrutiny. The district court concluded that "to the extent Section 514 suppresses the right of reliance parties to use works they exploited while the works were in the public domain," Section 514 was unconstitutional. *Golan v. Holder,* 611 F.Supp.2d 1165, 1177 (D.Colo. 2009). Consequently, the district court granted plaintiffs' motion for summary judgment, and denied the government's motion.

III. Government's Appeal (No. 09-1234)

In reviewing the constitutionality of a content-neutral regulation of speech, we apply "an intermediate level of scrutiny, because in most cases [such regulations] pose a less substantial risk of excising certain ideas or viewpoints from the public dialogue." *Id.* (internal citation omitted). Applying intermediate scrutiny, a content-neutral statute "will be sustained under the First Amendment if it advances important governmental interests unrelated to the suppression of free speech and does not burden substantially more speech than necessary to further those interests." *Turner Broad. Sys., Inc. v. FCC,* 520 U.S. 180, 189, 117 S. Ct. 1174, 137 L.Ed.2d 369 (1997) (*"Turner II "*).

The government argues on appeal that Section 514 is narrowly tailored to advancing three important governmental interests: (1) attaining indisputable compliance with international treaties and multilateral agreements, (2) obtaining legal protections for American copyright holders' interests abroad, and (3) remedying past inequities of foreign authors who lost or never obtained copyrights in the United States. We hold that the government has demonstrated a substantial interest in protecting American copyright holders' interests abroad, and Section 514 is narrowly tailored to advance that interest. Consequently, the district court erred in concluding that Section 514 violates plaintiffs' First Amendment rights.

A. Governmental Interest

1. Section 514 addresses a substantial or important governmental interest.

Copyright serves to advance both the economic and expressive interests of American authors. In addition to creating economic incentives that further expression, copyright also serves authors' First Amendment interests. "[F]reedom of thought and expression 'includes both the right to speak freely and the right to refrain from speaking at all.' " *Harper & Row Publishers, Inc. v. Nation Enter,* 471 U.S. 539 (1985) (quoting *Wooley v. Maynard,* 430 U.S. 705 (1977)). "Courts and commentators have recognized that copyright ... serve[s] this countervailing First Amendment value" of the freedom not to speak. *Harper & Row,* 471 U.S. at 560.

Plaintiffs contend that the government does not have an important interest in a "reallocation of speech interests" between American reliance parties and American copyright holders. However, the Supreme Court has recognized that not all First Amendment interests are equal. "The First Amendment securely protects the freedom to make--or decline to make--one's own speech; it bears less heavily when speakers assert the right to make other people's speeches." *Id.* Although plaintiffs have First Amendment interests, *see Golan I,* 501 F.3d at 1194, so too do American authors.

Securing foreign copyrights for American works preserves the authors' economic and expressive interests. These interests are at least as important or substantial as other interests that the Supreme Court has found to be sufficiently important or substantial to satisfy intermediate scrutiny. *See, e.g., Members of City Council v. Taxpayers for Vincent,* 466 U.S. 789, 807, 104 S. Ct. 2118, 80 L. Ed. 2d 772 (1984) ("The problem addressed by this ordinance--the visual assault ... presented by an accumulation of signs posted on public property--constitutes a significant substantive evil within the City's power to prohibit."). Accordingly, Section 514 advances an important or substantial governmental interest unrelated to the suppression of free expression.

2. Section 514 addresses a real harm.

The government's asserted interest cannot be merely important in the abstract--the statute must be directed at a real, and not merely conjectural, harm. *Turner I,* 512 U.S. at 664 (plurality opinion). Thus, we must examine whether Section 514 was "designed to address a real harm, and whether [it] will alleviate [that harm] in a material way." *See Turner II,* 520 U.S. at 195. In undertaking this review, we "must accord substantial deference to the predictive judgments of Congress. Our sole obligation is to assure that, in formulating its judgments, Congress has drawn reasonable inferences based on substantial evidence." *Id.* (quotations and citation omitted).

"[S]ubstantiality is to be measured in this context by a standard more deferential than we accord to judgments of an administrative agency." *Id.* This deferential standard is warranted for two important reasons. First, Congress is "far better equipped" as an institution "to amass and evaluate the vast amounts of data bearing upon the legislative questions." *Id.*(quotations and citation omitted). Second, we owe Congress "an additional measure of deference out of respect for its authority to exercise the legislative power." *Id.* at 196.

Even in the realm of First Amendment questions where Congress must base its conclusions upon substantial evidence, deference must be accorded to its findings as to the harm to be avoided and to the remedial measures adopted for that end, lest we infringe on traditional legislative authority to make predictive judgments....

Id.

Additionally, the other branches' judgments regarding foreign affairs warrant special deference from the courts. *See Citizens for Peace in Space,* 477 F.3d at 1221 ("Courts have historically given special deference to other branches in matters relating to foreign affairs, international relations, and national security; even when constitutional rights are invoked by a plaintiff."). The Supreme Court has "consistently acknowledged that the nuances of the foreign policy of the United States are much more the province of the Executive Branch and Congress than of [the courts]." *Crosby v. Nat'l Foreign Trade Council,* 530 U.S. 363 (2000) (quotations and alterations omitted). As such, we apply considerable deference to Congress and the Executive in making decisions that require predictive judgments in the areas of foreign affairs.

To be clear, we do not suggest that Congress's decisions regarding foreign affairs are entirely immune from the requirements of the First Amendment. *See Turner I,* 512 U.S. at 666 (plurality opinion) ("That Congress' predictive judgments are entitled to substantial deference does not mean, however, that they are insulated from meaningful judicial review altogether."); *see also Boos v. Barry,* 485 U.S. 312, 323, 108 S.Ct. 1157, 99 L.Ed.2d 333 (1988) ("[I]t is well established that no agreement with a foreign nation can confer power on the Congress, or on any other branch of Government, which is free from the restraints of the Constitution." (quotations and citation omitted)). Rather, we merely acknowledge that in undertaking our constitutional review of a content-neutral statute, Congress's predictive judgments are entitled to "substantial deference," *Turner II,* 520 U.S. at 195, and in this particular context, our review of Congress's predictive judgments is further informed by the special deference that Congress and the Executive Branch deserve in matters of foreign affairs.

Turning to the issue at hand, prior to enacting Section 514 of the URAA, Congress heard testimony addressing the interests of American copyright holders. In particular, American works were unprotected in several foreign countries, to the detriment of the United States' interests.

Congress had substantial evidence from which it could reasonably conclude that the ongoing harms to American authors were real and not merely conjectural. Around the globe, American works were being exploited without the copyright owners' consent and without providing compensation. Thus, there was a "substantial basis to support Congress' conclusion that a real threat justified enactment of" Section 514 of the URAA. *See Turner II*, 520 U.S. at 196.

3. Substantial evidence s upported the conclusion that Section 514 would alleviate these harms.

Next, we must determine whether there was substantial evidence from which Congress could conclude that Section 514 would alleviate these harms to American copyright holders. *See id.* at 213. At the Joint Hearings, Congress heard testimony that by refusing to restore copyrights in foreign works in the public domain, the United States was not in compliance with its obligations under the Berne Convention.

Further, the United States' trading partners had represented that they would restore American copyrights only if the United States restored foreign copyrights. Foreign countries were willing to provide, at most, reciprocal copyright protections to American works. Moreover, the United States had an opportunity to set an example for copyright restoration for other countries. Thus, if the United States wanted certain protections for American authors, it had to provide those protections for foreign authors.

Plaintiffs aver that Congress was presented with evidence regarding the need to restore copyrights generally, but that there was no evidence that Congress needed to provide limited protections for reliance parties. According to plaintiffs, there is "no support for the conclusion that enacting more stringent measures against reliance parties ... would have any impact whatsoever on the behavior of foreign countries." To the contrary, Congress heard testimony that the United States' chosen method and scope of copyright restoration would impact other nations that were similarly deciding how to restore copyrights.

In particular, Congress heard testimony that the United States could set an example regarding copyright restoration, and other countries might mirror the United States' approach. For example, Ira Shapiro, General

Counsel of the Office of the United States Trade Representative, testified that "the choices made in our implementation of the TRIPs agreement will set an example for other countries as governments decide on their own implementing legislation as well as influence future disputes over the obligations of the Agreement." Additionally, Eric Smith, speaking on behalf of a consortium of trade associations whose members represented both American copyright industries and reliance parties, testified as follows:

> The fact is that what the United States does in this area will carry great weight in the international community. If we interpret Article 18 and the TRIPS provisions to deny protection *or significantly limit its scope,* our trading partners-just now considering their own implementing legislation-will feel free to simply mirror our views. If the largest exporter of copyrighted material in the world takes the position that we have no, or only limited, obligations, the United States will have little credibility in convincing particularly the new nations with whom we are just starting copyright relations *to give us the expansive protection that we need.*

Congress heard testimony from a number of [other] witnesses that the United States' position on the scope of copyright restoration--which necessarily includes the enforcement against reliance parties--was critical to the United States' ability to obtain similar protections for American copyright holders.

Further, Congress squarely faced the need to balance the interests of American copyright holders and American reliance parties. In his opening remarks, Senator DeConcini stated:

> The conventional wisdom within the U.S. copyright community is that through the restoration of copyright protection to foreign authors we will get more than we give because U.S. authors will be able to retrieve far more works in foreign countries than foreign authors will retrieve here in the United States.
>
> ....
>
> ... [I]f we set out to restore copyright protection to foreign works, we must provide protection that is complete and meaningful. By the same token, we must ensure that copyright restoration provides

reliance users a sufficient opportunity to recoup their investment.

Congress also heard from Eric Smith, who testified that the bills under consideration would

> provide a careful balance between the need, on the one hand, to establish a "model" provision which other countries could follow in order to secure effective restoration of our copyrights abroad and the need, on the other hand, to balance the rights of foreign authors whose works are restored in the U.S. with the domestic users that may have relied on the public domain status of the work in making investments.

In spite of this testimony, plaintiffs contend that the government's interest is too speculative to satisfy intermediate scrutiny. Although we require "substantial evidence" in order to satisfy intermediate scrutiny, *see Turner I*, 512 U.S. at 667 (plurality opinion), the evidentiary requirement is not as onerous as plaintiffs would have us impose. The Supreme Court has cautioned that imposing too strict of an evidentiary requirement on Congress is "an improper burden for courts to impose on the Legislative Branch." *Turner II*, 520 U.S. at 213 (quotation omitted). An overly demanding "amount of detail is as unreasonable in the legislative context as it is constitutionally unwarranted. Congress is not obligated, when enacting its statutes, to make a record of the type that an administrative agency or court does to accommodate judicial review." *Id.*

"Sound policymaking often requires legislators to forecast future events and to anticipate the likely impact of these events based on deductions and inferences for which complete empirical support may be unavailable." *Turner I*, 512 U.S. at 665 (plurality opinion). Past conduct may be the best--and sometimes only--evidence available to Congress in making predictive judgments. We think that this is especially true in areas that involve predictions of foreign relations and diplomacy, where empirical data will rarely be available, and to which considerable deference is owed to Congress and the Executive.

Plaintiffs direct our attention to evidence in the Congressional record that contradicted the view that other countries would follow the United States' approach to copyright restoration. More specifically, Irwin Karp stated:

When these countries grant retroactivity, the theory goes, they will deny their reliance interests real protection--if we do so now. But this is only a theory, and an unlikely one. Most foreign countries, including the Commonwealth countries, already grant us retroactivity. They will not change their laws to restrict protection of their reliance parties. Nor will the few important countries who presently do not retroactively protect U.S. works[.] When they do grant retroactivity they can decide what protection they will grant to their reliance interests. There is nothing to stop them from adopting the British et al buy-out provision.

Although Congress was presented with evidence that its position on copyright restoration might not guarantee reciprocation, it does not follow that Section 514 is unconstitutional. "The Constitution gives to Congress the role of weighing conflicting evidence in the legislative process." *Turner II,* 520 U.S. at 199. Thus, we must determine "whether, given conflicting views ..., Congress had substantial evidence for making the judgment that it did." *Id.* at 208. In other words, "[t]he question is not whether Congress, as an objective matter, was correct to determine" that limited protections for reliance parties were "necessary" to garner similar protections from foreign countries. *See id.* at 211. "Rather, the question is whether the legislative conclusion was reasonable and supported by substantial evidence in the record before Congress." *Id.*

> In making that determination, we are not to reweigh the evidence *de novo,* or to replace Congress' factual predictions with our own. Rather, we are simply to determine if the standard is satisfied. If it is, summary judgment for [the government] is appropriate regardless of whether the evidence is in conflict.

Id.

Considering the deference that Congress is owed, particularly in areas of foreign relations, we conclude that Congress's judgments were supported by substantial evidence. The testimony before Congress indicated that the United States' historically lax position on copyright restoration had been an obstacle to the protection that the United States was seeking for its own copyright owners. Witnesses further testified that many countries would provide no greater protections to American authors than the United States gave to their foreign counterparts. There was also testimony that the chosen method of restoring foreign copyrights would have great weight in the international community and could induce other countries to follow the United States' lead, although Congress heard some testimony that other countries would not necessarily follow the United States' approach. Consequently, Congress was presented with substantial evidence that Section 514 would advance the government's interest in protecting American copyright holders "in a direct and effective way." The United States' ability to protect American works abroad would be achieved less effectively absent Section 514, and therefore, the government's interest is genuinely advanced by restoring foreign copyrights with limited protections for reliance parties such as plaintiffs.

B. Section 514 does not burden substantially more speech than necessary.

Under intermediate scrutiny, we must also determine whether Section 514 is narrowly tailored to further the government's interests. "Content-neutral regulations do not pose the same inherent dangers to free expression that content-based regulations do," and therefore, the government has a degree of latitude in choosing how to further its asserted interest. *Turner II,* 520 U.S. at 213 (quotations and citation omitted). Accordingly, "the [g]overnment may employ the means of its choosing so long as the regulation promotes a substantial governmental interest that would be achieved less effectively absent the regulation and does not burden substantially more speech than is necessary to further that interest." *Id.* at 213-14 (internal quotations, ellipses, and citation omitted). Further, the regulation need not be the least-restrictive alternative of advancing the government's interest. *Id.* at 217-18.

1. Section 514 is narrowly tailored.

The "[g]overnment may not regulate expression in such a manner that a substantial portion of the burden on speech does not serve to advance its goals." *Ward,* 491 U.S. at 799. "[T]he essence of narrow tailoring" is when a regulation "focuses on the source of the evils the [government] seeks to eliminate ... without at the same time banning or significantly restricting a substantial quantity of speech that does not create the same evils." *Id.* at 799 n. 7. That is, when "the burden imposed by [a regulation] is congruent to the benefits it affords," that regulation is narrowly tailored. *Turner II,* 520 U.S. at 215-16.

91

In the case at bar, the burdens imposed on the reliance parties are congruent with the benefits Section 514 affords American copyright holders. As discussed above, the government has a substantial interest in securing protections for American works in foreign countries. Further, Congress heard testimony that the United States could expect foreign countries to provide only as much protection to American copyright holders as the United States would provide to foreign copyright holders, and other countries might follow the United States' example. In other words, the United States needed to impose the same burden on American reliance parties that it sought to impose on foreign reliance parties. Thus, the benefit that the government sought to provide to American authors is congruent with the burden that Section 514 imposes on reliance parties. The burdens on speech are therefore directly focused to the harms that the government sought to alleviate. "This is the essence of narrow tailoring." *Ward v. Rock Against Racism,* 491 U.S. 781, 799 n. 7.

2. Alternatives do not undermine the narrow tailoring of Section 514.

Plaintiffs contend that "the Government could have complied with the Berne Convention while providing significantly stronger protection for the First Amendment interests of reliance parties like the Plaintiffs here." According to plaintiffs, Article 18 of the Berne Convention provides considerable discretion that allows the government to provide greater protections for reliance parties. The government responds that the Berne Convention requires only transitional protections for reliance parties.

The parties' arguments about what the Berne Convention requires and permits are beside the point. As discussed above, the government's interest is not limited to compliance with the Berne Convention. Rather, its interest includes securing protections for American copyright owners in foreign countries, which includes providing copyright protection against foreign reliance parties. Thus, it is immaterial whether, as plaintiffs contend, the government could have complied with the minimal obligations of the Berne Convention and granted stronger protections for American reliance parties. If Congress had provided stronger protections to American reliance parties such as plaintiffs, many foreign countries may have provided similar protections for their own reliance parties, thereby providing less protection for American authors. Thus, even assuming for purposes of this appeal that the United States could have provided stronger protections for American reliance parties while complying with the minimum requirements of the Berne Convention, Section 514 does not burden substantially more speech than necessary to further the government's interest.

With this in mind, we turn to plaintiffs' suggestion that there were less restrictive means of restoring foreign copyrights. Although no country has provided full, permanent exemptions for reliance parties, other countries have provided limited protections for reliance parties. The chief alternative discussed by plaintiffs and the district court is the United Kingdom model. *See Golan,* 611 F. Supp. 2d at 1174 ("Several member nations--including Germany, Hungary, the United Kingdom, Australia, and New Zealand--provide accommodations that are temporally permanent so long as certain conditions are met."); Appellees' Br. at 34 ("The provisions implemented by the United Kingdom and a dozen other signatories confirm what the text of Berne makes clear: permanent protection of reliance interests is permissible."). However, the United Kingdom model is not an obvious and substantially less restrictive alternative.

Under the United Kingdom model, a "reliance party is allowed to continue making those uses of the work it had made, or incurred commitments to make, before its copyright is restored. But the reliance party can be 'bought out' by the owner of the restored copyright." Irwin Karp, *Final Report, Berne Article 18 Study on Retroactive United States Copyright Protection for Berne and Other Works,* 20 Colum.-VLA J.L. & Arts 157, 180 (1996). Thus, copyright owners can "'buy back' their rights immediately after the entry into force of the law restoring copyright; and thus, there is no 'grace period'" similar to Section 514.

The United Kingdom model is not substantially less restrictive of speech than Section 514 of the URAA. In the United Kingdom, a copyright owner cannot enforce the copyright against a reliance party unless the owner "buys out" the reliance party. Under Section 514, a copyright owner cannot enforce the copyright against a reliance party unless the owner files notice with the Copyright Office or serves notice on a reliance party. 17 U.S.C. § 104A(d)(2). Moreover, under Section 514, reliance parties have twelve months to continue exploiting the works, although they cannot continue to make copies of the restored work. *Id.* § 104A(d)(2)(A)(ii)(III), (d)(2)(B)(ii)(III). Under the United Kingdom model, however, the reliance party's interests are immediately terminated

93

upon buy-out. Thus, under both systems, reliance parties receive qualified protection insofar as a reliance party can continue to exploit a work until the copyright owner does something: either buy out the reliance party (United Kingdom model) or file notice (Section 514). Ultimately, both approaches provide the copyright owner with the ability to terminate the reliance party's interests. The only significant difference is that under the United Kingdom model, the reliance party receives compensation from the owner, while under Section 514, the reliance party has a twelve month grace period to continue exploiting the work.

Further, the United Kingdom model is not far more protective of speech interests of reliance parties who have created derivative works, such as the late plaintiff Kapp. Section 514 allows these reliance parties to continue to use a derivative work as long as they pay "reasonable compensation" to the copyright owner. *See* 17 U.S.C. § 104A(d)(3)(A). The United Kingdom model, on the other hand, apparently provides no such protection for creators of derivative works. In a sense, the two models are mirror images of each other. Under Section 514, a reliance party can continue to exploit a derivative work as long as he pays compensation to the owner of the original copyright. In the United Kingdom, an author of a derivative work can continue to exploit the new work until the owner pays compensation to the reliance party.

We cannot say that one approach is clearly more protective of speech interests than the other. Although the United Kingdom model is arguably more protective of reliance parties' *economic* interests, we cannot say that it is substantially more protective of reliance parties' *expressive* interests. Moreover, even if the United Kingdom model is marginally more protective of speech interests,

> when evaluating a content-neutral regulation which incidentally burdens speech, we will not invalidate the preferred remedial scheme because some alternative solution is marginally less intrusive on a speaker's First Amendment interests. So long as the means chosen are not substantially broader than necessary to achieve the government's interest, the regulation will not be invalid simply because a court concludes that the government's interest could be adequately served by some less-speech-restrictive alternative.

94

Turner II, 520 U.S. at 217-18 (internal citations, quotations, and ellipses omitted).

At its core, plaintiffs' challenge to Section 514 "reflect[s] little more than disagreement over the level of protection" that reliance parties should receive. *See id.* at 224. Congress sought to balance the interests between American copyright holders and American reliance parties. In so doing, Congress crafted a nuanced statute that offered some protections for both of these competing interests. It is not our role to opine on the best method of striking this balance. A statute's "validity does not turn on a [court's] agreement with the responsible decisionmaker concerning the most appropriate method for promoting significant government interests." *Id.* at 218 (quotations and citation omitted). Plaintiffs may have preferred a different method of restoring copyrights in foreign works, but that is not what the Constitution requires; as long as the government has not burdened substantially more speech than necessary to further an important interest, the First Amendment does not permit us to second guess Congress's legislative choice. "We cannot displace Congress' judgment respecting content-neutral regulations with our own, so long as its policy is grounded on reasonable factual findings supported by evidence that is substantial for a legislative determination." *Id.* at 224.

We conclude that because Section 514 advances a substantial government interest, and it does not burden substantially more speech than necessary to advance that interest, it is consistent with the First Amendment. Accordingly, the district court erred in ruling that Section 514 violates plaintiffs' freedom of expression.

***

In sum, Congress acted within its authority under the Copyright Clause in enacting Section 514. *See id.* at 1187. Further, Section 514 does not violate plaintiffs' freedom of speech under the First Amendment because it advances an important governmental interest, and it is not substantially broader than necessary to advance that interest. Accordingly, we REVERSE the judgment of the district court and REMAND with instructions to grant summary judgment in favor of the government.

ADD THE FOLLOWING AT THE END OF NOTE 2 ON PAGE 469:

Do you agree with the court in *Perfect 10* that a search engine may be more transformative than a parody? Do you agree with the court's treatment of the superseding use? Note that this aspect of the decision also impacts the court's analysis of market harm.

INSERT THE FOLLOWING IN PLACE OF THE LAST PARAGRAPH OF NOTE 4 ON PAGES 471-472:

An interesting case to consider in relation to these questions is *Blackwell Publishing, Inc. v. Excel Research Group*,[1] where the company, pursuant to a contract with the university, took the coursepacks in question from members of the University of Michigan faculty, checked them for legibility, numbered the pages, and provided the copying equipment. Students requested the appropriate coursepack and used Excel's equipment to make copies for themselves. The District Court said that the company was liable for infringement both because its involvement was commercial and because the shop retained overall control of the copying process and made money from the activity as well.

INSERT THE FOLLOWING IN PLACE OF THE EXISTING NOTE 1 BEGINNING ON PAGE 473:

1. *Contributory infringement and vicarious liability.* Obviously there is a connection between the standard for copyright infringement generally and public access. This Assignment incorporates the doctrines of contributory infringement and vicarious liability in order to emphasize the impact of these doctrines on public access to copyrighted works. Under *Napster*, what is the impact of knowledge of the infringing use on the inquiry into contributory infringement? How does this relate to the contributory infringement issue in *Sony*? The vicarious liability section of *Napster* is important because this case is one of the first to set a standard of vicarious liability in the digital context. How does *Napster*'s standard apply to the Principal Problem? *Metro–Goldwyn–Mayer Studios, Inc. v. Grokster, Ltd.*,[2] however, shows that lack of knowledge may not immunize a defendant from liability if sufficient evidence of inducement is present.

---

[1] 661 F. Supp. 2d 786 (E.D. Mich. 2009).
[2] 545 U.S. 913 (2005).

96

The most recent major provider of software for peer-to-peer file sharing to be found liable on an inducement theory is LimeWire.[3]

Title II of the DMCA added section 512 to the Copyright Act. This provision addresses the vicarious liability of online service providers for copyright infringement. It creates several "safe harbors" for ISPs that limit liability for the following four categories of conduct by a service provider: 1) transitory communications—when providers merely act as data conduits by transmitting digital information from one point on a network to another at the request of a third party; 2) system caching—when providers, for a limited time period, store copies of material that has been made available online by someone other than the provider, and then transmitted to a subscriber at his or her direction; 3) for infringing material posted on the provider's system, so long as the service providers do not have actual knowledge of the infringement and act immediately upon notice to remove the infringing material; and 4) for services that direct users to a site containing infringing material by means of information location tools such as hyperlinks, online directories and search engines. The safe harbors provided by § 512 give providers immunity from monetary damages and restrict the availability of injunctive relief. The provision also includes a section governing the limitation of liability for nonprofit educational institutions. The scope of these safe harbor provisions is now being tested in the courts.[4]

In *Ellison v. Robertson*,[5] the court held that AOL's liability was limited under § 512(a), the first category listed above. In that case, Robertson uploaded a copyrighted work without permission onto USENET, so that anyone could access and copy the work. AOL was linked to USENET so the work became accessible to all of AOL's members. The court held that AOL qualified under the § 512(a) safe harbor because AOL's storage of the defendant's posts was an

---

[3] *Arista Records LLC v. LimeWire Group LLC*, No. 06 CV 5936, 2010 WL 2291485 at *13-21 (S.D.N.Y., May 25, 2010).

[4] It is interesting to note that the European Directive on Electronic Commerce, adopted by the European Community in 2000, adopts principles similar to those of Title II of the DMCA. Directive 2000/31/EC/ of the European Parliament and of the Council, 2000 O.J. (L 178) 1. See Neil A. Benchell, *The Digital Millennium Copyright Act: A Review of the Law and the Court's Interpretation*, 21 J. MARSHALL J. COMPUTER & INFO L. 1, 17 (2002).

[5] 189 F. Supp. 2d 1051 (C.D. Cal. 2002).

"intermediate and transient storage" that was not maintained on the system for a longer period than was reasonably necessary.[6]

On appeal, the Ninth Circuit reversed the district court's determination that, as matter of law, AOL had reasonably implemented a policy against repeat offenders as required by 512(i), a condition of eligibility for safe harbors generally.[7] With respect to the application of 512(a) specifically, however, the court determined that if a jury were to find that AOL did have such a policy and therefore qualified for the safe harbor exemptions, the district court's determination that AOL'S storage of the defendant's posts was intermediate and transient, and for a period no longer than necessary, should be affirmed.

In *Perfect 10, Inc. v. CCBill LLC*,[8] the Ninth Circuit construed § 512(c), the third safe harbor enumerated in the text. In that case, the court held that a copyright owner who notifies a Web hosting service about infringing content pursuant to this provision of the statute must provide a single notice containing all of the relevant information required under the DMCA: "The DMCA notification procedures place the burden of policing copyright infringement—identifying the potentially infringing material and adequately documenting infringement—squarely on the owners of the copyright."[9] The court also determined that one of the defendant service providers received no direct financial benefit attributable to the infringement and therefore fell within § 512(c)'s liability limitations for claims regarding direct, vicarious and contributory infringement.[10] In so concluding, the court held that "'direct financial benefit' should be interpreted consistent with the similarly-worded common law standard for vicarious copyright liability."[11]

Section 512(c) also was also at issue in a recently decided case against the operators of YouTube. Plaintiffs complained that tens of thousands of infringing video clips were uploaded on the site, and that the operator of YouTube had actual knowledge of that fact but failed to take

---

[6] Id. at 1070.
[7] See *Ellison v. Robertson*, 357 F.3d 1072 (9th Cir. 2004).
[8] 488 F.3d 1102 (9th Cir.), cert. den. 552 U.S. 1062 (2007).
[9] Id. at 113.
[10] 17 U.S.C. § 512(c)(1)(B)
[11] 488 F.3d at 1118.

steps to prevent such postings.[12] The Court ruled that to lose its safe harbor, the defendant would need actual knowledge of specific infringing items, not merely general awareness of the presence of infringing material on the site.

INSERT THE FOLLOWING ON PAGE 476 AFTER THE FIRST FULL PARAGRAPH:

In *Brilliance Audio, Inc. v. Haights Cross Communications, Inc.*,[13] the court held that a publisher of educational audiobooks (books on tape) did not commit copyright infringement by repackaging and renting a competitor's audiobooks.[14] The court held that in enacting the Record Rental Amendment Act, Congress intended to exclude only sound recordings of *musical works* from the ambit of the first sale doctrine.[15] Since the audiotapes were of *recitations of books*, and did not include music, the court held that the first sale doctrine shielded the defendant's activity. In contrast, the court concluded that the lower court had erred in dismissing the plaintiff's trademark claims on the ground that the defendant's repackaging and relabeling of the plaintiff's retail editions as library editions could result in a "material difference" so as to remove the sales from the ambit of trademark law's first sale doctrine[16] (see Assignment 4).

INSERT THE FOLLOWING AT THE END OF NOTE 2c ON PAGE 478:

Recently, the Court again granted certiorari in a case pitting § 109(a) against § 602(a).[17] This time, the goods in question were made abroad, sold to an authorized distributor abroad, and ultimately, after an additional transfer, found their way to the shelves of Costco in California. The issue this time is whether the application of the first sale doctrine to exhaust the

---

[12] *Viacom Int'l, Inc. v. YouTube, Inc.*, Nos. 07 Civ. 2103(LLS), 07 Civ. 3582(LLS), 2010 WL 2532404 (June 23, 2010).

[13] 474 F.3d 365 (6th Cir. 2007).

[14] Id. at 374.

[15] Id. at 372.

[16] Id. at 370-71.

[17] *Costco Wholesale Corp. v. Omega S.A.*, 130 S. Ct. 2089 (U.S. 2010) (granting certiorari).

copyright owner's rights is appropriate when both the manufacturer and initial sale took place abroad. The lower court ruled that application of § 109(a) under these circumstances would constitute an inappropriate extraterritorial application of U.S. law.[18]

INSERT THE FOLLOWING AT THE END OF NOTE 3a ON PAGE 479:

In 2006, the Librarian of Congress exempted six classes of works from the DMCA's prohibition on circumvention of access controls. Three of these exemptions were new, including one that allows consumers to bypass software controls on cell phone handsets. These controls prevent consumers from using their handsets on another service provider's network even after their contract with the original carrier expires.[19] Among the exemptions rejected was one for space-shifting that would have allowed circumvention of technological measures to copy audiovisual and musical works to other media or devices. The fourth rulemaking proceeding is currently underway.[20] In October, 2009, the Librarian extended the 2006 exemptions on an interim basis, recognizing that the 2009 rules could not be sent to Congress by their due date of October 27.[21] Although the Copyright Office had anticipated only a brief delay in issuing the new rules, they had not yet been promulgated when this Supplement went to press.

---

[18] *Omega S.A. v. Costco Wholesale Corp.*, 541 F.3d 982 (9th Cir. 2008).

[19] 71 Fed. Reg. 68,472, 68,473-78 (Nov. 27, 2006) (codified at 37 CFR pt. 201.40(b), (c)). Information about the 2006 rulemaking can be found at http://www.copyright.gov/1201/2006/index.html. A second exemption allows film scholars to bypass DVD encryption in order to compile film clips for educational use. The third one permits the circumvention of digital rights management software on CDs that controls access to lawfully purchased works and creates security flaws compromising the security of the end user's computer. Such circumvention is "for the purpose of good faith testing, investigating or correcting such security flaws or vulnerabilities." In addition, exemptions 2-4 delineated in footnote 56 on page 479 were renewed, but exemption 1 involving compilations of sites blocked by filtering software was dropped due to the proponents' failure to adduce current evidence of its relevance.

[20] 73 Fed. Reg. 79,425 (Dec. 29, 2008) (Exemption to Prohibition on Circumvention of Copyright Protection Systems for Access Control Technologies: Notice of Proposed Rulemaking).

[21] 74 Fed. Reg. 55,138 (Oct. 27, 2009).

INSERT THE FOLLOWING AS THE LAST PARAGRAPH OF NOTE 4 ON PAGE 484:

In *Cartoon Network LP v. CSC Holdings, Inc.*,[22] an individual subscriber could decide to record a cable television program on recording equipment resident with the cable company and then call it up when she was ready to watch it. The owners of the copyrights in the programming argued that the transmission of the recorded show to the viewer's own television was a public performance within clause (2) of the definition in §101. The Court found that as long at the transmission was of a "unique" copy of the work in question (as opposed to the repeated transmission from a single copy as was the case in Redd Horne), a "public" performance had not occurred.[23]

The growing importance of the Internet as a means of both legitimate and infringing transmission of copyrighted works also raises questions about the meaning of "public performance." In *United States v. American Society of Composers, Authors and Publishers*,[24] the court held in a case of first impression that a musical work downloaded through the Internet involves the right of reproduction rather than the public performance right. At issue in this case was whether AOL, Yahoo and others needed public performance licenses from ASCAP to cover instances in which their users downloaded musical files embodying musical compositions within ASCAP's repertoire. Recall that authors grant ASCAP and other performing rights societies the right to license public performances of compositions (see Note 7 in the casebook on page 487). The court distinguished downloaded music files from streamed music, reasoning that downloading involves the transmission of data to be saved by the recipient and played at a later time rather than a performance by the sender.[25] The court construed the statute to treat the reproduction involved in downloading music separately from the performance involved in streaming, while acknowledging that there might in theory be instances in which transmission over the Internet involves both.[26] See also the Insert on page 104 of this Supplement, "following at the end of page 489," for a

---

[22] 536 F.3d 121 (2d Cir. 2008), cert. denied sub nom. *Cable News Network, Inc. v. CSC Holdings, Inc.*, 129 S. Ct. 2890 (2009).

[23] Id. at 138.

[24] 485 F. Supp. 2d 438 (S.D.N.Y. 2007).

[25] Id. at 443-44.

[26] Id. at 447.

discussion of legislative reforms urged by the register of copyrights to address the similar issue of distinguishing public performances of sound recordings (covered under § 114) and distributions of phonorecords of musical works (covered under § 115).

INSERT AS LAST SENTENCE OF FIRST PARAGRAPH OF NOTE 9 ON PAGE 488:

Legislation currently pending before Congress would eliminate the distinction, requiring that over-the-air broadcasters also pay for performing sound recordings.[27]

INSERT AS A NEW NOTE 9a ON PAGE 489:

9a. *The Family Entertainment and Copyright Act.* Congress recently passed the Family Entertainment and Copyright Act (FEC Act) of 2005. This amendment contains provisions that allow private parties to avoid undesirable content while viewing authorized copies of movies. The act accomplishes this by amending 17 U.S.C. § 110, which exempts certain types of behavior from infringement. The FEC Act allows both the removal of certain sections of movies presented in a private household during viewing and the creation of software that performs this action, as long as the software does not create a fixed copy of the altered version.[28] The act also amends 15 U.S.C.A. § 1114 to remove from liability for trademark infringement actions that fall under 17 U.S.C. § 110(11).

Given the increasing popularity of DVD movies over the last few years, a few services have emerged which attempt to make movies more "family friendly." There are two common ways of achieving this goal. Several companies, such as ClearPlay, release special "filters" for selected movies which bypass graphic scenes and mute undesirable sounds during playback of any copy of the filtered movie. A different approach is used by companies such as CleanFlicks, which provide not just a filter, but provide the end customer with an edited version of the movie already recorded on a DVD ready to be played back. Representatives of the movie

---

[27] Performance Rights Act, H.R. 848, 111th Cong. (2009); Performance Rights Act, S. 379, 111th Cong. (2009).
[28] See § 110(11).

industry sued providers of these family friendly films soon after these businesses started.[29]

The FEC Act attempts to balance concerns of the motion picture industry as well as those of the commercial filtering businesses. Most importantly, the act excludes from copyright and trademark infringement products which "make imperceptible" limited portions of motion pictures. However, there are critical limits to this exclusion. First, the filtering of content must take place during private home viewing and the filtered content must come from an authorized original.[30] Second, no fixed copy of the altered version may be created, and when a portion of the content is made imperceptible, it cannot be replaced by other content – it must be either muted or skipped.[31] Under further changes to the Lanham Act, if a manufacturer of filtering products complies with provisions which exclude it from copyright liability, that same manufacturer benefits from an exclusion of liability under trademark law, as well.[32] Manufacturers of devices which incorporate the filtering technology are likewise immune from suit, as long as notice is given before the display of any edited work.[33]

The FEC Act therefore gives a limited allowance to the creators of filtering technology. Lawsuits against ClearPlay and some other manufacturers were dismissed in light of these new provisions.[34] Since the law is narrowly drawn, providers of actual sanitized movies, such as CleanFlicks, have not benefitted from the passage of this act.[35]

INSERT THE FOLLOWING BEFORE THE LAST FULL PARAGRAPH ON PAGE 489 AS PART OF NOTE 10:

---

[29] The claims leveraged against the providers of filtering technologies included many different claims such as copyright infringement through creation of an unauthorized derivative work, false designation of origin, distortion and dilution in violation of the Lanham Act, and other claims.

[30] § 110(11) (2005).

[31] Id.

[32] 15 USCA § 1114(3)(A) (2005).

[33] 15 USCA § 1114(3)(B) (2005).

[34] *Huntsman v. Soderbergh*, No. Civ.A02CV01662RPMMJW, 2005 WL 1993421 (D. Colo. Aug. 17, 2005).

[35] *CleanFlicks v. Soderbergh*, 433 F. Supp. 2d 1236 (D. Colo. 2006).

Pursuant to this amendment, the Librarian of Congress was vested with power to create and appoint Copyright Arbitration Panels ("CARP's") whose purpose was to set compulsory licenses. The CARP's were convened when necessary and had membership that could vary depending on the session. Parties who had dealt with CARP's had complained about a lack of clear procedure in this area, as well as inconsistencies in the results reached by panels.[36] In 2004, Congress amended Chapter 8 of the Copyright Act replacing the CARP's with three full-time Copyright Royalty Judges.[37] Each judge is appointed by the Librarian of Congress, serves for a term of six years, and is required to be an attorney with significant arbitration experience.[38] The Act further clarifies procedures in front of the newly established arbitration courts.

INSERT THE FOLLOWING AT THE END OF PAGE 489:

The growth of online business models for distributing copyrighted works raises new questions regarding the compulsory licensing provisions. At present, confusion exists over whether certain online transmissions of digital music files by streaming should be treated solely as performances under § 114 or also as distributions covered by § 115. As a result, providers are facing royalty demands by dual entities. Currently, the register of copyrights is struggling to resolve some of these questions by promulgating a rule outlining the transmission events which trigger § 115. An interim regulation is now in place,[39] while consideration of the final form of the regulation continues.[40] Note that *United States v. American Society of Composers, Authors and Publishers* (see insert to Note 4, above) raised a related issue of whether music downloads should be considered reproductions or public performances of the *musical compositions* under 106(4).[41]

---

[36] See H.R. REP. 108-408 Section 3: "Background and Need for Legislation."

[37] § 801(a) (2005).

[38] § 802(a)-(c) (2005).

[39] *Compulsory License for Making and Distributing Phonorecords, Including Digital Phonorecord Deliveries: Interim Rule and Request for Comments*, 73 FED. REG. 66,173 (Nov. 7, 2008).

[40] See http://www.copyright.gov/docs/section115/.

[41] 485 F. Supp. 2d 438 (S.D.N.Y. 2007).

ASSIGNMENT 12—REMEDIES

INSERT THE FOLLOWING AFTER THE FIRST PARAGRAPH ON PAGE 493:

In 2005, Congress again acted to amend federal criminal law in the copyright area. As part of the Family Entertainment and Copyright Act (FEC Act), Congress expanded Section 506 to include an additional definition of criminal copyright infringement. As the introductory material to this Assignment indicates, following the 1997 NET Act, there were two distinct ways of violating a copyright criminally (see pages 492-93 in Casebook). The FEC creates yet a third way: criminal copyright infringement occurs when a defendant posts to a public computer network a work that is scheduled for commercial release, if the defendant knew or should have known that the work was scheduled for commercial release.[1] This amendment covers a wide gamut of works, including computer programs, musical works, and motion pictures.[2] In order to facilitate this criminal provision, a new registration process for pre-release work is authorized by the act.[3] Beyond expanding the pre-existing criminal copyright provisions, the FEC Act also creates a new federal crime which prohibits unauthorized recording of a motion picture presentation in a movie theater.[4] For additional discussion of FEC, see Note 9a in Assignment 11 of this Supplement.

The most recent addition to the remedies for copyright infringement is the Prioritizing Resources and Organization for Intellectual Property Act of 2008 (known as the Pro IP Act), P.L. 110-403, enacted on Oct. 13, 2008. The statute permits courts in civil cases to order impoundment, not only of the alleged infringing articles, but of records relating to their manufacture and sale. It also creates a new executive position for an Intellectual Property Enforcement Coordinator and increases the resources devoted by the Justice Department and the F.B.I. to criminal enforcement.

---

[1] § 506(a)(1)(C) (2005).
[2] § 506(a)(3)(A) (2005).
[3] § 408(f)(2) (2005).
[4] 18 U.S.C. 2319B (2005) (providing for three years in prison if there was no financial gain and five years with a financial gain for a first offense; subsequent offenses are doubled).

INSERT THE FOLLOWING AT THE BEGINNING OF THE FIRST PARAGRAPH ON PAGE 517:

In *WB Music Corp. v. RTV Communication Group*,[5] the court held that statutory damages for infringing compilations of separate copyrighted works should be based on the number of infringed works rather than the number of infringing compilations.

---

[5] 445 F.3d 538 (2d Cir. 2006).

ASSIGNMENT 13—PREEMPTION OF STATE LAWS: THE RIGHT OF PUBLICITY AND MISAPPROPRIATION

INSERT AT THE END OF NOTE 8 ON PAGE 561:

In *C.B.C. Distribution and Marketing, Inc. v. Major League Baseball Advanced Media, L.P.*,[1] the Eighth Circuit Court of Appeals concluded that commercial use by CBC of the names and statistics of players in offering fantasy baseball products to the public was not an actionable violation of the players' rights of publicity. In explaining its conclusion, the Court wrote that "the information used in CBC's fantasy baseball games is all readily available in the public domain, and it would be strange law that a person would not have a first amendment right to use information that is available to everyone. It is true that CBC's use of the information is meant to provide entertainment, but [s]peech that entertains, like speech that informs, is protected by the First Amendment because [t]he line between the informing and the entertaining is too elusive for the protection of that basic right."[2] The opinion went on to express skepticism about the significance of the kind of interest asserted by the players. They were not attempting to vindicate their right to earn a living ("major league baseball players are rewarded, and handsomely, too, for their participation in games and can earn additional large sums from endorsements and sponsorship arrangements,"[3] the majority observed); nor did the case raise problems of possible consumer confusion. Claims of natural rights and other non-monetary arguments were, in the Court's view, insufficient to overcome CBC's interest in making use of public domain information.[4]

---

[1] 505 F.3d 818 (8th Cir. 2007), cert. denied, 128 S. Ct. 2872 (2008).

[2] Id. at 823.

[3] Id. at 824.

[4] Id. The disagreement over how to deal with factual information in the context of fantasy sports games continues. In *Keller v. Electronic Arts, Inc.*, No. 4:09-cv-01967-CW, 2010 WL 530108 (N.D. Cal. Feb. 8, 2010), a district court ruled in favor of the plaintiff (a college football player) who complained that use of an athlete's biographical data and appearance to create a virtual player for simulated games was a violation of his publicity rights.

ASSIGNMENT 14—PATENT PROTECTION: INTRODUCTION

INSERT AT THE END OF FOOTNOTE 1 ON PAGE 564:

If they meet the requirements discussed in this and later chapters, plants may also be covered by utility patents. *J.E.M. AG Supply, Inc. v. Pioneer Hi-Bred International, Inc.*, 534 U.S. 124 (2001).

INSERT AT THE END OF FOOTNOTE 16 ON PAGE 575:

The more recent interpretation of the written description requirement – that it can be used separately from the enablement requirement to establish invalidity even when priority is not at issue – has been extremely controversial. However, it has been reaffirmed in an en banc ruling of the Federal Circuit. *Ariad Pharms., Inc. v. Eli Lilly & Co.*, 598 F. 3d 1336 (Fed. Cir. 2010).

INSERT FOLLOWING THE LAST PARAGRAPH ON PAGE 588:

4. PATENT REFORM LEGISLATION

The last few years have seen the introduction of several bills aimed at significant reform of the patent system.[1] As of this writing none of these bills has been enacted by Congress. Some of the important changes proposed in various versions of patent reform legislation include:

> (1) Priority accorded to the first inventor to file a patent application, rather than to the first to invent. (See Assignment 20.) The change to first to file would necessitate major changes to § 102, which determines what prior art is considered in assessing novelty, nonobviousness, and statutory bars to patentability. (See Assignments 17-19.)

---

[1] See, e.g. H.R. 2795, 109th Cong. (1st Sess. 2005); H.R. 5096 109th Cong. (2d Sess. 2006); H.R. 1908, 110th Cong. (1st Sess. 2007); S. 1145, 110th Cong. (1st Sess, 2007); H.R. 1260, 111th Cong. (1st Sess. 2009); S. 515, 111th Cong. (1st Sess. 2009) (reintroduced in 2010 as an "amendment in the nature of a substitute").

(2) Inventiveness judged on a standard closer to absolute novelty; there would no longer be an explicit distinction between U.S. and foreign knowledge and use. (See Assignment 17.)

(3) New systems for insuring patent quality. For example, the public might have an expanded right to submit information relevant to patent examination to the PTO prior to allowance; after issuance, it might be possible, within specific time periods, to bring an inter partes post-grant opposition proceeding challenging the validity of a patent. (See Assignment 14, Section 2.)

(4) Subjective elements in litigation—including claims of inequitable conduct before the PTO (see Assignment 14, p. 582), or willful infringement—revised or eliminated. (See Assignment 23.)

(5) Best mode requirement eliminated (See Assignment 14, pp. 574-575.)

(6) Changes to the determination of damages in cases in which the infringed patent plays a minor role in the overall product or process at issue. (See Assignment 23.)

The parentheticals indicate the portions of this casebook to which the changes would be most relevant. We now consider some of the issues raised by the proposed reforms.

Proposed Changes to Patent Prosecution. Proposals including an inter partes post-grant opposition procedure, expanded publication of patent applications, and an expanded public right to submit prior art information prior to allowance are aimed particularly at improving the PTO's ability to assess the inventiveness of applications in fields, such as software and business methods, in which patent searches may not be effective means of uncovering the most relevant prior art. They are intended to enlist the assistance of the applicant's competitors and other members of the public in identifying prior art in a relatively inexpensive and early forum.

The proposals include expanded opportunities for third party *pre-grant submissions* of prior art bearing on validity. Under the current rule, 37 C.F.R. § 1.99, submissions must be made within a short time-span, are limited to patents and publications, and cannot include an explanation. In contrast, some reform proposals would give third parties a longer time period, allow them to submit evidence of "knowledge or use, or public use or sale," and have them explain the applicability of each reference.

A related pilot project, based on a proposal by New York Law School professor Beth Noveck, attempts to use a "peer production" model to uncover pertinent prior art. Applications are posted on a website so that members of the relevant technical community can suggest and rank prior art. Up to ten pieces of prior art identified in this way can be submitted to USPTO examiners for their consideration. Information about the project is available at http://www.peertopatent.org.

Some version of *post-grant opposition procedure*, a formal means for third parties to challenge patents for a period of time after issuance, has also been included in most legislative proposals. Oppositions could be instituted within a specified time after the grant or reissue of a patent. In some versions of the proposal, a party receiving notice of infringement or otherwise experiencing economic harm due to a particular patent would have an opportunity to bring a later opposition proceeding. An opposition proceeding would have two phases: first, the Patent Office could dismiss any request lacking "substantial merit"; second, a panel of administrative law judges would hear the merits of the challenge. There would be limited discovery; with permission, oral argument; and appeal to the Federal Circuit.

Proposed Changes to Patent Litigation and Remedies. Besides proposing changes at the prosecution stage, patent reform legislation has also addressed several litigation issues, such as requiring that damages be based upon the contribution of the patented invention to the overall value of an infringing product or that royalty awards be based on a comparison to available non-infringing substitutes, limiting the ability of patentees to "forum shop" for patent-friendly venues or providing for a stay of injunctive relief pending appeal. Following the lead of recent Federal Circuit case law (see discussion in Note 2, p. 878 and associated supplementary material) some of the proposals also limit the circumstances under which triple damages may be awarded for *willful infringement*, for example by requiring a showing of reckless disregard of an explicit notice of infringement. Under the reform, any notice sufficient to establish willfulness would also be enough to allow the alleged infringer to initiate a declaratory judgment suit so that the issue of infringement can be decided in a timely manner. (With respect to the standard for bringing a declaratory judgment action for invalidity in a patent case, see also the discussion of the Supreme Court's decision in *MedImmune, Inc. v. Genentech, Inc.*[2] in Assignment 23.)

First Inventor to File.   The move to first-to-file from the current U.S. first to invent system has been proposed many times and is the common approach of major international patent regimes such as those of Europe and Japan. A change to first inventor to file would drastically change the scope of "prior art" relevant to determining whether a patent is allowed (see Assignments 17 and 19) and would essentially eliminate the question of "priority" (the subject of Assignment 20) and the need for "interference" proceedings to determine who invented first. Up until now the first-to-file proposal has always failed because small inventors have a big lobby that successfully appeals to romantic notions about "can-do" entrepreneurs working alone in their garages late at night, preserving America's technological edge.   In the past, these inventors have argued that first-to-invent puts them on a level playing field with large R&D firms, which have ample funds to file patent applications quickly. However, empirical evidence shows that small inventors do not actually benefit much from first-to-invent because well-heeled firms are also better situated to prove their dates of invention in an interference and—if that fails—to find invalidating prior art when the small inventor asserts its patent in court. University technology transfer offices will also play a role in future debates about first to file and first to invent. Some universities consider themselves handicapped relative to large R&D firms in getting their applications filed quickly, but they do not suffer from the same evidentiary problems as small inventors. Faculty members have their eyes on various prizes, so they tend to keep careful records of when they invented.

The advantages of first to file are significant: moving to that system would harmonize our law with that of other nations and it would eliminate the need to engage in virtually all of the analysis in Assignment 20, along

---

[2] 549 U.S. 118 (2007).

with the expensive interference practice that analysis entails. Further, some versions of first to file would provide inventors who lose the race to the PTO with a consolation prize by amending § 273 and providing an *"earlier inventor"* defense for all inventions (not just business methods, see p. 617), to any inventor who reduced the subject matter of the patent to practice and commercially used it or made significant preparations to use it before the filing date of the patent. Put more simply, the first-to-invent could continue to use the invention for its own purposes even if another inventor filed first.

ASSIGNMENT 15—SUBJECT MATTER

REPLACE THE PRINCIPAL PROBLEM ON PAGES 591-592 WITH THE DISCUSSION OF THE CASES IN NOTES 6c AND d BELOW. REPLACE PAGES 593-619 WITH THE FOLLOWING (WHICH INCLUDES CONDENSED VERSIONS OF *CHAKRABARTY* AND *STATE STREET BANK*):

Diamond v. Chakrabarty

Supreme Court of the United States, 1980.
447 U.S. 303.

■ MR. CHIEF JUSTICE BURGER delivered the opinion of the Court.

We granted certiorari to determine whether a live, human-made micro-organism is patentable subject matter under 35 U.S.C.A. § 101.

I

In 1972, respondent Chakrabarty, a microbiologist, filed a patent application, assigned to the General Electric Co. The application asserted 36 claims related to Chakrabarty's invention of "a bacterium from the genus Pseudomonas containing therein at least two stable energy-generating plasmids, each of said plasmids providing a separate hydrocarbon degradative pathway." This human-made, genetically engineered bacterium is capable of breaking down multiple components of crude oil. Because of this property, which is possessed by no naturally occurring bacteria, Chakrabarty's invention is believed to have significant value for the treatment of oil spills.

Chakrabarty's patent claims were of three types: first, process claims for the method of producing the bacteria; second, claims for an inoculum comprised of a carrier material floating on water, such as straw, and the new bacteria; and third, claims to the bacteria themselves. The patent examiner allowed the claims falling into the first two categories, but rejected claims for the bacteria. His decision rested on two grounds: (1) that micro-organisms are "products of nature," and (2) that as living things they are not patentable subject matter under 35 U.S.C. § 101.

113

Chakrabarty appealed the rejection of these claims to the Patent Office Board of Appeals, and the Board affirmed the Examiner on the second ground. Relying on the legislative history of the 1930 Plant Patent Act, in which Congress extended patent protection to certain asexually reproduced plants, the Board concluded that § 101 was not intended to cover living things such as these laboratory created micro-organisms.

The Court of Customs and Patent Appeals, by a divided vote, reversed.

* * *

II

The Constitution grants Congress broad power to legislate to "promote the Progress of Science and useful Arts, by securing for limited Times to Authors and Inventors the exclusive Right to their respective Writings and Discoveries." Art. I, § 8, cl. 8. The patent laws promote this progress by offering inventors exclusive rights for a limited period as an incentive for their inventiveness and research efforts. The authority of Congress is exercised in the hope that "[t]he productive effort thereby fostered will have a positive effect on society through the introduction of new products and processes of manufacture into the economy, and the emanations by way of increased employment and better lives for our citizens." *Kewanee Oil Co. v. Bicron Corp.*, 416 U.S.470, 480 (1974).

The question before us in this case is a narrow one of statutory interpretation requiring us to construe 35 U.S.C. § 101, which provides:

> "Whoever invents or discovers any new and useful process, machine, manufacture, or composition of matter, or any new and useful improvement thereof, may obtain a patent therefore, subject to the conditions and requirements of this title."

Specifically, we must determine whether respondent's micro-organism constitutes a "manufacture" or "composition of matter" within the meaning of the statute.

III

In cases of statutory construction we begin, of course, with the language of the statute. And "unless otherwise defined, words will be interpreted as taking their ordinary, contemporary common meaning." We have also cautioned that courts "should not read into the patent laws limitations and conditions which the legislature has not expressed."

Guided by these canons of construction, this Court has read the term "manufacture" in § 101 in accordance with its dictionary definition to mean "the production of articles for use from raw or prepared materials by giving to these materials new forms, qualities, properties, or combinations, whether by hand-labor or by machinery." *American Fruit Growers, Inc. v. Brogdex Co.*, 283 U.S. 1, 11 (1931). Similarly, "composition of matter" has been construed consistent with its common usage to include "all compositions of two or more substances and ... all composite articles, whether they be the results of chemical union, or of mechanical mixture, or whether they be gases, fluids, powders or solids." *Shell Development Co. v. Watson*, 149 F.Supp. 279, 280 (D.D.C.1957). In choosing such expansive terms as "manufacture" and "composition of matter," modified by the comprehensive "any," Congress plainly contemplated that the patent laws would be given wide scope.

The relevant legislative history also supports a broad construction. The Patent Act of 1793, authored by Thomas Jefferson, defined statutory subject matter as "any new and useful art, machine, manufacture, or composition of matter, or any new or useful improvement [thereof]." Act of Feb. 21, 1793, § 1, 1 Stat. 319. The Act embodied Jefferson's philosophy that "ingenuity should receive a liberal encouragement." 5 Writings of Thomas Jefferson 75–76 (Washington ed. 1871). Subsequent patent statutes in 1836, 1870, and 1874 employed this same broad language. In 1952, when the patent laws were recodified, Congress replaced the word "art" with "process," but otherwise left Jefferson's language intact. The Committee Reports accompanying the 1952 Act inform us that Congress intended statutory subject matter to "include anything under the sun that is made by man." S. Rep. No. 1979, 82d Cong., 2d Sess., 5 (1952); HR Rep. No. 1923, 82d Cong., 2d Sess., 6 (1952).

This is not to suggest that § 101 has no limits or that it embraces every discovery. The laws of nature, physical phenomena, and abstract ideas have been held not patentable. Thus, a new mineral discovered in the earth or a new plant found in the wild is not patentable subject matter. Likewise, Einstein could not patent his celebrated law that $E=mc^2$; nor could Newton have patented the law of gravity. Such discoveries are "manifestations of ... nature, free to all men and reserved exclusively to none." *Funk Brothers Seed Co. v. Kalo Inoculant Co.*, 333 U.S. 127, 130 (1948).

Judged in this light, respondent's micro-organism plainly qualifies as patentable subject matter. His claim is not to a hitherto unknown natural phenomenon, but to a nonnaturally occurring manufacture or composition of matter—a product of human ingenuity "having a distinctive name, character [and] use." The point is underscored dramatically by comparison of the invention here with that in *Funk*. There, the patentee had discovered that there existed in nature certain species of root-nodule bacteria which did not exert a mutually inhibitive effect on each other. He used that discovery to produce a mixed culture capable of inoculating the seeds of leguminous plants. Concluding that the patentee had discovered "only some of the handiwork of nature," the Court ruled the product nonpatentable:

> "Each of the species of root-nodule bacteria contained in the package infects the same group of leguminous plants which it always infected. No species acquires a different use. The combination of species produces no new bacteria, no change in the six species of bacteria, and no enlargement of the range of their utility. Each species has the same effect it always had. The bacteria perform in their natural way. Their use in combination does not improve in any way their natural functioning. They serve the ends nature originally provided and act quite independently of any effort of the patentee."

Here, by contrast, the patentee has produced a new bacterium with markedly different characteristics from any found in nature and one having the potential for significant utility. His discovery is not nature's handiwork, but his own; accordingly it is patentable subject matter under § 101.

IV

116

Two contrary arguments are advanced, neither of which we find persuasive.

(A) [The Court rejected the argument that the legislation of the Plant Patent Act and the Plant Variety Protection Act precludes granting utility patents on living things.]

(B)

The petitioner's second argument is that micro-organisms cannot qualify as patentable subject matter until Congress expressly authorizes such protection. His position rests on the fact that genetic technology was unforeseen when Congress enacted § 101. From this it is argued that resolution of the patentability of inventions such as respondents should be left to Congress. The legislative process, the petitioner argues, is best equipped to weigh the competing economic, social, and scientific considerations involved, and to determine whether living organisms produced by genetic engineering should receive patent protection. In support of this position, the petitioner relies on our recent holding in *Parker v. Flook*, 437 U.S. 584 (1978), and the statement that the judiciary "must proceed cautiously when ... asked to extend patent rights into areas wholly unforeseen by Congress." *Id.* at 596.

It is, of course, correct that Congress, not the courts, must define the limits of patentability; but it is equally true that once Congress has spoken it is "the province and duty of the judicial department to say what the law is." *Marbury v. Madison*, 1 Cranch 137, 177 (1803). Congress has performed its constitutional role in defining patentable subject matter in § 101; we perform ours in construing the language Congress has employed. In so doing, our obligation is to take statutes as we find them, guided, if ambiguity appears, by the legislative history and statutory purpose. Here, we perceive no ambiguity. The subject-matter provisions of the patent law have been cast in broad terms to fulfill the constitutional and statutory goal of promoting "the Progress of Science and the useful Arts" with all that means for the social and economic benefits envisioned by Jefferson. Broad general language is not necessarily ambiguous when congressional objectives require broad terms.

This Court frequently has observed that a statute is not to be confined to the "particular application[s] ... contemplated by the legislators." This is especially true in the field of patent law. A rule that unanticipated inventions are without protection would conflict with the core concept of the patent law that anticipation undermines patentability. Mr. Justice Douglas reminded that the inventions most benefiting mankind are those that "push back the frontiers of chemistry, physics, and the like." *Great A. & P. Tea Co. v. Supermarket Corp.*, 340 U.S. 147, 154 (1950) (concurring opinion). Congress employed broad general language in drafting § 101 precisely because such inventions are often unforeseeable.

To buttress his argument, the petitioner, with the support of amicus, points to grave risks that may be generated by research endeavors such as respondents. The briefs present a gruesome parade of horribles. Scientists, among them Nobel laureates, are quoted suggesting that genetic research may pose a serious threat to the human race, or, at the very least, that the dangers are far too substantial to permit such research to proceed apace at this time. We are told that genetic research and related technological developments may spread pollution and disease, that it may result in a loss of genetic diversity, and that its practice may tend to depreciate the value of human life. These arguments are forcefully, even passionately, presented; they remind us that, at times, human ingenuity seems unable to control fully the forces it creates—that with Hamlet, it is sometimes better "to bear those ills we have than fly to others that we know not of."

It is argued that this Court should weigh these potential hazards in considering whether respondent's invention is patentable subject matter under § 101. We disagree. The grant or denial of patents on micro-organisms is not likely to put an end to genetic research or to its attendant risks. The large amount of research that has already occurred when no researcher had sure knowledge that patent protection would be available suggests that legislative or judicial fiat as to patentability will not deter the scientific mind from probing into the unknown any more than Canute could command the tides. Whether respondent's claims are patentable may determine whether research efforts are accelerated by the hope of reward or slowed by want of incentives, but that is all.

What is more important is that we are without competence to entertain these arguments—either to brush them aside as fantasies generated by fear of the unknown, or to act on them. The choice we are urged to make is a matter of high policy for resolution within the legislative process after the kind of investigation, examination, and study that legislative bodies can provide and courts cannot. That process involves the balancing of competing values and interests, which in our democratic system is the business of elected representatives. Whatever their validity, the contentions now pressed on us should be addressed to the political branches of the Government, the Congress and the Executive, and not to the courts.

Accordingly, the judgment of the Court of Customs and Patent Appeals is Affirmed.

■ [The dissenting opinion of JUSTICE BRENNAN, joined by JUSTICES WHITE and MARSHALL, is omitted.]

State Street Bank & Trust Co. v. Signature Financial Group, Inc.

United States Court of Appeals for the Federal Circuit, 1998.
149 F.3d 1368.

■ RICH, CIRCUIT JUDGE.

Signature Financial Group, Inc. (Signature) [assignee of U.S. Patent No. 5,193,056 (the '056 patent), which issued to R. Todd Boes] appeals from the decision of the United States District Court for the District of Massachusetts granting a motion for summary judgment in favor of State Street Bank & Trust Co. (State Street), finding the '056 invalid on the ground that the claimed subject matter is not encompassed by 35 U.S.C. § 101 (1994). See *State Street Bank & Trust Co. v. Signature Financial Group, Inc.,* 927 F.Supp. 502, 38 USPQ2d 1530 (D.Mass.1996). We reverse and remand because we conclude that the patent claims are directed to statutory subject matter.

DISCUSSION

The patented invention relates generally to a system that allows an administrator to monitor and record the financial information flow and make all calculations necessary for maintaining a partner fund financial services configuration. A partner fund financial services configuration essentially allows several mutual funds, or "Spokes," to pool their investment funds into a single portfolio, or "Hub," allowing for consolidation of, inter alia, the costs of administering the fund combined with the tax advantages of a partnership.

[T]he [district] court concluded that the claimed subject matter fell into one of two alternative judicially-created exceptions to statutory subject matter. The court refers to the first exception as the "mathematical algorithm" exception and the second exception as the "business method" exception.

The "Mathematical Algorithm" Exception

The Supreme Court has identified three categories of subject matter that are unpatentable, namely "laws of nature, natural phenomena, and abstract ideas." [*Diamond v. Diehr*, 450 U.S. 175, 815 (1981).] Of particular relevance to this case, the Court has held that mathematical algorithms are not patentable subject matter to the extent that they are merely abstract ideas. Unpatentable mathematical algorithms are identifiable by showing they are merely abstract ideas constituting disembodied concepts or truths that are not "useful." From a practical standpoint, this means that to be patentable an algorithm must be applied in a "useful" way.

Today, we hold that the transformation of data, representing discrete dollar amounts, by a machine through a series of mathematical calculations into a final share price, constitutes a practical application of a mathematical algorithm, formula, or calculation, because it produces "a useful, concrete and tangible result"—a final share price momentarily fixed for recording and reporting purposes and even accepted and relied upon by regulatory authorities and in subsequent trades.

The Business Method Exception

As an alternative ground for invalidating the '056 patent under § 101, the court relied on the judicially-created, so-called "business method" exception to statutory subject matter. We take this opportunity to lay this ill-conceived exception to rest. The business method exception has never been invoked by this court, or the CCPA, to deem an invention unpatentable. Application of this particular exception has always been preceded by a ruling based on some clearer concept of Title 35 or, more commonly, application of the abstract idea exception based on finding a mathematical algorithm.

This case is no exception. The district court announced the precepts of the business method exception as set forth in several treatises, but noted as its primary reason for finding the patent invalid under the business method exception as follows:

> If Signature's invention were patentable, any financial institution desirous of implementing a multi-tiered funding complex modeled (sic) on a Hub and Spoke configuration would be required to seek Signature's permission before embarking on such a project. This is so because the '056 Patent is claimed [sic] sufficiently broadly to foreclose virtually any computer-implemented accounting method necessary to manage this type of financial structure.

927 F.Supp. 502, 516. Whether the patent's claims are too broad to be patentable is not to be judged under § 101, but rather under §§ 102, 103 and 112. Assuming the above statement to be correct, it has nothing to do with whether what is claimed is statutory subject matter.

CONCLUSION

The appealed decision is reversed and the case is remanded to the district court for further proceedings consistent with this opinion.

Bilski v. Kappos
Supreme Court of the United States, 2010.
2010 U.S. LEXIS 5521

■ JUSTICE KENNEDY delivered the opinion of the Court, except as to Parts II-B-2 and II-C-2. (JUSTICE SCALIA does not join Parts II-B-2 and II-C-2.)

The question in this case turns on whether a patent can be issued for a claimed invention designed for the business world. The patent application claims a procedure for instructing buyers and sellers how to protect against the risk of price fluctuations in a discrete section of the economy. Three arguments are advanced for the proposition that the claimed invention is outside the scope of patent law: (1) it is not tied to a machine and does not transform an article; (2) it involves a method of conducting business; and (3) it is merely an abstract idea. The Court of Appeals ruled that the first mentioned of these, the so-called machine-or-transformation test, was the sole test to be used for determining the patentability of a "process" under the *Patent Act*, 35 U.S.C. § 101.

I

Petitioners' application seeks patent protection for a claimed invention that explains how buyers and sellers of commodities in the energy market can protect, or hedge, against the risk of price changes. The key claims are claims 1 and 4. Claim 1 describes a series of steps instructing how to hedge risk. Claim 4 puts the concept articulated in claim 1 into a simple mathematical formula. Claim 1 consists of the following steps:

> "(a) initiating a series of transactions between said commodity provider and consumers of said commodity wherein said consumers purchase said commodity at a fixed rate based upon historical averages, said fixed rate corresponding to a risk position of said consumers;

> "(b) identifying market participants for said commodity having a counter-risk position to said consumers; and

> "(c) initiating a series of transactions between said commodity provider and said market participants at a second fixed rate such that said series of market participant transactions balances the risk position of said series of consumer transactions." App. 19-20.

The remaining claims explain how claims 1 and 4 can be applied to allow energy suppliers and consumers to minimize the risks resulting from fluctuations in market demand for energy. The patent examiner rejected petitioners' application, explaining that it "'is not implemented on a specific apparatus and merely manipulates [an] abstract idea and solves a purely mathematical problem without any limitation to a practical application, therefore, the invention is not directed to the technological arts.'" The Board of Patent Appeals and Interferences affirmed, concluding that the application involved only mental steps that do not transform physical matter and was directed to an abstract idea.

The United States Court of Appeals for the Federal Circuit heard the case en banc and affirmed. The case produced five different opinions. Students of patent law would be well advised to study these scholarly opinions.

Chief Judge Michel wrote the opinion of the court. The court rejected its prior test for determining whether a claimed invention was a patentable "process" under § 101 -- whether it produces a "'useful, concrete, and tangible result'." The court held that "[a] claimed process is surely patent-eligible under § 101 if: (1) it is tied to a particular machine or apparatus, or (2) it transforms a particular article into a different state or thing." The court concluded this "machine-or-transformation test" is "the sole test governing § 101 analyses," and thus the "test for determining patent eligibility of a process under § 101," Applying the machine-or-transformation test, the court held that petitioners' application was not patent eligible.

Three judges wrote dissenting opinions. Judge Mayer argued that petitioners' application was "not eligible for patent protection because it is directed to a method of conducting business." He urged the adoption of a "technological standard for patentability." Judge Rader would have found petitioners' claims were an unpatentable abstract idea. Only Judge Newman disagreed with the court's conclusion that petitioners' application was outside of the reach of § 101. She did not say that the application should have been granted but only that the issue should be remanded for further proceedings to determine whether the application qualified as patentable under other provisions.

II

A

Section 101 defines the subject matter that may be patented under the Patent Act:

> "Whoever invents or discovers any new and useful process, machine, manufacture, or composition of matter, or any new and useful improvement thereof, may obtain a patent therefore, subject to the conditions and requirements of this title."

Section 101 thus specifies four independent categories of inventions or discoveries that are eligible for protection: processes, machines, manufactures, and compositions of matter. "In choosing such expansive terms . . . modified by the comprehensive 'any,' Congress plainly contemplated that the patent laws would be given wide scope." *Diamond v. Chakrabarty,* 447 U.S. 303, 308 (1980). Congress took this permissive approach to patent eligibility to ensure that "'ingenuity should receive a liberal encouragement.'" *Id.,* at 308-309. The Court's precedents provide three specific exceptions to § 101's broad patent-eligibility principles: "laws of nature, physical phenomena, and abstract ideas." The concepts covered by these exceptions are "part of the storehouse of knowledge of all men . . . free to all men and reserved exclusively to none." *Funk Brothers Seed Co. v. Kalo Inoculant Co.,* 333 U.S. 127, 130 (1948).

The § 101 patent-eligibility inquiry is only a threshold test. Even if an invention qualifies as a process, machine, manufacture, or composition of matter, in order to receive the Patent Act's protection the claimed invention must also satisfy "the conditions and requirements of this title." § 101. Those requirements include that the invention be novel, see § 102, nonobvious, see § 103, and fully and particularly described, see § 112.

The present case involves an invention that is claimed to be a "process" under § 101. Section 100(b) defines "process" as:

> "process, art or method, and includes a new use of a known process, machine, manufacture, composition of matter, or material."

The Court first considers two proposed categorical limitations on "process" patents under § 101 that would, if adopted, bar petitioners' application in the present case: the machine-or-transformation test and the categorical exclusion of business method patents.

B

1

Under the Court of Appeals' formulation, an invention is a "process" only if: "(1) it is tied to a particular machine or apparatus, or (2) it transforms a particular article into a different state or thing. This Court has "more than once cautioned that courts 'should not read into the patent laws limitations and conditions which the legislature has not expressed.'" *Diamond v. Diehr,* 450 U.S. 175, 182 (1981). In patent law, as in all statutory construction, "[u]nless otherwise defined, 'words will be interpreted as taking their ordinary, contemporary, common meaning.'" *Diehr, supra,* at 182.

Any suggestion in this Court's case law that the Patent Act's terms deviate from their ordinary meaning has only been an explanation for the exceptions for laws of nature, physical phenomena, and abstract ideas.

124

This Court has not indicated that the existence of these well-established exceptions gives the Judiciary *carte blanche* to impose other limitations that are inconsistent with the text and the statute's purpose and design. Concerns about attempts to call any form of human activity a "process" can be met by making sure the claim meets the requirements of § 101.

Adopting the machine-or-transformation test as the sole test for what constitutes a "process" (as opposed to just an important and useful clue) violates these statutory interpretation principles. The Court is unaware of any "'ordinary, contemporary, common meaning,' of the definitional terms "process, art or method" that would require these terms to be tied to a machine or to transform an article. "When a statute includes an explicit definition, we must follow that definition."

The Court of Appeals incorrectly concluded that this Court has endorsed the machine-or-transformation test as the exclusive test. It is true that *Cochrane v. Deener*, 94 U.S. 780, 788 (1877), explained that a "process" is "an act, or a series of acts, performed upon the subject-matter to be transformed and reduced to a different state or thing." More recent cases, however, have rejected the broad implications of this dictum; and, in all events, later authority shows that it was not intended to be an exhaustive or exclusive test. This Court's precedents establish that the machine-or-transformation test is a useful and important clue, an investigative tool, for determining whether some claimed inventions are processes under § 101. The machine-or-transformation test is not the sole test for deciding whether an invention is a patent-eligible "process."

2

It is true that patents for inventions that did not satisfy the machine-or-transformation test were rarely granted in earlier eras, especially in the Industrial Age. But times change. Technology and other innovations progress in unexpected ways.

The machine-or-transformation test may well provide a sufficient basis for evaluating processes similar to those in the Industrial Age -- for example, inventions grounded in a physical or other tangible form. But there are reasons to doubt whether the test should be the sole criterion for determining the patentability of inventions in the Information Age. As numerous *amicus* briefs argue, the machine-or-transformation test would create uncertainty as to the patentability of software, advanced diagnostic medicine techniques, and inventions based on linear programming, data compression, and the manipulation of digital signals. In the course of

125

applying the machine-or-transformation test to emerging technologies, courts may pose questions of such intricacy and refinement that they risk obscuring the larger object of securing patents for valuable inventions without transgressing the public domain. As a result, in deciding whether previously unforeseen inventions qualify as patentable "process[es]," it may not make sense to require courts to confine themselves to asking the questions posed by the machine-or-transformation test. Section 101's terms suggest that new technologies may call for new inquiries.

It is important to emphasize that the Court today is not commenting on the patentability of any particular invention, let alone holding that any of the above-mentioned technologies from the Information Age should or should not receive patent protection. This Age puts the possibility of innovation in the hands of more people and raises new difficulties for the patent law. With ever more people trying to innovate and thus seeking patent protections for their inventions, the patent law faces a great challenge in striking the balance between protecting inventors and not granting monopolies over procedures that others would discover by independent, creative application of general principles. Nothing in this opinion should be read to take a position on where that balance ought to be struck.

C

1

Section 101 similarly precludes the broad contention that the term "process" categorically excludes business methods. The Court is unaware of any argument that the "'ordinary, contemporary, common meaning,'" of "method" excludes business methods. Nor is it clear how far a prohibition on business method patents would reach, and whether it would exclude technologies for conducting a business more efficiently.

The argument that business methods are categorically outside of § 101's scope is further undermined by the fact that federal law explicitly contemplates the existence of at least some business method patents. Under 35 U.S.C. § 273(b)(1), if a patent-holder claims infringement based on "a method in [a] patent," the alleged infringer can assert a defense of prior use. For purposes of this defense alone, "method" is defined as "a method of doing or conducting business." § 273(a)(3). In other words, by allowing this defense the statute itself acknowledges that there may be business method patents. A conclusion that business methods are not patentable in any circumstances would render § 273 meaningless. This would violate the canon against interpreting any statutory provision in a manner that would render another provision superfluous. Finally, while § 273 appears to leave open the possibility of some business method patents, it does not suggest broad patentability of such claimed inventions.

2

Interpreting § 101 to exclude all business methods simply because business method patents were rarely issued until modern times revives many of the previously discussed difficulties. At the same time, some business method patents raise special problems in terms of vagueness and suspect validity. *See eBay Inc. v. MercExchange, L. L. C.*, 547 U.S. 388, 397 (2006) (KENNEDY, J., concurring). The Information Age empowers people with new capacities to perform statistical analyses and mathematical calculations with a speed and sophistication that enable the design of protocols for more efficient performance of a vast number of business tasks. If a high enough bar is not set when considering patent applications of this sort, patent examiners and courts could be flooded with claims that would put a chill on creative endeavor and dynamic change.

In searching for a limiting principle, this Court's precedents on the unpatentability of abstract ideas provide useful tools. Indeed, if the Court of Appeals were to succeed in defining a narrower category or class of patent applications that claim to instruct how business should be conducted, and then rule that the category is unpatentable because, for instance, it represents an attempt to patent abstract ideas, this conclusion might well be in accord with controlling precedent. But beyond this or some other limitation consistent with the statutory text, the Patent Act leaves open the possibility that there are at least some processes that can be fairly described as business methods that are within patentable subject matter under § 101.

III

Even though petitioners' application is not categorically outside of § 101 under the two broad and atextual approaches the Court rejects today, that does not mean it is a "process" under § 101. Petitioners seek to patent both the concept of hedging risk and the application of that concept to energy markets. Rather than adopting categorical rules that might have wide-ranging and unforeseen impacts, the Court resolves this case narrowly on the basis of this Court's decisions in *Benson*, *Flook*, and *Diehr*, which show that petitioners' claims are not patentable processes because they are attempts to patent abstract ideas. Indeed, all members of the Court agree that the patent application at issue here falls outside of § 101 because it claims an abstract idea.

In *Benson*, the Court considered whether a patent application for an algorithm to convert binary-coded decimal numerals into pure binary code was a "process" under § 101. 409 U.S., at 64-67. The Court first explained that "'[a] principle, in the abstract, is a fundamental truth; an original cause; a motive; these cannot be patented, as no one can claim in either of them an exclusive right.'" The Court then held the application at issue was not a "process," but an unpatentable abstract idea. "It is conceded that one may not patent an idea. But in practical effect that would be the result if the formula for converting . . . numerals to pure binary numerals were patented in this case." A contrary holding "would wholly pre-empt the mathematical formula and in practical effect would be a patent on the algorithm itself."

In *Flook*, the Court considered the next logical step after *Benson*. The applicant there attempted to patent a procedure for monitoring the conditions during the catalytic conversion process in the petrochemical and oil-refining industries. The application's only innovation was reliance on a mathematical algorithm. 437 U.S., at 585-586. *Flook* held the invention was not a patentable "process." The Court conceded the invention at issue, unlike the algorithm in *Benson*, had been limited so that it could still be freely used outside the petrochemical and oil-refining industries. Nevertheless, *Flook* rejected "[t]he notion that post-solution activity, no matter how conventional or obvious in itself, can transform an unpatentable principle into a patentable process. The Court concluded that the process at issue there was "unpatentable under § 101, not because it contain[ed] a mathematical algorithm as one component, but because once that algorithm [wa]s assumed to be within the prior art, the application, considered as a whole, contain[ed] no patentable invention." As the Court later explained, *Flook* stands for the proposition that the prohibition against patenting abstract ideas "cannot be circumvented by attempting to limit the use of the formula to a particular technological environment" or adding "insignificant postsolution activity." *Diehr*, 450 U.S., at 191-192.

Finally, in *Diehr*, the Court established a limitation on the principles articulated in *Benson* and *Flook*. The application in *Diehr* claimed a previously unknown method for "molding raw, uncured synthetic rubber into cured precision products," using a mathematical formula to complete some of its several steps by way of a computer. 450 U.S., at 177. *Diehr* explained that while an abstract idea, law of nature, or mathematical formula could not be patented, "an *application* of a law of nature or mathematical formula to a known structure or process may well be deserving of patent protection." *Diehr* emphasized the need to consider the invention as a whole, rather than "dissect[ing] the claims into old and new elements and then . . . ignor[ing] the presence of the old elements in the analysis." Finally, the Court concluded that because the claim was not "an attempt to patent a mathematical formula, but rather [was] an industrial process for the molding of rubber products," it fell within § 101's patentable subject matter.

In light of these precedents, it is clear that petitioners' application is not a patentable "process." Claims 1 and 4 in petitioners' application explain the basic concept of hedging, or protecting against risk. The concept of hedging, described in claim 1 and reduced to a mathematical formula in claim 4, is an unpatentable abstract idea, just like the algorithms at issue in *Benson* and *Flook*. Allowing petitioners to patent risk hedging would pre-empt use of this approach in all fields, and would effectively grant a monopoly over an abstract idea.

Petitioners' remaining claims are broad examples of how hedging can be used in commodities and energy markets. *Flook* established that limiting an abstract idea to one field of use or adding token postsolution components did not make the concept patentable. That is exactly what the remaining claims in petitioners' application do. These claims attempt to patent the use of the abstract idea of hedging risk in the energy market and then instruct the use of well-known random analysis techniques to help establish some of the inputs into the equation. Indeed, these claims add even less to the underlying abstract principle than the invention in *Flook* did, for the *Flook* invention was at least directed to the narrower domain of signaling dangers in operating a catalytic converter.

* * *

Today, the Court once again declines to impose limitations on the Patent Act that are inconsistent with the Act's text. The patent application here can be rejected under our precedents on the unpatentability of abstract ideas. The Court, therefore, need not define further what constitutes a patentable "process," beyond pointing to the definition of that term provided in § 100(b) and looking to the guideposts in *Benson*, *Flook*, and *Diehr*.

129

And nothing in today's opinion should be read as endorsing interpretations of § 101 that the Court of Appeals for the Federal Circuit has used in the past. *See, e.g., State Street,* 149 F.3d at 1373. It may be that the Court of Appeals thought it needed to make the machine-or-transformation test exclusive precisely because its case law had not adequately identified less extreme means of restricting business method patents, including (but not limited to) application of our opinions in *Benson, Flook,* and *Diehr.* In disapproving an exclusive machine-or-transformation test, we by no means foreclose the Federal Circuit's development of other limiting criteria that further the purposes of the Patent Act and are not inconsistent with its text.

The judgment of the Court of Appeals is affirmed.

■ JUSTICE STEVENS, with whom JUSTICE GINSBURG, JUSTICE BREYER, and JUSTICE SOTOMAYOR join, concurring in the judgment.

In the area of patents, it is especially important that the law remain stable and clear. The only question presented in this case is whether the so-called machine-or-transformation test is the exclusive test for what constitutes a patentable "process" under 35 U.S.C. § 101. It would be possible to answer that question simply by holding, as the entire Court agrees, that although the machine-or-transformation test is reliable in most cases, it is not the *exclusive* test.

I agree with the Court that, in light of the uncertainty that currently pervades this field, it is prudent to provide further guidance. But I would take a different approach. Rather than making any broad statements about how to define the term "process" in § 101 or tinkering with the bounds of the category of unpatentable, abstract ideas, I would restore patent law to its historical and constitutional moorings.

For centuries, it was considered well established that a series of steps for conducting business was not, in itself, patentable. In the late 1990's, the Federal Circuit and others called this proposition into question. Congress quickly responded to a Federal Circuit decision with a stopgap measure designed to limit a potentially significant new problem for the business community. It passed the First Inventors Defense Act of 1999 (codified at 35 U.S.C. § 273), which provides a limited defense to claims of patent infringement, for "method[s] of doing or conducting business." Following several more years of confusion, the Federal Circuit changed course, overruling recent decisions and holding that a series of steps may constitute a patentable process only if it is tied to a machine or transforms an article into a different state or thing. This "machine-or-transformation test" excluded general methods of doing business as well as, potentially, a variety of other subjects that could be called processes.

The Court correctly holds that the machine-or-transformation test is not the sole test for what constitutes a patentable process; rather, it is a critical clue.[a] But the Court is quite wrong, in my view, to suggest that any series of steps that is not itself an abstract idea or law of nature may constitute a "process" within the meaning of § 101. The language in the Court's opinion to this effect can only cause mischief. The wiser course would have been to hold that petitioners' method is not a "process" because it describes only a general method of engaging in business transactions -- and business methods are not patentable. More precisely, although a process is not patent-ineligible simply because it is useful for conducting business, a claim that merely describes a method of doing business does not qualify as a "process" under § 101.

I

***

II

Before explaining in more detail how I would decide this case, I will comment briefly on the Court's opinion. The opinion is less than pellucid in more than one respect, and, if misunderstood, could result in confusion or upset settled areas of the law.

***

[I]n its discussion of an issue not contained in the questions presented -- whether the particular series of steps in petitioners' application is an abstract idea -- the Court uses language that could suggest a shift in our approach to that issue. Although I happen to agree that petitioners seek to patent an abstract idea, the Court does not show how this conclusion follows "clear[ly]," from our case law. The patent now before us is not for

---

[a] Even if the machine-or-transformation test may not define the scope of a patentable process, it would be a grave mistake to assume that anything with a "'useful, concrete and tangible result,'" *State Street Bank & Trust v. Signature Financial Group, Inc.*, 149 F.3d 1368, 1373 (CA Fed. 1998), may be patented.

"[a] principle, in the abstract," or a "fundamental truth." *Parker v. Flook,* 437 U.S. 584, 589 (1978). Nor does it claim the sort of phenomenon of nature or abstract idea that was embodied by the mathematical formula at issue in *Gottschalk v. Benson, 409* U.S. 63, 67 (1972), and in *Flook.*

The Court construes petitioners' claims on processes for pricing as claims on "the basic concept of hedging, or protecting against risk," and thus discounts the application's discussion of what sorts of data to use, and how to analyze those data, as mere "token postsolution components." In other words, the Court artificially limits petitioners' claims to hedging, and then concludes that hedging is an abstract idea rather than a term that describes a category of processes including petitioners' claims. Why the Court does this is never made clear. One might think that the Court's analysis means that any process that utilizes an abstract idea is *itself* an unpatentable, abstract idea. But we have never suggested any such rule, which would undermine a host of patentable processes. It is true, as the Court observes, that petitioners' application is phrased broadly. But claim specification is covered by § 112, not § 101; and if a series of steps constituted an unpatentable idea merely because it was described without sufficient specificity, the Court could be calling into question some of our own prior decisions. At points, the opinion suggests that novelty is the clue. But the fact that hedging is "'long prevalent in our system of commerce,'", cannot justify the Court's conclusion, as "the proper construction of § 101 . . . does not involve the familiar issu[e] of novelty" that arises under § 102. *Flook,* 437 U.S., at 588. At other points, the opinion for a plurality suggests that the analysis turns on the category of patent involved (courts should use the abstract-idea rule as a "too[l]" to set "a high enough bar" "when considering patent applications of this sort"). But we have never in the past suggested that the inquiry varies by subject matter.

The Court, in sum, never provides a satisfying account of what constitutes an unpatentable abstract idea. Indeed, the Court does not even explain if it is using the machine-or-transformation criteria. The Court essentially asserts its conclusion that petitioners' application claims an abstract idea. This mode of analysis (or lack thereof) may have led to the correct outcome in this case, but it also means that the Court's musings on this issue stand for very little.

III

I agree with the Court that the text of § 101 must be the starting point of our analysis. As I shall explain, however, the text must not be the end point as well.

Section 101 undoubtedly defines in "expansive terms" the subject matter eligible for patent protection, as the statute was meant to ensure that "'ingenuit[ies] receive a liberal encouragement.'" *Diamond v. Chakrabarty,* 447 U.S. 303, 308-309 (1980). Nonetheless, not every new invention or discovery may be patented. Certain things are "free for all to use." *Bonito Boats, Inc. v. Thunder Craft Boats, Inc.,* 489 U.S. 141, 151.

The text of the Patent Act does not on its face give much guidance about what constitutes a patentable process. The statute defines the term "process" as a "process, art or method [that] includes a new use of a known process, machine, manufacture, composition of matter, or material." § 100(b). But, this definition is not especially helpful, given that it also uses the term "process" and is therefore somewhat circular.

As lay speakers use the word "process," it constitutes any series of steps. But it has always been clear that, as used in § 101, the term does not refer to a "'process' in the ordinary sense of the word," *Flook,* 437 U.S., at 588. Rather, the term "process" (along with the definitions given to that term) has long accumulated a distinctive meaning in patent law. When the term was used in the 1952 Patent Act, it was neither intended nor understood to encompass *any* series of steps or any *way* to do any *thing.*

IV

Because the text of § 101 does not on its face convey the scope of patentable processes, it is necessary, in my view, to review the history of our patent law in some detail. This approach yields a much more straightforward answer to this case than the Court's. As I read the history, it strongly supports the conclusion that a method of doing business is not a "process" under § 101.

***

Our recent case law reinforces my view that a series of steps for conducting business is not a "process" under § 101. Since Congress passed the 1952 Act, we have never ruled on whether that Act authorizes patents on business methods. But we have cast significant doubt on that proposition by giving substantial weight to the machine-or-transformation test, as general methods of doing business do not pass that test. And more recently, Members of this Court have noted that patents on business

133

methods are of "suspect validity." *eBay Inc. v. MercExchange, L. L. C.,* 547 U.S. 388, 397 (2006) (KENNEDY, J., concurring).

* * *

Since at least the days of Assyrian merchants, people have devised better and better ways to conduct business. Yet it appears that neither the Patent Clause, nor early patent law, nor the current § 101 contemplated or was publicly understood to mean that such innovations are patentable. Although it may be difficult to define with precision what is a patentable "process" under § 101, the historical clues converge on one conclusion: A business method is not a "process." And to the extent that there is ambiguity, we should be mindful of our judicial role. "[W]e must proceed cautiously when we are asked to extend patent rights" into an area that the Patent Act likely was not "enacted to protect," *Flook,* 437 U.S., at 596, 593, lest we create a legal regime that Congress never would have endorsed, and that can be repaired only by disturbing settled property rights.

V

Despite the strong historical evidence that a method of doing business does not constitute a "process" under § 101, petitioners nonetheless argue -- and the Court suggests in dicta-- that a subsequent law, the First Inventor Defense Act of 1999, "must be read together" with § 101 to make business methods patentable. This argument utilizes a flawed method of statutory interpretation and ignores the motivation for the 1999 Act.

In 1999, following a Federal Circuit decision that intimated business methods could be patented, Congress moved quickly to limit the potential fallout. Congress passed the 1999 Act, which provides a limited defense to claims of patent infringement, regarding certain "method[s] of doing or conducting business," § 273(a)(3).

It is apparent, both from the content and history of the Act, that Congress did not in any way ratify *State Street* (or, as petitioners contend, the broadest possible reading of *State Street*). The Act merely limited one potential effect of that decision: that businesses might suddenly find themselves liable for innocently using methods they assumed could not be patented. The Act did not purport to amend the limitations in § 101 on eligible subject matter.

In light of its history and purpose, I think it obvious that the 1999 Congress would never have enacted § 273 if it had foreseen that this Court would rely on the provision as a basis for concluding that business methods are patentable. Section 273 is a red herring; we should be focusing our attention on § 101 itself.

VI

The constitutionally mandated purpose and function of the patent laws bolster the conclusion that methods of doing business are not "processes" under § 101.

The Constitution allows Congress to issue patents "[t]o promote the Progress of . . . useful Arts," Art. I, § 8, cl. 8. This clause "is both a grant of power and a limitation." *Graham*, 383 U.S., at 5. It "reflects a balance between the need to encourage innovation and the avoidance of monopolies which stifle competition without any concomitant advance in the 'Progress of Science and useful Arts.'" *Bonito Boats*, 489 U.S., at 146. "This is the standard expressed in the Constitution and it may not be ignored. And it is in this light that patent validity 'requires reference to [the] standard written into the Constitution.'" *Graham*, 383 U.S., at 6.

Thus, although it is for Congress to "implement the stated purpose of the Framers by selecting the policy which in its judgment best effectuates the constitutional aim," *Graham*, 383 U.S., at 6, we interpret ambiguous patent laws as a set of rules that "wee[d] out those inventions which would not be disclosed or devised but for the inducement of a patent," *id., at 11*, and that "embod[y]" the "careful balance between the need to promote innovation and the recognition that imitation and refinement through imitation are both necessary to invention itself and the very lifeblood of a competitive economy," *Bonito Boats*, 489 U.S., at 146. And absent a discernible signal from Congress, we proceed cautiously when dealing with patents that press on the limits of the "'standard written into the constitution,'" *Graham*, 383 U.S., at 6, 86 S. Ct. 684, for at the "fringes of congressional power," "more is required of legislatures than a vague delegation to be filled in later," *Barenblatt v. United States*, 360 U.S. 109, *139-140 (1959)* (BLACK, J., dissenting). We should not casually risk exceeding the constitutional limitation on Congress' behalf.

Without any legislative guidance to the contrary, there is a real concern that patents on business methods would press on the limits of the "standard expressed in the Constitution," *Graham*, 383 U.S., at 6, more likely stifling progress than "promot[ing]" it. *U.S. Const.*, Art. I, § 8, cl. 8. I recognize that not all methods of doing business are the same, and that therefore the constitutional "balance," *Bonito Boats*, 489 U.S., at 146, may

135

vary within this category. Nevertheless, I think that this balance generally supports the historic understanding of the term "process" as excluding business methods. And a categorical analysis fits with the purpose, as Thomas Jefferson explained, of ensuring that "'every one might know when his actions were safe and lawful,'" *Graham*, 383 U.S., at 10.

On one side of the balance is whether a patent monopoly is necessary to "motivate the innovation," *Pfaff v. Wells Electronics, Inc.*, 525 U.S. 55, 63 (1998). Although there is certainly disagreement about the need for patents, scholars generally agree that when innovation is expensive, risky, and easily copied, inventors are less likely to undertake the guaranteed costs of innovation in order to obtain the mere possibility of an invention that others can copy. Both common sense and recent economic scholarship suggest that these dynamics of cost, risk, and reward vary by the type of thing being patented. And the functional case that patents promote progress generally is stronger for subject matter that has "historically been eligible to receive the protection of our patent laws," *Diehr*, 450 U.S., at 184, than for methods of doing business.

Many have expressed serious doubts about whether patents are necessary to encourage business innovation. Despite the fact that we have long assumed business methods could not be patented, it has been remarked that "the chief business of the American people, is business." Federal Express developed an overnight delivery service and a variety of specific methods (including shipping through a central hub and online package tracking) without a patent. Although counterfactuals are a dubious form of analysis, I find it hard to believe that many of our entrepreneurs forwent business innovation because they could not claim a patent on their new methods.

"[C]ompanies have ample incentives to develop business methods even without patent protection, because the competitive marketplace rewards companies that use more efficient business methods." Innovators often capture advantages from new business methods notwithstanding the risk of others copying their innovation. Some business methods occur in secret and therefore can be protected with trade secrecy. And for those methods that occur in public, firms that innovate often capture long-term benefits from doing so, thanks to various first mover advantages, including lockins, branding, and networking effects. Business innovation, moreover, generally does not entail the same kinds of risk as does more traditional, technological innovation. It generally does not require the same

136

"enormous costs in terms of time, research, and development," *Bicron,*
416 U.S., at 480, and thus does not require the same kind of
"compensation to [innovators] for their labor, toil, and expense," *Seymour
v. Osborne*, 78 U.S. 516 (1871).

Nor, in many cases, would patents on business methods promote
progress by encouraging "public disclosure." Many business methods are
practiced in public, and therefore a patent does not necessarily encourage
the dissemination of anything not already known. And for the methods
practiced in private, the benefits of disclosure may be small: Many such
methods are distributive, not productive -- that is, they do not generate any
efficiency but only provide a means for competitors to one-up each other
in a battle for pieces of the pie. And as the Court has explained, "it is hard
to see how the public would be benefited by disclosure" of certain
business tools, since the nondisclosure of these tools "encourages
businesses to initiate new and individualized plans of operation," which
"in turn, leads to a greater variety of business methods." *Bicron*, 416 U.S.,
at 483.

In any event, even if patents on business methods were useful for
encouraging innovation and disclosure, it would still be questionable
whether they would, on balance, facilitate or impede the progress of
American business. For even when patents encourage innovation and
disclosure, "*too much* patent protection can impede rather than 'promote
the Progress of . . . useful Arts.'" *Laboratory Corp. of America Holdings v.
Metabolite Laboratories, Inc.,* 548 U.S. 124, 126-127 (2006) (BREYER, J.,
dissenting from dismissal of certiorari). Patents "can discourage research
by impeding the free exchange of information," for example, by forcing
people to "avoid the use of potentially patented ideas, by leading them to
conduct costly and time-consuming searches of existing or pending
patents, by requiring complex licensing arrangements, and by raising the
costs of using the patented" methods. Although "[e]very patent is the grant
of a privilege of exacting tolls from the public," *Great Atlantic*, 340 U.S.,
at 154 (DOUGLAS, J., concurring), the tolls of patents on business methods
may be especially high. The primary concern is that patents on business
methods may prohibit a wide swath of legitimate competition and
innovation. As one scholar explains, "it is useful to conceptualize
knowledge as a pyramid: the big ideas are on top; specific applications are

137

at the bottom."[b] The higher up a patent is on the pyramid, the greater the social cost and the greater the hindrance to further innovation.

***

The constitutional standard for patentability is difficult to apply with any precision, and Congress has significant discretion to "implement the stated purpose of the Framers by selecting the policy which in its judgment best effectuates the constitutional aim," *Graham*, 383 U.S., at 6. But Congress has not, either explicitly or implicitly, determined that patents on methods of doing business would effectuate this aim. And as I understand their practical consequences, it is hard to see how they would.

VII

The Constitution grants to Congress an important power to promote innovation. In its exercise of that power, Congress has established an intricate system of intellectual property. The scope of patentable subject matter under that system is broad. But it is not endless. In the absence of any clear guidance from Congress, we have only limited textual, historical, and functional clues on which to rely. Those clues all point toward the same conclusion: that petitioners' claim is not a "process" within the meaning of § 101 because methods of doing business are not, in themselves, covered by the statute. In my view, acknowledging as much would be a far more sensible and restrained way to resolve this case. Accordingly, while I concur in the judgment, I strongly disagree with the Court's disposition of this case.

■ JUSTICE BREYER, with whom JUSTICE SCALIA joins as to Part II, concurring in the judgment.

I

II

In addition to the Court's unanimous agreement that the claims at issue here are unpatentable abstract ideas, it is my view that the following four points are consistent with both the opinion of the Court and JUSTICE STEVENS' opinion concurring in the judgment:

---

[b] Rochelle C. Dreyfuss, *Are Business Methods Patents Bad for Business?*, 16 SANTA CLARA COMPUTER & HIGH TECH. L.J. 263, 276 (2000); Merges & Nelson, *On the Complex Economics of Patent Scope*, 90 COLUM. L. REV. 839, 873–78 (1990).

First, although the text of § 101 is broad, it is not without limit. "[T]he underlying policy of the patent system [is] that 'the things which are worth to the public the embarrassment of an exclusive patent,' . . . must outweigh the restrictive effect of the limited patent monopoly." *Graham v. John Deere Co. of Kansas City,* 383 U.S. 1, 10-11 (1966).The Court has thus been careful in interpreting the Patent Act to "determine not only what is protected, but also what is free for all to use." *Bonito Boats, Inc. v. Thunder Craft Boats, Inc.,* 489 U.S. 141, 151 (1989). In particular, the Court has long held that "[p]henomena of nature, though just discovered, mental processes, and abstract intellectual concepts are not patentable" under § 101, since allowing individuals to patent these fundamental principles would "wholly pre-empt" the public's access to the "basic tools of scientific and technological work." *Gottschalk v. Benson,* 409 U.S. 63, 67, 72, (1972).

Second, in a series of cases that extend back over a century, the Court has stated that "[t]ransformation and reduction of an article to a different state or thing is *the clue* to the patentability of a process claim that does not include particular machines." *Diehr, supra,* at 184. Application of this test, the so-called "machine-or-transformation test," has thus repeatedly helped the Court to determine what is "a patentable 'process.'" *Flook,* supra, at 589.

Third, while the machine-or-transformation test has always been a "useful and important clue," it has never been the "sole test" for determining patentability. Rather, the Court has emphasized that a process claim meets the requirements of § 101 when, "considered as a whole," it "is performing a function which the patent laws were designed to protect (*e.g.,* transforming or reducing an article to a different state or thing)." *Diehr, supra,* at 192. The machine-or-transformation test is thus an *important example* of how a court can determine patentability under § 101, but the Federal Circuit erred in this case by treating it as the *exclusive test.*

Fourth, although the machine-or-transformation test is not the only test for patentability, this by no means indicates that anything which produces a "'useful, concrete, and tangible result,'" *State Street Bank & Trust Co. v. Signature Financial Group, Inc.,* 149 F.3d 1368, 1373 (CA Fed. 1998), is patentable. Indeed, the introduction of the "useful, concrete, and tangible result" approach to patentability, associated with the Federal Circuit's *State Street* decision, preceded the granting of patents that "ranged from the somewhat ridiculous to the truly absurd." *In re Bilski,*

545 F.3d 943, 1004 (CA Fed. 2008) (MAYER, J., dissenting) (citing patents on, *inter alia*, a "method of training janitors to dust and vacuum using video displays," a "system for toilet reservations," and a "method of using color-coded bracelets to designate dating status in order to limit 'the embarrassment of rejection'"). To the extent that the Federal Circuit's decision in this case rejected that approach, nothing in today's decision should be taken as disapproving of that determination.

In sum, it is my view that, in reemphasizing that the "machine-or-transformation" test is not necessarily the *sole* test of patentability, the Court intends neither to de-emphasize the test's usefulness nor to suggest that many patentable processes lie beyond its reach.

III

With these observations, I concur in the Court's judgment.

Association for Molecular Pathology v. USPTO

United States District Court for the Southern District of New York, 2010
2010 U.S. Dist. LEXIS 35418

■ ROBERT W. SWEET, DISTRICT JUDGE.

Plaintiffs Association for Molecular Pathology, et al. (collectively "Plaintiffs") have moved for summary judgment pursuant to Rule 56, Fed. R. Civ. P., to declare invalid fifteen claims (the "claims-in-suit") contained in seven patents (the "patents-in-suit") relating to the human BRCA1 and BRCA2 genes (Breast Cancer Susceptibility Genes 1 and 2) (collectively, "BRCA1/2") under each of (1) the Patent Act, 35 U.S.C. § 101, (2) Article I, Section 8, Clause 8 of the United States Constitution, and (3) the First and Fourteenth Amendments of the Constitution because the patent claims cover products of nature, laws of nature and/or natural phenomena, and abstract ideas or basic human knowledge or thought.

[T]he challenged patent claims are directed to (1) isolated DNA containing all or portions of the BRCA1 and BRCA2 gene sequence and (2) methods for "comparing" or "analyzing" BRCA1 and BRCA2 gene sequences to identify the presence of mutations correlating with a predisposition to breast or ovarian cancer. Plaintiffs' challenge to the validity of these claims, and the arguments presented by the parties and amici, have presented a unique and challenging question:

Are isolated human genes and the comparison of their sequences patentable?

The claims-in-suit directed to "isolated DNA" containing human BRCA1/2 gene sequences reflect the USPTO's practice of granting patents on DNA sequences so long as those sequences are claimed in the form of "isolated DNA." This practice is premised on the view that DNA should be treated no differently from any other chemical compound, and that its purification from the body, using well-known techniques, renders it patentable by transforming it into something distinctly different in character. Many, however, including scientists in the fields of molecular biology and genomics, have considered this practice a "lawyer's trick" that circumvents the prohibitions on the direct patenting of the DNA in our bodies but which, in practice, reaches the same result. The resolution of these motions is based upon long recognized principles of molecular biology and genetics: DNA represents the physical embodiment of biological information, distinct in its essential characteristics from any other chemical found in nature. It is concluded that DNA's existence in an "isolated" form alters neither this fundamental quality of DNA as it exists in the body nor the information it encodes. Therefore, the patents at issue directed to "isolated DNA" containing sequences found in nature are unsustainable as a matter of law and are deemed unpatentable subject matter under 35 U.S.C. § 101.

III. THE FACTS

A. The Development of Genetics as a Field of Knowledge

In 1944, scientists determined that the chemical compound known as deoxyribonucleic acid, or DNA, served as the carrier for genetic information by demonstrating that DNA extracted from one strain of bacteria and transferred to another strain could transfer certain characteristics found in the first strain.

On April 25, 1953, James Watson and Francis Crick published their determination of the famous double-helix structure of DNA in the journal *Nature*. Dr. Crick subsequently contributed to the decryption of the genetic code and proposed "the central dogma" of molecular biology: (1) information is encoded in a segment of DNA, i.e., a gene; (2) transmitted through a molecule called RNA; and then (3) utilized to direct the creation of a protein, the building block of the body.

Our understanding of the DNA contained within our cells has since grown at an exponential rate and has included the landmark completion of the first full-length sequence of a human genome, containing 25,000 genes, as a result of the work performed by the Human Genome Project from 1990 to 2003. Access to the information encoded in our DNA has presented expansive new possibilities for future biomedical research and the development of novel diagnostic and therapeutic approaches. How this genomic information is best harnessed for the greater good presents difficult questions touching upon innovation policy, social policy, medical ethics, economic policy, and the ownership of what some view as our common heritage.

B. Molecular Biology and Gene Sequencing

An understanding of the basics of molecular biology is required to resolve the issues presented and to provide the requisite insight into the fundamentals of the genome, that is, the nature which is at the heart of the dispute between the parties.

1. DNA

DNA is a chemical molecule composed of repeating chemical units known as "nucleotides" or "bases." DNA is composed of four standard nucleotides: adenine, thymine, cytosine, and guanine. As shorthand, scientists denote nucleotides by the first letter of the names of their bases: "A" for adenine; "G" for guanine; "T" for thymine; and "C" for cytosine. These nucleotide units are composed of several chemical elements, namely carbon, hydrogen, oxygen, nitrogen, and phosphorus, and are linked together by chemical bonds to form a strand, or polymer, of the DNA molecule.

2. Extracted and purified DNA

Native DNA may be extracted from its cellular environment, including the associated chromosomal proteins, using any number of well-established laboratory techniques. A particular segment of DNA, such as a gene, contained in the extracted DNA may then be excised from the genomic DNA in which it is embedded to obtain the purified DNA of interest. DNA molecules may also be chemically synthesized in the laboratory.

Although the parties use the term "isolated DNA" to describe DNA that is separated from proteins and other DNA sequences, the term "isolated DNA" possesses a specific legal definition reflecting its use in the patents-in-suit. To avoid any confusion for purposes of this fact recitation, the term "extracted DNA" will be used to refer to DNA that has been removed from the cell and separated from other non-DNA materials in the cell (e.g., proteins); "purified DNA" will be used to refer to extracted DNA which has been further processed to separate the particular segment of DNA of interest from the other DNA in the genome; and "synthesized DNA" will be used to refer to DNA which has been synthesized in the laboratory.

Purified or synthesized DNA may be used as tools for biotechnological applications for which native DNA cannot be used. For example, unlike native DNA, purified or synthesized DNA may be used as a "probe," which is a diagnostic tool that a molecular biologist uses to target and bind to a particular segment of DNA, thus allowing the target DNA sequence to be detectable using standard laboratory machinery. Purified or synthesized DNA can also be used as a "primer" to sequence a target DNA, a process used by molecular biologists to determine the order of nucleotides in a DNA molecule, or to perform polymerase chain reaction ("PCR") amplification, a process which utilizes target-DNA specific primers to duplicate the quantity of target DNA exponentially.

The DNA molecule being used as a probe or a primer binds, or "hybridizes," to a specific nucleotide sequence of a DNA target molecule, such as the *BRCA1* or *BRCA2* gene. The utility of purified *BRCA1/2* DNA molecules as biotechnological tools therefore relies on their ability to selectively bind to native or isolated *BRCA1/2* DNA molecules, which ability is a function of the isolated DNA's nucleotide sequence.

C. The Development of the Patents-in-Suit

Breast cancer is the most frequently diagnosed cancer worldwide and is the leading cause of cancer death for women in Britain and the second leading cause of cancer death for women in the United States. Ovarian cancer is the eighth most common cancer in women and causes more deaths in the Western world than any other gynecologic cancer.

Throughout the 1980s, organizations dedicated to breast cancer awareness began efforts to increase public and governmental awareness of the breast cancer epidemic. In 1991, the U.S. Department of Defense created a research program devoted to breast cancer research. Over the years this funding has grown from less than $ 90 million during the fiscal year 1990 to more than $ 2.1 billion during the fiscal year 2008.

In September 1994, the group at Myriad, along with researchers from the National Institute for Environmental Health Sciences ("NIEHS") (a subdivision of the NIH), the University of Utah, McGill University, and Eli Lilly and Company announced that they had sequenced the *BRCA1* gene. In addition to funding the six NIEHS researchers who participated in the identification of *BRCA1*, the NIH had also provided approximately $ 2 million in funding to the University of Utah. According to one analysis, the NIH contributed one-third of the funding for the identification of *BRCA1*.

Following the isolation of *BRCA1*, scientists continued to search for a second gene also believed to be linked with breast and ovarian cancer. Myriad collaborated with several research groups, including scientists at the University of Laval in Quebec, Canada, the Hospital for Sick Children in Toronto, Canada, and the University of Pennsylvania in their search for this second gene. It also collaborated with a team of researchers led by Dr. Stratton at the ICR which, in November 1995, identified a mutation in breast cancer patients that appeared to be located in the as-yet unpublished *BRCA2* gene. Dr. Stratton ended the collaboration with Myriad upon learning of Myriad's plans to patent the *BRCA2* gene sequence.

On December 21, 1995, Myriad filed for patents on the *BRCA2* gene in both the U.S. and Europe. The next day, the Stratton group published its identification of the *BRCA2* gene in the journal *Nature*, and Myriad submitted the sequence of *BRCA2* to GenBank, an international depository of gene sequence information. Subsequent analysis of the *BRCA2* sequence from the Stratton group indicated that while they had correctly sequenced the primary portion of the *BRCA2* gene, their published sequence had errors in both ends of the *BRCA2* gene. Nonetheless, the consensus among the scientific community is that the Stratton group, rather than Myriad, was the first to sequence the *BHCA2* gene.

The isolation of the *BRCA1/2* genes required considerable effort on the part of Myriad and its collaborators as well as ingenuity in overcoming technical obstacles associated with the isolation process. However, the process and techniques used were well understood, widely used, and fairly uniform insofar as any scientist engaged in the search for a gene would likely have utilized a similar approach.

D. Application of the Patents-in-Suit

Mutations in the *BRCA1/2* genes correlate with an increased risk of breast and ovarian cancer. Women with *BRCA1* and *BRCA2* mutations face up to an 85% cumulative risk of breast cancer, as well as up to a 50% cumulative risk of ovarian cancer. In addition, among the 10-15% of ovarian cancer cases that are inherited genetically, 80% of women diagnosed under the age of 50 carry mutations in their *BRCA1* genes and 20% carry mutations in their *BRCA2* genes. The women with inherited *BRCA1* mutations have a 40-52% cumulative risk of ovarian cancer by the time they reach 70 years old. For women with inherited *BRCA2* mutations, the risk is approximately 15-25%. Male carriers of mutations are also at an increased risk for breast and prostate cancer.

The existence of *BRCA1/2* mutations is therefore an important consideration in the provision of clinical care for breast and/or ovarian cancer. This information is useful for women who are facing difficult decisions regarding whether or not to undergo prophylactic surgery, hormonal therapy, chemotherapy, and other measures. Testing results for the *BRCA1/2* genes can be an important factor in structuring an appropriate course of cancer treatment, since certain forms of chemotherapy can be more effective in treating cancers related to *BRCA1/2* mutations.

1. Myriad's *BRCA1/2* testing

Myriad offers multiple forms of *BRCA1/2* testing to the general public. Its standard test [is] called Comprehensive BRACAnalysis. In 2006, Myriad began offering a supplemental test to Comprehensive BRACAnalysis called the BRACAnalysis Rearrangement Test ("BART").

2. Funding for Myriad's *BRCA1/2 tests*

The Myriad tests are available to clinicians and patients at a cost of over $ 3000 per test. In 2008, the total cost to Myriad of providing these tests was $ 32 million with resulting revenues of $ 222 million. In Ontario, where the regional public healthcare plan is ignoring Myriad's patent, the testing for breast cancer is performed for a third of Myriad's cost. Plaintiffs have noted several instances where women have been unable to obtain funding for all of Myriad's testing services.

Myriad's BART test is not covered by a number of insurers, and unless a patient is one of a limited number of "high risk patients" who meet certain clinical criteria established by Myriad, a patient must pay an extra fee for BART testing. As a result of the cost of BART testing, the test is unavailable to women who would otherwise choose to utilize the test.

Myriad has pursued Medicaid coverage for years, but has been unable to secure "participating provider" status in 25 states which would allow it to offer testing to that state's Medicaid patients. Myriad also has a financial assistance program which provides free testing to low-income and uninsured patients who meet certain economic and clinical requirements. In addition, Myriad provides free testing to independent non-profit institutions. Currently, 90% of the tests Myriad performs are covered by insurance at over 90% of the test cost.

A number of researchers, clinicians, and molecular pathologists have the personnel, equipment, and expertise to sequence and analyze genes, including the BRCA1 and BRCA2 genes, at a lower cost than Myriad's testing.

E. Disputed Issues

1. The impact of Myriad's patents on *BRCA1/2* testing

According to Plaintiffs, Myriad's patents and its position as the sole provider of BRCA1/2 testing has hindered the ability of patients to receive the highest-quality breast cancer genetic testing and has impeded the development of improvements to BRCA1/2 genetic testing. According to Plaintiffs, other labs are in a position to offer more comprehensive testing than Myriad's standard testing services and would use newer [and additional] testing methods with improved testing quality and efficiency.

According to Myriad, however, its full sequencing test has been recognized as the "gold standard" for BRCA1/2 mutation testing, and it continues to improve its testing process. According to Myriad, BRCA1/2 studies conducted by outside researchers confirmed that the BART test exhibited superior performance over other methods for mutation detection, including the MLPA kit often used by academic researchers.

Plaintiffs contend that as a result of the patents-in-suit, BRCA1/2 genetic testing is one of the very few tests performed as part of breast cancer care and prevention for which a doctor or patient cannot get a second confirmatory test done through another laboratory. According to Myriad, absent any doubts regarding the accuracy of the original test, resequencing the patient's genes by another laboratory would be an unnecessary waste of resources, and Myriad has never prohibited a second interpretation of the results of its diagnostic tests. In addition, there are multiple laboratories available to conduct confirmatory BRCA1/2 testing pursuant to patent licenses granted by Myriad. That confirmatory testing, however, is limited to the confirmation of certain, specific positive test results; the remaining types of positive test results as well as all negative test results are excluded from such testing services.

Whether the patents at issue impact the testing for *BRCA1/2* mutations favorably or unfavorably is an issue of factual dispute not resolvable in the context of the instant motions.

2. The impact of gene patents on the advancement of science and medical treatment

There exists a deep disagreement between the parties concerning the effects of gene patents on the progression of scientific knowledge. According to Plaintiffs, data sharing is the key to the future of genetic discoveries and bioinformatics, and gene patents impede research aimed at identifying the role of genes in medical conditions. Plaintiffs assert that this understanding has wide acceptance, noting that from the beginning of the Human Genome project, most scientists and even some private companies recognized the importance of keeping the genome freely available to all. For example, in 1994, the pharmaceutical company Merck funded a massive drive to generate gene sequences and place them into public databases, thereby making them difficult to patent. In 1996, a group of 50 of the most prominent geneticists who were involved with the sequencing of the human genome adopted the Bermuda principles which included the mandate that all "human genome sequence information should be freely available and in the public domain in order to encourage research and development and to maximize its benefit to society." The proliferation of intellectual property rights directed to genetic material has also been postulated to contribute to a phenomenon dubbed "the tragedy of the anti-commons," in which numerous competing patent rights held by independent parties prevents any one party from engaging in productive innovation.

According to Dr. Fiona Murray ("Dr. Murray"), who received a grant to research the impact of gene patenting on scientific research and commercialization, 4382 of the 23,688 genes listed in the database of the National Center for Biotechnology Information ("NCBI") - nearly 20% of human genes - are explicitly claimed as United States intellectual property.

147

Plaintiffs have cited other studies to demonstrate the chilling effect of gene patents on the advancement of both genetic research and clinical testing. A survey of laboratory directors in the United States conducted by Dr. Mildred Cho (the "Cho study") found that 53% decided not to develop a new clinical test because of a gene patent or license, and 67% believed that gene patents decreased their ability to conduct research. This correlated with a study conducted by the American Society of Human Genetics that reported that 46% of respondents felt that patents had delayed or limited their research. The Cho study also revealed [] that nine labs had ceased performing BRCA1/2 genetic testing as a result of the patents-in-suit. In addition [], labs have avoided or refrained from developing tests for BRCA1 and BRCA2 as a result of the patents held by Myriad. Studies of other gene patents have also revealed that labs frequently stop developing or offering clinical tests for disease as a result of gene patents.

Researchers, clinicians, and pathologists are aware that Myriad has sent cease and desist letters in connection with the patents-in-suit and that Myriad prohibits clinical testing of the BRCA1/2 genes. Myriad also does not permit researchers to tell patients involved in research the results of their BRCA1/2 testing, leaving physicians involved in breast cancer care and research unable to meet their ethical obligations to provide genetic test results to research subjects, when requested. The AMA has also expressed its belief that the "[t]he use of patents ... or other means to limit the availability of medical procedures places significant limitation on the dissemination of medical knowledge, and is therefore unethical." In addition, others have argued that human genes are the common heritage of mankind whose use should not be restricted by patent grants.

Plaintiffs also assert that gene patents impede the development of improved genetic testing. For example, as new sequencing technologies offer the possibility of faster and less expensive sequencing of a patient's genes, patents on one or more genes may impede scientists' ability to develop a comprehensive test for complex diseases or provide a person with an analysis of his or her entire genome. In addition, Plaintiffs assert that gene patents interfere with the ability of physicians and researchers to investigate complex diseases. For example, BRCA1/2 may be associated with cancers other than breast and ovarian cancer, but so long as the patents on these genes remain, no one will be able to include these genes in tests for other disease predispositions. Gene patents similarly impede the development and improvement of tests for diseases by geneticists.

148

Plaintiffs further assert that gene patents are not necessary to create incentives for initial discoveries or the development of commercial applications, including diagnostic tests. Patents have not been necessary for the rapid introduction of genetic testing, as evidenced by genetic testing that has been offered prior to the issuance of a patent. In support of this assertion, Plaintiffs cite a study of gene patents issued in the United States for genetic diagnostics that showed that 67% of these patents were issued for discoveries funded by the U.S. government. Similarly, another study showed that 63% of patents on gene sequences resulted from federally supported research. As previously noted, the NIH provided $ 2 million in research grants to the University of Utah, or approximately one-third of the total funding, for the identification of the *BRCA1* sequence.

Myriad has contested these assertions and disputes the idea that patenting of isolated human DNA conflicts with the advancement of science. According to Myriad, the quid pro quo of the patent system is that inventors, in exchange for a limited period of patent exclusivity, must provide a sufficient description of the patented invention so that others may improve upon it. Furthermore, according to Myriad, its policy and practice has been and still is to allow scientists to conduct research studies on BRCA1 and BRCA2 freely, the result of which has been the publication of over 5,600 research papers on BRCA1 and over 3,000 research papers on BRCA2, representing the work of over 18,000 scientists.

According to Myriad, patents on isolated DNA, including the patents-in-suit, actually promote research and advance clinical development to the benefit of patients. In support, Myriad has cited a survey published in 2009 by the BIO of 150 biotechnology member companies in the therapeutic and diagnostic healthcare industry stating that the majority of companies (61%) generally in-licensed projects that are in the pre-clinical or Phase I stage of development, and thus still require substantial R&D investment and commercialization risk by the licensee. A substantial majority (77%) of the respondents without approved products indicated that they expect to spend 5-15 years and over $ 100 million developing a commercial product. Myriad asserts that these expenditures dwarf any initial research funding by the federal government. Therefore, Myriad asserts that absent the promise of a period of market exclusivity provided by patents and the infusion of venture and risk capital derived there from, companies such as Myriad that capitalize on innovation simply would not be created and their products would not be brought to market or the clinic.

As the declarations submitted by the parties make clear, there exists a sharp dispute concerning the impact of patents directed to isolate DNA on genetic research and consequently the health of society. As with the dispute concerning the effect of the patents-in-suit on *BRCA1/2* genetic testing, the resolution of these disputes of fact and policy are not possible within the context of these motions.

B. 35 U.S.C. § 101 and Its Scope

In interpreting [35 U.S.C. § 101, the Supreme Court has observed that "Congress plainly contemplated that the patent laws would be given wide scope." *Diamond v. Chakrabarty,* 447 U.S. 303, 308 (1980). However, this broad reading of § 101 and statutory patent eligibility is not without limits. Specifically, the Supreme Court has recognized three categories of subject-matter that fall outside the scope of § 101: "The laws of nature, physical phenomena, and abstract ideas have been held not patentable" *Chakrabarty,* 447 U.S. at 309; *see also Diamond v. Diehr,* 450 U.S. 175, 185 (1981). "The rule that the discovery of a law of nature cannot be patented rests, not on the notion that natural phenomena are not processes, but rather on the more fundamental understanding that they are not the kind of 'discovery' that the statute was enacted to protect." *Parker v. Flook,* 437 U.S. 584, 593.

The exclusion of products of nature as patentable subject matter under § 101 also reflects the Supreme Court's recognition that "[p]henomena of nature, though just discovered, mental processes, and abstract intellectual concepts are not patentable, as they are the basic tools of scientific and technological work." *Gottschalk v. Benson,* 409 U.S. 63, 67 (1972). Thus, as Justice Breyer has observed, "the reason for this exclusion is that sometimes too *much* patent protection can impede rather than 'promote the Progress of Science and useful Arts,' the constitutional objective of patent and copyright protection." *Lab. Corp. of Am. Holdings v. Metabolite Labs., Inc.,* 548 U.S. 124, 126-27 (2006) (BREYER, J., dissenting). For these reasons, "manifestations of laws of nature [are] free to all men and reserved exclusively to none." *Funk Bros. Seed Co. v. Kalo Inoculant Co.,* 333 U.S. 127, 130 (1948).

The inquiry into an invention's patent eligibility is a fundamental one, and as such, "[t]he obligation to determine what type of discovery is sought to be patented must precede the determination of whether that discovery is, in fact, new or obvious." *Flook,* 437 U.S. at 593. Consistent with this approach, the courts have rejected patent claims even when the purported invention was highly beneficial or novel, or the research and work that went into identifying it was costly or time-consuming.

C. The Composition Claims Are Invalid Under 35 U.S.C. § 101

As noted, the issue presented by the instant motions with respect to the composition claims is whether or not claims directed to isolated DNA containing naturally-occurring sequences fall within the products of nature exception to § 101. Based upon the reasons set forth below, it is concluded that the composition claims-in-suit are excepted.

1.

* * *

2. Patentable subject matter must be "markedly different" from a product of nature

Supreme Court precedent has established that products of nature do not constitute patentable subject matter absent a change that results in the creation of a fundamentally new product. In *American Fruit Growers*, the Supreme Court rejected patent claims covering fruit whose skin had been treated with mold-resistant borax. Acknowledging that the "complete article is not found in nature," and "treatment, labor and manipulation" went into producing the fruit, the Court nonetheless held that the fruit did not become an "article of manufacture" unless it "possesses a new or distinctive form, quality, or property" compared to the naturally-occurring article." 283 U.S. at 11. The Court went on to observe:

> Manufacture implies a change, but every change is not manufacture, and yet every change in an article is the result of treatment, labor, and manipulation. But something more is necessary . . . . There must be transformation; a new and different article must emerge having a distinctive name, character, or use.

Similarly, in *Funk Brothers*, the Supreme Court considered whether a mixture of several naturally-occurring species of bacteria was patentable. 333 U.S. at 128-31. Each species of bacteria in the mixture could extract nitrogen from the air for plant usage. While the patent holder had created a mixture by selecting and testing for strains of bacteria that did not

151

mutually inhibit one another, the Court concluded that the patent holder "did not create a state of inhibition or of non-inhibition in the bacteria. Their qualities are the work of nature. Those qualities are of course not patentable."

Most recently, the Supreme Court addressed the application of § 101 to product claims in *Diamond v. Chakrabarty,* 447 U.S. 303.

[a] In *Chakrabarty,* the Court considered whether a "live, human-made micro-organism is patentable subject matter under 35 U.S.C. § 101." The microorganism in question was a bacterium that had been genetically engineered to break down multiple components of crude oil and possessed considerable utility in the treatment of oil spills. In concluding that the man-made bacterial strain was patentable, the Court observed that the claim "is not to a hitherto unknown natural phenomenon, but to a nonnaturally occurring manufacture or composition of matter - a product of human ingenuity 'having a distinctive name, character [and] use.'" The Court went on to contrast the Chakrabarty bacterium with the bacterial mixture at issue in Funk Brothers, stating that in Chakrabarty's case, "the patentee has produced a new bacterium with markedly different characteristics from any found in nature and one having the potential for significant utility. His discovery is not nature's handiwork, but his own . . . ." This requirement that an invention possess "markedly different characteristics" for purposes of *§ 101* reflects the oft-repeated requirement that an invention have "a new or distinctive form, quality, or property" from a product of nature. *Am. Fruit Growers,* 283 U.S. at 11.

Courts have also specifically held that "purification" of a natural compound, without more, is insufficient to render a product of nature patentable. In *The American Wood-Paper Co. v. The Fibre Disintegrating Co.,* 90 U.S. 566 (1874), the Supreme Court held that refined cellulose, consisting of purified pulp derived from wood and vegetable, was unpatentable because it was "an extract obtained by the decomposition or disintegration of material substance." As the Court observed:

---

[a] Although *Chakrabarty* is often cited for the proposition that "anything under the sun that is made by man" is patentable, that phrase is a misleading quotation from the legislative history of the Patent Act of 1952. The full quote clearly acknowledges the statutory limitations to patentable subject matter "A person may have 'invented' a machine or a manufacture, which may include anything under the sun made by man, but it is not necessarily patentable under *section 101* unless the conditions of the title are fulfilled " H.R. Rep. No. 1923, 82d Cong, 2d Sess. 6 (1952).

There are many things well known and valuable in medicine or in the arts which may be extracted from divers[e] substances. But the extract is the same, no matter from what it has been taken. A process to obtain it from a subject from which it has never been taken may be the creature of invention, but the thing itself when obtained cannot be called a new manufacture.

Similarly, in *Cochrane v. Badische Anilin & Soda Fabrik*, 111 U.S. 293 (1884), the Court rejected a patent on an artificial version of a natural red dye called alizarine that was produced by manipulating another compound through acid, heat, water or distillation. Although the artificial version of the dye was of a brighter hue than the naturally occurring dye, the Court concluded that "[c]alling it artificial alizarine did not make it a new composition of matter, and patentable as such . . . ."

In *General Electric*, 28 F.2d at 642, the Third Circuit Court of Appeals considered the patentability of purified tungsten, which possessed superior characteristics and utility over its brittle, naturally-occurring form. The court first noted that "[i]f it is a natural thing then clearly, even if [the patentee] was the first to uncover it and bring it into view, he cannot have a patent for it because a patent cannot be awarded for a discovery or for a product of nature, or for a chemical element." The court went on to state:

> Naturally we inquire who created pure tungsten. Coolidge? No. It existed in nature and doubtless has existed there for centuries. The fact that no one before Coolidge found it there does not negative its origin or existence. ·
>
> The second part of the claim reads: "Having ductility and high tensile strength." Did Coolidge give those qualities to "substantially pure tungsten"? We think not for it is now conceded that tungsten pure is ductile cold. If it possess that quality now it is certain that it possessed it always.

The Court of Customs and Patent Appeals, the precursor to the Federal Circuit Court of Appeals, subsequently relied on General Electric in rejecting patents claiming purified uranium and vanadium. Similarly, in Ex Parte Latimer, the Patent Commissioner refused to allow a patent on pine needle fibers that were better suited for textile production, even though it was necessary to remove the needle from its sheath and other resinous material. 1889 Dec. Comm'r Pat. 123, 125 (1889).

Myriad argues that purification of "'naturally occurring' compounds that 'do not exist in nature in pure form' renders such compounds patent-eligible." However, Myriad cites no Supreme Court authority that would rebut the authorities presented by Plaintiffs, nor do the cited cases support Myriad's position.

Myriad has relied heavily on the holding of the Honorable Learned Hand in *Parke-Davis & Co. v. H.K. Mulford Co.*, 189 F. 95 (S.D.N.Y. 1911). In Parke-Davis, Judge Hand considered a challenge to the validity of a patent claiming an adrenaline compound that had been isolated and purified from animal suprarenal glands. It had been known that suprarenal glands in powdered form had hemostatic, blood-pressure-raising and astringent properties, but could not be used for those purposes in gross form. The isolated adrenaline, however, possessed the desired therapeutic properties and could be administered to humans.

Although Myriad argues that the holding in Parke-Davis establishes that the purification of a natural product necessarily renders it patentable, the opinion, read closely, fails to support such a conclusion. The question before the court in Parke-Davis was one of novelty (a modern-day § 102 question), not of patentable subject matter (the § 101 question before this Court). In framing the issue, Judge Hand observed that, "[the validity of the claims] is attacked, first, because they are *anticipated* in the art; and second, for a number of technical grounds which I shall take up in turn." He went on to conclude that the patented purified extract was not, in fact, different from the prior art "only for a degree of purity," but rather was a different chemical substance from that found in the prior art. (observing that "no one had ever isolated a substance [adrenaline] which was not in salt form" and that "the [claimed] base [form of adrenaline] was an original production of [the patentee's]"). Thus, Judge Hand held that the purified adrenaline was not anticipated by the prior art, namely, the ground paradrenal gland that was known to possess certain beneficial properties.

Only after concluding that the claimed purified adrenaline was novel over the prior art did Judge Hand offer, as dicta, the statement to which Myriad cites: "But, even if it were merely an extracted product without change, there is no rule that such products are not patentable." While the accuracy of this statement at the time was written is dubious in light of

154

American Wood-Paper (to which Judge Hand did not cite) it is certainly no longer good law in light of subsequent Supreme Court cases, which, as noted above, require that a claimed invention possess "markedly different characteristics" over products existing in nature in order for it to constitute patentable subject matter. *Chakrabarty*, 447 U.S. at 310; *see also Funk Bros.*, 333 U.S. at 130-32. By the same token, Judge Hand's suggestion that a claimed invention was patentable since it was a "new thing commercially and therapeutically," *Parke-Davis*, 189 F. at 103, is firmly contradicted by subsequent case law establishing that "it is improper to consider whether a claimed element or step in a process is novel or nonobvious, since such considerations are separate requirements" when evaluating whether a claim is patent-eligible subject matter. *Prometheus*, 581 F.3d at 1343. Such an approach would also be inconsistent with the Supreme Court's rejection of the patentability of the commercially useful mixture of bacteria in Funk Brothers, the refined cellulose in American Wood-Paper, and the electromagnetic communication devices in *O'Reilly v. Morse*, 56 U.S. (15 How.) 62 (1853).

Finally, *Merck & Co., Inc. v. Olin Mathieson Chem. Corp.*, 253 F.2d 156, cited by Myriad, is entirely consistent with the principle set forth in *Funk Brothers* and *American Fruit Growers* that something derived from a product of nature must "possess a new or distinctive form, quality, or property" in order to become patentable subject matter. *Am. Fruit Growers*, 283 U.S. at 11. In Merck, the Fourth Circuit considered the validity of a patent claiming a Vitamin B12 composition useful for treating pernicious anemia. Although naturally occurring Vitamin B[12] produced in cows had known therapeutic properties and was commercially available, the court found the purified B[12] composition, which was obtained from a microorganism, patentable. In upholding the validity of the patent, the court held:

> Every slight step in purification does not produce a new product. What is gained may be the old product, but with a greater degree of purity. Alpha alumina purified is still alpha alumina, *In re Ridgway*, 76 F.2d 602, [] and ultramarine from which floatable impurities have been removed is still ultramarine, *In re Merz*, 97 F.2d 599.

155

Because the court concluded that the purified B[12] was more than a "mere advance in the degree of purity of a known product," it determined that the claimed invention was entitled to patent protection.

In sum, the clear line of Supreme Court precedent and accompanying lower court authorities, stretching from American Wood-Paper through to Chakrabarty, establishes that purification of a product of nature, without more, cannot transform it into patentable subject matter. Rather, the purified product must possess "markedly different characteristics" in order to satisfy the requirements of § 101.

3. The claimed isolated DNA is not "markedly different" from native DNA

The question thus presented by Plaintiffs' challenge to the composition claims is whether the isolated DNA claimed by Myriad possesses "markedly different characteristics" from a product of nature. *Chakrabarty*, 447 U.S. at 310. In support of its position, Myriad cites several differences between the isolated DNA claimed in the patents and the native DNA found within human cells. None, however, establish the subject matter patentability of isolated *BRCA1/2* DNA.

The central premise of Myriad's argument that the claimed DNA is "markedly different" from DNA found in nature is the assertion that "[i]solated DNA molecules should be treated no differently than other chemical compounds for patent eligibility," and that the alleged "difference in the structural and functional properties of isolated DNA" render the claimed DNA patentable subject matter.

Myriad's focus on the chemical nature of DNA, however, fails to acknowledge the unique characteristics of DNA that differentiate it from other chemical compounds. As Myriad's expert Dr. Joseph Straus observed: "Genes are of double nature: On the one hand, they are chemical substances or molecules. On the other hand, they are physical carriers of information, i.e., where the actual biological function of this information is coding for proteins. Thus, inherently genes are multifunctional." This informational quality is unique among the chemical compounds found in our bodies, and it would be erroneous to view DNA as "no different[]" than other chemicals previously the subject of patents.

Myriad's argument that all chemical compounds, such as the adrenaline at issue in *Parke-Davis*, necessarily convey some information ignores the biological realities of DNA in comparison to other chemical compounds in the body. The information encoded in DNA is not information about its *own* molecular structure incidental to its biological function, as is the case with adrenaline or other chemicals found in the body. Rather, the information encoded by DNA reflects its primary biological function: directing the synthesis of other molecules in the body -- namely, proteins, "biological molecules of enormous importance" which "catalyze biochemical reactions" and constitute the "major structural materials of the animal body." *O'Farrell*, 853 F.3d at 895-96. DNA, and in particular the ordering of its nucleotides, therefore serves as the physical embodiment of laws of nature - those that define the construction of the human body. Any "information" that may be embodied by adrenaline and similar molecules serves no comparable function, and none of the declarations submitted by Myriad support such a conclusion. Consequently, the use of simple analogies comparing DNA with chemical compounds previously the subject of patents cannot replace consideration of the distinctive characteristics of DNA.

In light of DNA's unique qualities as a physical embodiment of information, none of the structural and functional differences cited by Myriad between native BRCA1/2 DNA and the isolated BRCA1/2 DNA claimed in the patents-in-suit render the claimed DNA "markedly different." This conclusion is driven by the overriding importance of DNA's nucleotide sequence to both its natural biological function as well as the utility associated with DNA in its isolated" form. The preservation of this defining characteristic of DNA in its native and isolated forms mandates the conclusion that the challenged composition claims are directed to unpatentable products of nature.

Myriad argues that the § 101 inquiry into the subject matter patentability of isolated DNA should focus exclusively on the differences alleged to exist between native and isolated DNA, rather than considering the similarities that exist between the two forms of DNA. Setting aside the fact that considerations such as novelty are irrelevant for § 101 purposes, Myriad offers no authorities supporting such an approach. To the contrary, the Supreme Court has held that "[i]n determining the eligibility of [a] claimed process for patent protection under § 101, [the] claims must be considered as a whole." *Diehr,* 450 U.S. at 188. Similarly, the Federal Circuit has expressly held that "[i]n the final analysis under § 101, the claimed invention, as a whole, must be evaluated for what it is." *In re Grams,* 888 F.2d 835, 839 (Fed. Cir. 1989).

Were Myriad's approach the law, it is difficult to discern how any invention could fail the test. For example, the bacterial mixture in *Funk Brothers* was unquestionably different from any preexisting bacterial mixture; yet the Supreme Court recognized that a patent directed to the mixture, considered as a whole, did no more than patent "the handiwork of nature." 333 U.S. at 131. There will almost inevitably be some identifiable differences between a claimed invention and a product of nature; the appropriate § 101 inquiry is whether, considering the claimed invention as a whole, it is sufficiently distinct in its fundamental characteristics from natural phenomena to possess the required "distinctive name, character, [and] use." *Chakrabarty*, 447 U.S. at 309-10.

None of Myriad's arguments establish the distinctive nature of the claimed DNA. Myriad's argument that the functional differences between native and isolated DNA demonstrates that they are "markedly different" relies on the fact that isolated DNA may be used in applications for which native DNA is unsuitable, namely, in "molecular diagnostic tests (e.g., as probes, primers, templates for sequencing reactions), in biotechnological processes (e.g. production of pure *BRCA1* and *BRCA2* protein), and even in medical treatments (e.g. gene therapy)."

Isolated DNA's utility as a primer or a molecular probe (for example, for Southern blots) arises from its ability to "target and interact with other DNA molecules," that is, the ability of a given DNA molecule to bind exclusively to a specific DNA target sequence. However, the basis for this utility is the fact that the isolated DNA possesses the identical nucleotide sequence as the target DNA sequence, thus allowing target specific hybridization between the DNA primer and the portion of the target DNA molecule possessing the corresponding sequence. In contrast, another 24 nucleotide segment of DNA possessing the same nucleotide composition but a different nucleotide sequence would not have the same utility because it would be unable to hybridize to the proper location in the *BRCA1* gene. Indeed, Myriad implicitly acknowledges this fact when it states that the usefulness of isolated DNA molecules "is based on their ability to target and interact with other DNA molecules, which is a function of *their own individual structure and chemistry*." Therefore, the cited utility of the isolated DNA as a primer or probe is primarily a function of the nucleotide sequence identity between native and isolated *BRCA1/2 DNA*.

Similarly, the utility of isolated DNA as a sequencing target relies on the preservation of native DNA's nucleotide sequence. The entire premise behind Myriad's genetic testing is that the claimed isolated DNA retains, in all relevant respects, the identical nucleotide sequence found in native DNA. The use of isolated *BRCA1/2* DNA in the production of BRCA1/2 proteins or in gene therapy also relies on the identity between the native DNA sequences and the sequences contained in the isolated DNA molecule. Were the isolated *BRCA1/2 sequences* different in any significant way, the entire point of their use - the production of BRCA1/2 proteins - would be undermined.

While the absence of proteins and other nucleotide sequences is currently required for DNA to be useful for the cited purposes, the purification of native DNA does not alter its essential characteristic - its nucleotide sequence - that is defined by nature and central to both its biological function within the cell and its utility as a research tool in the lab. The requirement that the DNA used be "isolated" is ultimately a technological limitation to the use of DNA in this fashion, and a time may come when the use of DNA for molecular and diagnostic purposes may not require such purification. The nucleotide sequence, however, is the defining characteristic of the isolated DNA that will always be required to provide the sequence-specific targeting and protein coding ability that allows isolated DNA to be used for the various applications cited by Myriad. For these reasons, the use of isolated DNA for the various purposes cited by Myriad does not establish the existence of differences "in kind" between native and isolated DNA that would establish the subject matter patentability of what is otherwise a product of nature.

Finally, the isolated *BRCA1/2 DNA* claimed in Myriad's patents bears comparison to the bacterial mixture in Funk Brothers. In explaining why the claimed mixture of bacteria did not constitute an invention, the Court observed that the first part of the claimed invention was the "[d]iscovery of the fact that certain strains of each species of these bacteria can be mixed without harmful effect to the properties of either" which was "a discovery of their qualities of non-inhibition. It is no more than the discovery of some of the handiwork of nature and hence is not patentable." 333 U.S. at 131. The Court went on to observe that the second part of the claimed invention was "[t]he aggregation of select strains of the several species into one product[,] an application of that newly-discovered natural principle. But however ingenious the discovery of that natural principle may have been, the application of it is hardly more than an advance in the packaging of the inoculants."

According to Myriad, the invention claimed in its patents required the identification of the specific segments of chromosomes 17 and 13 that correlated with breast and ovarian cancer (*BRCA1* and *BRCA2*) followed by the isolation of these sequences away from other genomic DNA and cellular components. Like the discovery of the mutual non-inhibition of the bacteria in Funk Brothers, discovery of this important correlation was a discovery of the handiwork of nature - the natural effect of certain mutations in a particular segment of the human genome. And like the aggregation of bacteria in Funk Brothers, the isolation of the *BRCA1* and *BRCA2* DNA, while requiring technical skill and considerable labor, was simply the application of techniques well-known to those skilled in the art. The identification of the *BRCA1* and *BRCA2* gene sequences is unquestionably a valuable scientific achievement for which Myriad deserves recognition, but that is not the same as concluding that it is something for which they are entitled to a patent.

Because the claimed isolated DNA is not markedly different from native DNA as it exists in nature, it constitutes unpatentable subject matter under 35 U.S.C. § 101.

E. The Constitutional Claims Against the USPTO Are Dismissed

With the holding that the patents are invalid, the Plaintiffs have received the relief sought in the Complaint and the doctrine of constitutional avoidance precludes this Court from reaching the constitutional claims against the USPTO.

VIII. CONCLUSION

For the reasons set forth above, Plaintiffs' motion for summary judgment is granted in part, Myriad's motion for summary judgment is denied, the USPTO's motion for judgment on the pleadings is granted, and the claims-in-suit are declared invalid pursuant to 35 U.S.C. § 101.

NOTES

1. *Ideas vs. embodiments: A longstanding line-drawing dilemma.* The difficulty in drawing a line between an idea, or a principle of nature, and its embodiment became evident early in patent law's history. In particular,

160

consider two early cases, *O'Reilly v. Morse*,[1] involving the patent on the telegraph, and *Dolbear v. American Bell Telephone Co.* ("*The Telephone Cases*").[2] Morse's claim read as follows:

> "Eighth. I do not propose to limit myself to the specific machinery ... described in the foregoing specification and claims; the essence of my invention being the use of the motive power of the electric or galvanic current, which I call electro-magnetism, however developed, for making or printing intelligible characters (letters or signs), at any distances ... "

Bell claimed:

> "The method of, and apparatus for, transmitting vocal or other sounds telegraphically, as herein described, by causing electrical undulations, similar in form to the vibrations of the air accompanying the said vocal or other sounds, substantially as set forth."

As to *Morse,* the Supreme Court said:

> "If this claim can be maintained, it matters not by what process or machinery the result is accomplished. For aught that we now know some future inventor, in the onward march of science, may discover a mode of writing or printing at a distance by means of the electric or galvanic current, without using any part of the "If this claim can be maintained, it matters not by what process or machinery the result is accomplished. For aught that we now know some future inventor, in the onward march of science, may discover a mode of writing or printing at a distance by means of the electric or galvanic current, without using any part of the process or combination set forth in the plaintiff's specification.... But yet if it is covered by this patent the inventor could not use it, nor the public have the benefit of it without the permission of this patentee."[3]

---

[1] 56 U.S. (15 How.) 62 (1854).
[2] 126 U.S. 1 (1888).
[3] 56 U.S. (15 How.) at 113.

161

In contrast, in *The Telephone Cases,* the Court held:

> "The patent for the art does not necessarily involve a patent for the particular means employed for using it. Indeed, the mention of any means ... is only necessary to show that the art can be used...."[4]

Admittedly, Bell drafted his claim so that it would appear limited to "undulations." In contrast, Morse made very clear that his claim was meant to be broad. Yet both claims seem equally drawn to principles: in Morse's case, the principle of using the wave properties of electromagnetism to transmit signs; in Bell's, the principle of using its oscillations to transmit sound. And so, the Supreme Court's concern that Morse was tying up basic building blocks of knowledge and extending the reach of his claim to those who were not utilizing his insight seems equally applicable to Bell.

To be sure, *The Telephone Cases* tried to distinguish *Morse*:

> "In the present case the claim is not for the use of a current of electricity in its natural state as it comes from the battery, but for putting a continuous current in a closed circuit into a certain specified condition suited to the transmission of vocal and other sounds, and using it in that condition for that purpose."[5]

However, the argument is somewhat less than convincing.[6]

Rather than indulge in similar talmudic distinctions, the lower courts invented a series of "rules of thumb" to help draw the line between principles and the embodiments. Among the inventions considered unpatentable were business systems,[7] printed matter,[8] functions-of-

---

[4] 126 U.S. at 533.

[5] Id. at 534.

[6] See, e.g., DONALD S. CHISUM, PATENTS § 1.03[2].

[7] In *In re Wait*, 73 F.2d 982 (C.C.P.A.1934), for example, the applicant claimed a process for the exchange of stocks and commodities that obviated the need for a broker. The court rejected the claims as drawn to non-statutory subject matter, holding:

> The process, when analyzed carefully, appears to comprise, in its essence, nothing more than the advertising of, or giving publicity to, offers of purchase or sale by one party, the acceptance thereof by another, and the making of a record of the transaction followed by a withdrawal of the offer. Surely these are, and

machines,[9] mental steps,[10] and methods dependent on human reactions.[11] Although later courts rightly rejected these doctrines as too simplistic,[12]

---

always have been, essential steps in all dealings of this nature, and even conceding, without holding, that some methods of doing business might present patentable novelty, we think such novelty is lacking here.

73 F.2d at 983. See also, e.g., *Hotel Security Checking Co. v. Lorraine Co.*, 160 F. 467 (2d Cir.1908).

[8] See, e.g., *Ex parte Gwinn*, 112 U.S.P.Q. (BNA) 439 (P.Bd.App. 1955).

[9] *Wyeth v. Stone*, 30 F. Cas. 723 (No. 18,107) (C.C.D. Mass.1840) is a good example. The patentee had invented a new machine to cut ice. His patent read: "It is claimed, as new, to cut ice of a uniform size, by means of an apparatus worked by any other power than human." Justice Story (riding Circuit) invalidated the claim, stating:

It is a claim for an art or principle in the abstract, and not for any particular method of machinery, by which ice is to be cut. No man can have a right to cut ice by all means or methods, or by all or any sort of apparatus, although he is not the inventor of any or all such means, methods, or apparatus. A claim broader than the actual invention of the patentee is, for that very reason, upon the principles of the common law, utterly void ...

30 F. Cas. at 730. Later courts distinguished between claims drawn to particular machines and claims drawn to the "function of the machine." See, e.g., *Corning v. Burden*, 56 U.S. (15 How.) 252, 14 L.Ed. 683 (1853).

[10] *Halliburton Oil Well Cementing Co. v. Walker*, 146 F.2d 817 (9th Cir.1944), is most often cited. There, the court invalidated Walker's patent on a method for determining the location of an obstruction in a well, noting:

In substance, Walker's method here claimed consists in setting down three knowns in a simple equation and from them determining or computing an unknown. The three knowns are: (a) the distance from the well head to the tubing catcher (for example); (b) the length of time it takes an echo to return from that obstruction; and (c) the length of time it takes an echo to return from the fluid surface. From these three knowns can then be determined the distance of the fluid surface from the well head.

* * *

It must be remembered that this is purely a method patent. No apparatus is claimed. Given an apparatus for initiating an impulse wave in a well and a means for differentiating between and for recording echoes returned from obstruction in it, anybody with a rudimentary knowledge of arithmetic will be able to do what Walker claims a monopoly of doing. If his method were patentable it seems to us that the patentee would have a monopoly much broader than would the patentee of a particular apparatus....

146 F.2d at 821–22.

[11] See, e.g., *Ex parte Turner*, 1894 Dec. Comm'r Pat. 36, 38

[12] See, e.g., *Application of Tarczy–Hornoch*, 397 F.2d 856 (C.C.P.A.1968) (overruling the function-of-machine doctrine). Cf. *Cincinnati Traction Co. v. Pope*, 210 Fed. 443 (C.C.A.6 1913) (casting some doubt on the printed-matter doctrine and the business-method doctrine).

the dispute between Supreme Court Justices in *Bilski* illustrates that line drawing remains a difficult problem.

2. *Software Patentability.* Because the early mental-steps doctrine considered any series of steps that *could* be performed in a person's head unpatentable, it was clear from the dawn of the computer era that software would pose problems to patent law. But surprisingly, the first Court to consider software patentability put its objection in more general terms. Thus, in *Gottschalk v. Benson*,[13] the issue was whether a computerized method for converting numerals expressed as binary-coded decimals into pure binary numerals was a patentable process. The Court held it was not. Justice Douglas explained:

> "It is conceded that one may not patent an idea. But in practical effect, that would be the result if the formula for converting binary code to pure binary were patented in this case. The mathematical formula involved here has no substantial practical application except in connection with a digital computer, which means that if the judgment below is affirmed, the patent would wholly pre-empt the mathematical formula and in practical effect would be a patent on the algorithm itself."[14]

After the defeat in *Benson*, many patent applicants changed their strategies. Instead of applying for patents on mathematical manipulations, they tried to conform their claims to the process paradigm described by *Cochrane v. Deener*, 94 U.S. 780 (1877). That tack was first reviewed by the Supreme Court in *Parker v. Flook*.[15] In that case, the claims were drawn to a physical reaction: the catalytic conversion of hydrocarbons. The process used a computer program to continuously monitor a set of variables, compare changes in the variables, and signal abnormalities so that the reaction could be stopped. Flook was careful to stress the chemical changes occurring in the course of using his program rather than focus on the operation of the program itself. Nonetheless, the Court held the claim unpatentable, saying that a "conventional, post-solution application" that

---

[13] 409 U.S. 63 (1972).

[14] Id. at 71–72. Justice Douglas defined "algorithm" as "[a] procedure for solving a given type of mathematical problem," id. at 65.

[15] 437 U.S. 584 (1978).

was well known in the art could not turn a rule of nature into patentable subject matter.

Four years later, in *Diamond v. Diehr*,[16] the Court returned to the question, but this time it provided an answer more favorable to those who thought patent rights necessary to the continued vitality of the computer field. The invention at issue in *Diehr* was a process for curing rubber in a mold. The essentials of the process were commonly used in the rubber manufacturing industry, but it was not efficient as it was difficult to calculate when the rubber should be released from the mold. Diehr's solution coupled a standard device for measuring temperature to a computer programmed to use the well-known Arrhenius rate equation to continuously calculate the curing time from the temperature and signal when the curing process was finished. The Court found that:

> "The 'Arrhenius' equation is not patentable in isolation, but when a process for curing rubber is devised which incorporates in it a more efficient solution of the equation, that process is at the very least not barred at the threshold by § 101."[17]

Despite the promise *Diehr* held for computer patents, implementing its holding proved difficult. The striking similarity between the processes at issue in *Flook* and *Diehr*, coupled with *Diehr*'s failure to articulate a standard for drawing the elusive line between ideas and embodiments, spawned much confusion and several lines of cases leading up to the broad interpretation of patentable subject matter in *State Street Bank* and the reigning in of that interpretation in *Bilski*. Where do software patents stand after *Bilski*? Do you see a difference between how software patents are likely to be treated under the Supreme Court's approach and the "machine or transformation" test?

3. *Business methods.* One of the old rules of thumb held business methods unpatentable. Although use of thumbs to decide abstract issues was long questionable, prior to the software cases there was general agreement that business methods were not among the technologies to which patent law was directed. Once processes using programs became patentable, however, business methods dependent on software were drawn

---

[16] 450 U.S. 175 (1981).
[17] Id. at 188.

into the fold. In *Paine, Webber, Jackson & Curtis, Inc. v. Merrill, Lynch, Pierce, Fenner & Smith, Inc.*,[18] for example, the court upheld the patent on a "Cash Management Account" that used a computer to track clients' deposits in a brokerage securities account, a money market fund, and a Visa charge/checking account.

State Street Bank unequivocally rejected the business method exception, permitting the patenting of business methods even when they did not involve computers. Was this wise? Michael Milken made a fortune selling high risk bonds offering substantial interest. These "junk bonds" proved very popular in the market; many acquisitions have been financed with them. How much more would Milken have made had he been able to patent junk bonds or the process of using them to raise capital? Should the airline that first thought up frequent flyer miles have gained an even greater competitive advantage by patenting the practice of awarding them? How about protection for the tools of other professions: should sports moves—pitches, end-zone wiggles, high jumps—be patentable? Novel legal theories?[19] The next technique for avoiding the strictures of campaign finance reform? A method of launching a research project?[20] Where do business method patents fit in to the various justifications for awarding patents?

4. *The "useful, concrete, and tangible result" test.* How well did the "useful, concrete, and tangible result" test for patentable subject matter deal with the concern that fundamental relationships will become subject to private ownership? Did it do enough to prevent patentees from tying up applications of principles of nature, including applications they have not invented? In this connection, note that the patentee's right of action is not confined to literal infringement. As with copyright's substantial similarity test and trademark's confusing similarity test, patentees can assert rights against those who use "equivalents" of their inventions. See Assignment 21. Thus, claims meeting the requirements of *State Street Bank* were often quite broad.

---

[18] 564 F. Supp. 1358 (D.Del. 1983).

[19] See John R. Thomas, *The Patenting of the Liberal Professions*, 40 B.C. L. REV. 1139 (1999).

[20] Cf., e.g., U.S. Patent 6,584,450, Method and apparatus for renting items, which was awarded to Netflix for its method for renting a fixed number of items (such as three DVDs) at a time.

At the same time, however, the "useful, concrete, and tangible result" test meant that highly abstract lines did not need to be drawn at a time when the significance of an invention (both commercial and scientific) was unknowable. If it becomes clear that a patent is overly broad, the public domain can be protected in other ways. First, an application could be rejected for failure to meet the specification requirement: as the Introductory Assignment explained, § 112 requires the patentee to provide a written description of the invention and enough information about it to enable persons with skill in the art to practice the invention. In *Fiers v. Revel,* the court held that a description of how to isolate DNA was inadequate as a "written description" within the meaning of the statute on the ground that a less stringent rule would allow patentees "to preempt the future before it has arrived."[21] Second, § 112 can be used to reject an attempt to enforce a patent against a later-discovered technology that was not enabled by the disclosure.[22] Third, narrow tests of infringement could be adopted.

Nonetheless, concern that the *State Street Bank* approach had led to an explosion of overly broad, vague, and unnecessary patent claims led up to the Federal Circuit's decision to reverse course and reign in the patentable subject matter doctrine in *Bilski,* as well as the Supreme Court's attention to the issue.

5. *Bilski at the Supreme Court.* The Supreme Court's opinion is complex. All of the Justices rejected the Federal Circuit's attempt to define patentable subject matter using the "machine or transformation" test alone. Were they right to do so? What are the weaknesses of that test? It also seems that all of the Justices reject the Federal Circuit's earlier "useful, concrete, and tangible result" test. Where does that leave the doctrine? Is patentable subject matter likely to be more or less difficult to demonstrate after the Supreme Court's ruling? Where does the patentability of business methods stand after Bilski? Note that four Justices (Justice Stevens and those who joined his concurrence) would have banned business method patents altogether. Four others (all of the Justices in the majority except for Justice Scalia), while unwilling to ban

---

[21] 984 F.2d 1164, 1171 (Fed. Cir. 1993).
[22] Arguably, this is exactly how this problem is being handled in the biotechnology context. See, e.g., *Enzo Biochem, Inc. v. Gen–Probe Inc.,* 323 F.3d 956 (Fed. Cir. 2002); *Fiers v. Revel,* 984 F.2d 1164 (Fed. Cir. 1993).

business method patents categorically, expressed rather serious reservations about them, noting that "[i]f a high enough bar is not set when considering patent applications of this sort, patent examiners and courts could be flooded with claims that would put a chill on creative endeavor and dynamic change" and suggesting rather tepidly "the possibility that there are at least some processes that can be fairly described as business methods that are within patentable subject matter under § 101." Would it have been better from a social perspective to adopt an outright ban on business method patents? From the perspective of a business person? The USPTO had rejected the *Bilski* patent based on a "technological arts" test similar to the test for patentable subject matter employed in Europe. Would a distinction between "technology" and other human endeavors (presumably including "business") be better justified or more workable than the approach we are left with after *Bilski*?

6. *Biologicals. Chakrabarty* established that a living thing that is a "nonnaturally occurring manufacture or composition of matter" may be patentable. It also reiterated, as did *Bilski*, the longstanding doctrine that "laws of nature, physical phenomena, and abstract ideas" are not patentable. *Bilski* focused on the "abstract ideas" prong of these judge-made subject matter exemptions. However, equally difficult line-drawing questions arise in determining the scope of "laws of nature" and "physical phenomena." Like abstract ideas, laws of nature and physical phenomena are "the basic tools of scientific and technological work." *Gottschalk v. Benson,* 409 U.S. 63, 67 (1972). Thus, for example, cell lines and DNA (whether naturally occurring or artificially produced) are not only commercial products, they are also the tools of basic biological research. Indeed patents on biological products present obstacles to biologists. They may hinder innovation and ensnare an inventor who uses a patented product in ways not enabled by the patentee. In addition, as with the computer cases, applicants for patents on the "new" biologicals have had to deal with some old "rules of thumb."

   a. *Material derived from living organisms.* An early case here is *Funk Brothers Seed Co. v. Kalo Inoculant Co.,*[23] discussed in *Chakrabarty.* The invention was a culture of nitrogen-fixing bacteria used to inoculate plant seeds. Many strains of bacteria were prepared in a laboratory and combined in order to make a product useful to a broad

---

[23] 333 U.S. 127, 130 (1948).

168

range of plants. The Supreme Court held the preparation not patentable on the ground that each bacterium is a "manifestation of laws of nature, free to all men and reserved exclusively to none."[24]

Funk's apparent unwillingness to extend patent protection to artificially-enhanced naturally occurring materials was, however, short lived. In 1947, after years of unsuccessful efforts, researchers of Merck & Co. isolated the active substance that gave cow liver its therapeutic benefits to anemia patients. A patent issued on the successful product, termed vitamin B_{12}. In *Merck & Co. v. Olin Mathieson Chemical Corp.*[25] the Fourth Circuit upheld the validity of the patent over a challenge that the product was naturally occurring. In the course of the opinion, the court rejected the argument that vitamin B_{12} was not patentable subject matter because it was merely a purification of living materials:

> The fact ... that a new and useful product is the result of processes of extraction, concentration and purification of natural materials does not defeat its patentability.
>
> The compositions of the patent here ... never existed before; there was nothing comparable to them. If we regard them as a purification of the active principle in natural fermentates, the natural fermentates are quite useless, while the patented compositions are of great medicinal and commercial value. The step from complete uselessness to great and perfected utility is a long one. That step is no mere advance in the degree of purity of a known product.[26]

Of course, prior to *Chakrabarty*, *Funk* could also have been read as prohibiting the patenting of living things. But since *Chakrabarty*, the PTO

---

[24] Id. at 130.

[25] 253 F.2d 156 (4th Cir.1958).

[26] 253 F.2d at 163. In support, the court quoted from Judge Learned Hand's opinion in *Parke–Davis & Co. v. H. K. Mulford Co.*, 189 Fed. 95 (S.D.N.Y.1911), aff'd, 196 F. 496 (2d Cir.1912), upholding a patent on "Adrenalin," a substance isolated and purified from suprarenal glands of living animals.

has taken the position that all non-human living things that are artificially produced are patentable.[27]

b. *Medicine.* The seminal case is *Morton v. New York Eye Infirmary*,[28] which invalidated the patent on ether as used to anesthetize surgical patients. This was probably the single most important discovery in the science of surgery, for no matter how successful a procedure, there had always been a danger that a patient would die of shock. In finding the patent invalid, the *Morton* court cited several grounds: ether was known, the effect of inhaling it was known, and the invention was dependent on human reaction. Furthermore, at the time of *Morton,* the Patent Act did not provide for process patents in the manner of § 101. Nonetheless, there is a strong suspicion that the real ground for *Morton* was the notion that life-saving procedures should not be privately owned. Indeed, one of the first significant medical substances to be patented was the scarlet fever vaccine, and the decision to patent it was greeted with substantial criticism on precisely this ground. Interestingly, the inventors, George and Gladys Dick, tried to defend their action on humanitarian grounds, claiming that the patent enabled them to control quality.[29] And although numerous decisions have upheld patents on medicines since *Morton,*[30] the debate over the propriety of patents in the field has not abated.[31]

c. *DNA patents.* As is clear from *Association of Molecular Pathology v. USPTO,* the patenting of DNA sequences continues to be highly controversial. Not surprisingly, Judge Sweet's ruling has been appealed to the Federal Circuit. That appeal is pending as of this writing. Whatever the Federal Circuit decides in the case, a petition for certiorari to

---

[27] See, e.g., *Ex parte Allen,* 2 U.S.P.Q.2d (BNA) 1425 (Bd.Pat.App. & Int. 1987) (upholding a patent on a polyploid pacific oyster); U.S. Pat. No. 4,736,866 (patent on the so-called "Harvard mouse").

[28] 17 F. Cas. 879 (C.C.S.D.N.Y. 1862).

[29] See Charles Weiner, *Patenting and Academic Research: Historical Case Studies, in* OWNING SCIENTIFIC AND TECHNICAL INFORMATION (V. Weil and J. Snapper, eds., Rutgers Univ. Press 1989).

[30] See, e.g., *Ex parte Scherer,* 103 U.S.P.Q. (BNA) 107 (P.T.O. Bd. App.1954); *Dick v. Lederle Antitoxin Laboratories,* 43 F.2d 628 (S.D.N.Y.1930). See generally, Gregory Burch, *Ethical Considerations in the Patenting of Medical Processes,* 65 TEX. L. REV. 1139 (1987).

[31] See, e.g., BRUCE NUSSBAUM, GOOD INTENTIONS: HOW BIG BUSINESS AND THE MEDICAL ESTABLISHMENT ARE CORRUPTING THE FIGHT AGAINST AIDS, ALZHEIMER'S, CANCER, AND MORE (Penguin Books 1990).

the Supreme Court is virtually inevitable given the high stakes involved in the case.

d. *Medical test patents*. Patents with broad-based claims involving testing for medically significant correlations between disease and relevant biological indicators have been highly controversial in recent years. These patents raise difficult issues involving the line between artificial phenomena and scientific principles or phenomena of nature. The questions are similar to, but distinct from, the issues about abstract ideas raised in cases such as *Bilski*.

The Supreme Court came close to opining on the issue in the case of *Laboratory Corp. of America v. Metabolite Laboratories.*[32] That case involved a patent claim directed to "A method for detecting a deficiency of cobalamin or folate in warm-blooded animals comprising the steps of: assaying a body fluid for an elevated level of total homocysteine; and correlating an elevated level of total homocysteine in said body fluid with a deficiency of cobalamin or folate." The inventors of the patent had developed a specific test for detecting an elevated level of total homocysteine, which was covered by other claims in the patent. They had also discovered the scientific fact that high levels of homocysteine were correlated with deficiencies of the vitamins cobalamin (B_{12}) and folate (folic acid). The claim at issue in the case was interpreted by the court to cover any instance in which a physician used *any test* to detect an elevated level of total homocysteine and then recognized that the elevated level suggested a vitamin deficiency.

The Supreme Court granted certiorari to consider whether a claim covering such a "correlation" is viable. The case was widely seen as raising important questions about the line between patentable processes and unpatentable "laws of nature" and about the patentability of business methods. After the case was fully briefed and argued, the Court dismissed the writ as improvidently granted. The respondent rested its successful, if unusual, argument for dismissal of the writ on procedural grounds and on the fact that the Federal Circuit had not addressed the patentable subject matter questions in its opinion below. The dismissal of the writ prompted a strong dissent by JUSTICE BREYER, joined by JUSTICES STEVENS and SOUTER, who would have held the claim unpatentable.

---

[32] 126 S. Ct. 2921 (2006).

In his dissent, JUSTICE BREYER distinguished the limitation on patenting laws of nature from other limitations on patentability and focused on the "dangers of overprotection":

> The justification for the principle does not lie in any claim that "laws of nature" are obvious, or that their discovery is easy, or that they are not useful. . . . Rather, the reason for the exclusion is that sometimes too much patent protection can impede rather than "promote the Progress of Science and useful Arts," the constitutional objective of patent and copyright protection.[33]

According to JUSTICE BREYER, the exclusion of laws of nature from patentability "reflects a basic judgment that protection in such cases, despite its potentially positive incentive effects, would too often severely interfere with, or discourage, development and the further spread of useful knowledge itself."[34] JUSTICE BREYER also raised significant questions about the *State Street Bank* case, stating that though *State Street Bank* "does say that a process is patentable if it produces a 'useful, concrete, and tangible result'," "this Court has never made such a statement and, if taken literally, the statement would cover instances where this Court has held to the contrary."

Though the Supreme Court dismissed its grant of certiorari in *Lab Corp. v. Metabolite*, two other cases involving medical processes – and coming to opposite results -- were the subjects of petitions for certiorari to the Supreme Court that were pending at the time of the *Bilski* decision. The Supreme Court granted certiorari in both cases solely for the purpose of vacating the Federal Circuit's rulings and remanding for consideration in light of the *Bilski* opinion.[35] In *Prometheus Laboratories v. Mayo Collaborative*, 581 F.3d 1336 (Fed. Cir. 2008), the Federal Circuit originally upheld claims to a method for testing the effectiveness of certain medications for gastrointestinal disorders. The broadest claims cover a physician administering a drug, using *any* testing method to

---

[33] Id. (BREYER, J., dissenting).

[34] Id.

[35] *Mayo Collaborative Servs. v. Prometheus Labs., Inc.*, 2010 U.S. LEXIS 5537 (U.S. June 29, 2010); *Classen Immunotherapies, Inc. v. Biogen IDEC*, 2010 U.S. LEXIS 5533 (U.S. June 29, 2010).

measure the levels of relevant drug metabolites in a patient, and then considering whether to adjust the dosage of the corresponding drug. An exemplary claim is:

> A method of optimizing therapeutic efficacy for treatment of an immune-mediated gastrointestinal disorder, comprising:
> (a) administering a drug providing 6-thioguanine to a subject having said immune-mediated gastrointestinal disorder; and
> (b) determining the level of 6-thioguanine in said subject having said immune-mediated gastrointestinal disorder, wherein the level of 6-thioguanine less than about 230 pmol per 8x108 red blood cells indicates a need to increase the amount of said drug subsequently administered to said subject and wherein the level of 6-thioguanine greater than about 400 pmol per 8x108 red blood cells indicates a need to decrease the amount of said drug subsequently administered to said subject.

In *Classen Immunotherapies, Inc. v. Biogen IDEC*, 304 Fed. Appx. 866 (Fed. Cir. 2008), on the other hand, the Federal Circuit affirmed a district court ruling that the following was not a claim to patentable subject matter:

> A method of determining whether an immunization schedule affects the incidence or severity of a chronic immune-mediated disorder in a treatment group of mammals, relative to a control group of mammals, which comprises immunizing mammals in the treatment group of mammals with one or more doses of one or more immunogens, according to said immunization schedule, and comparing the incidence, prevalence, frequency or severity of said chronic immune-mediated disorder or the level of a marker of such a disorder, in the treatment group, with that in the control group

At this writing, the Federal Circuit has yet to reconsider these cases. Depending on what the Federal Circuit does on remand, either or both is likely to be the subject of yet another petition for certiorari. If these cases are taken up by the Supreme Court, what should the outcome be? Do these patents claim abstract ideas? Scientific principles? What would be the social consequences of allowing (or not allowing) such claims?

7. *The property analogy.* Another manifestation of the concern over granting exclusive rights in biological materials is evident in the debate over whether the law should consider body parts as property. Some people argue that recognizing such rights would be a species of slavery.[36] Another rationale for rejecting the property analogy is that ownership of rights to body parts will impede research.

Consider, for example, *Moore v. Regents of University of California.*[37] John Moore had had his spleen removed at UCLA Medical Center as part of his treatment for hairy-cell leukemia. Doctors required him to return to the Center from his home in Seattle on a number of occasions so they could take further samples of blood, blood serum, skin, bone marrow aspirate, and sperm. Unbeknownst to him, these samples were used not for treatment, but to grow a cell line of his T-lymphocytes, which was later patented and subject to lucrative licensing agreements. Moore sued on, among other things, a theory of tortious conversion, asserting that the samples and cell line were his property. In rejecting his claim, the court stated:

> "The extension of conversion law into this area will hinder research by restricting access to the necessary raw materials. Thousands of human cell lines already exist in tissue repositories, such as the American Type Culture Collection and those operated by the National Institutes of Health and the American Cancer Society. These repositories respond to tens of thousands of requests for samples annually. Since the patent office requires the holders of patents on cell lines to make samples available to anyone, many patent holders place their cell lines in repositories to avoid the administrative burden of responding to requests. At present, human cell lines are routinely copied and distributed to other researchers for experimental purposes, usually free of charge.

---

[36] Cf. *Davis v. Davis*, 842 S.W.2d 588 (Tenn.1992) (rejecting the notion that frozen embryos are property), *cert. denied sub nom. Stowe v. Davis*, 507 U.S. 911 (1993). See generally, Kevin D. DeBre', Note, *Patents on People and the U.S. Constitution: Creating Slaves or Enslaving*, 16 HASTINGS CONST. L.Q. 221 (1989). Indeed, when the PTO announced that it would examine claims to non-human animals, it stated that it regarded claims to human beings as prohibited by the Constitution, presumably the Thirteenth Amendment, see Nonnaturally Occurring Non–Human Animals are Patentable Under § 101, 33 Pat. Trademark & Copyright J. 884 (1987).

[37] 51 Cal. 3d 120, 271 Cal. Rptr. 146, 793 P.2d 479 (1990) (en banc).

This exchange of scientific materials, which still is relatively free and efficient, will surely be compromised if each cell sample becomes the potential subject matter of a lawsuit.

"To expand liability by extending conversion law into this area would have a broad impact. The House Committee on Science and Technology of the United States Congress found that '49 percent of the researchers at medical institutions surveyed used human tissues or cells in their research.' Many receive grants from the National Institute of Health for this work. In addition, 'there are nearly 350 commercial biotechnology firms in the United States actively engaged in biotechnology research and commercial product development and approximately 25 to 30 percent appear to be engaged in research to develop a human therapeutic or diagnostic reagent.... Most, but not all, of the human therapeutic products are derived from human tissues and cells, or human cell lines or cloned genes.' "

8. *Dealing with new technological arenas.* Even if a particular new type of technology is indisputably patentable, the recognition of new categories of patentable subject matter can create significant transition problems. The PTO must hire examiners with enough experience in the new field to examine applications effectively. If the field is newly recognized, but not entirely new, then the PTO must also develop a library of prior art against which to determine claims of novelty and nonobviousness. Sometimes new examining approaches are also necessary. For example, because business methods are often put directly into practice (rather than described in journals), there is a paucity of public documentation available anywhere. As a result, the Office has been criticized for not citing relevant prior art and for issuing patents on methods long in use.[38] The PTO has instituted a series of checks to make sure examining in this field is accurate.[39] For a time, the industry took matters into its own hands and created a website that offered rewards for locating invalidating prior art. The site was apparently unsuccessful.[40] Commentators have suggested

---

[38] See, e.g., Rochelle C. Dreyfuss, *Are Business Method Patents Bad For Business?*, 16 SANTA CLARA COMPUTER & HIGH TECH. L.J. 263 (2000). For a contrasting view on the value of business method patents, see Robert P. Merges, *The Uninvited Guest: Patents on Wall Street*, available at http://papers.ssrn.com/sol3/papers.cfm?abstract_id=410900.

[39] See http://www.uspto.gov/web/offices/com/sol/actionplan.html.

[40] It was found at www.bountyquest.com.

other changes in the patent-granting system to reduce the number of invalid or overbroad patents.[41]

In time, the problems in the new fields of software, business methods, and biotechnology will surely abate. However, in the interim, there is considerable uncertainty, and that has ramifications of its own. When the validity or the scope of issued patents is unclear, investors may hesitate to invest, for they would not want to find themselves on the wrong end of a successful infringement suit. Those who choose to participate in the field may begin to patent "defensively." That is, they may apply for patents not because they want to protect their investments in technologies they plan to use, but rather because they need bargaining chips—patents that they can cross license, or counterclaims that they can assert, should anyone sue them for infringement. This vicious cycle of patenting and defensive patenting creates even more work for the PTO and—arguably—further chills entry into the field because every potential participant must then negotiate her way through a thicket of patents to determine whether she can freely pursue her business objectives. If she can't, then considerable negotiation may be required to put together the needed package of patent rights.[42]

Finally, even after it is clear that a field should be the subject of patent protection, there may be specific issues meriting special treatment. For example, in the wake of cases expanding the subject matter of patents, Congress enacted two provisions limiting their scope. To cope with the possibility that a business method patent will issue on a method already in use, Congress enacted the First Inventor Defense, also known as a prior user right. This is a defense to infringement in favor of any person who:

> "acting in good faith, actually reduced the subject matter [of a business method patent] to practice at least one year before the effective filing date of such patent, and commercially used the subject matter before the effective filing date of such patent."[43]

---

[41] See, e.g., Robert P. Merges, *As Many as Six Impossible Patents Before Breakfast: Property Rights for Business Concepts and Patent System Reform*, 14 BERKELEY TECH. L.J. 577 (1999).

[42] See Michael A. Heller & Rebecca S. Eisenberg, *Can Patents Deter Innovation? The Anticommons in Biomedical Research*, 280 SCIENCE 698 (1998).

[43] § 273(b)(1).

In order to prevent the first inventor from competing away all patent profits, the defense can be asserted only by the party who established the defense and it can only be used with respect to the specific subject matter claimed.[44] The Supreme Court majority in *Bilski* relied in part on the enactment of this statute in holding that there is no categorical exclusion of business methods from patentable subject matter.

Another example is a special provision enacted after it became clear that medical procedures (such as new types of incisions) were patentable subject matter. Congress became concerned that these patents would limit access to, and increase the price of, important medical methods, without any indication that physicians and surgeons needed a patent incentive to perfect their methods. Instead of changing the subject matter provisions of the statute, an amendment was made to the damages provision. It provides that a medical practitioner's performance of certain medical activities that constitute infringement cannot be the basis for monetary or injunctive relief against the medical practitioner or a health related care entity.[45] The *Prometheus* and *Classen* cases discussed in Note 6d continue to raise similar issues for the medical profession.

In the same vein, some have argued that special legislation should be enacted to bar patents on biological research tools or to create a defense to infringement when these tools are used for noncommercial purposes.[46] Others suggest that in the software and business method areas, special treatment should be accorded to industrial standards—inventions that an entire industry must share for compatibility or other reasons.[47]

9. *Non-utility patents.* The focus of this case book is on utility patents, but it is important to recognize that the law provides patent, or patent-like, protection to two other kinds of subject matter, plants and designs.

a. *Plants.* Plants are protected under two different statutes. The Plant Patent Act, §§ 161–164 of the Patent Act, creates rights in new and

---

[44] § 273(b)(6) & (b)(3)(C).

[45] § 287(c).

[46] See, e.g., Rebecca S. Eisenberg, *Technology Transfer And The Genome Project: Problems With Patenting Research Tools*, 5 RISK: HEALTH SAFETY & ENV'T 163 (1994).

[47] See Janice M. Mueller, *Patenting Industry Standards*, 34 J. MARSHALL L. REV. 897 (2001); Mark Lemley, *Standardizing Government Standard–Setting Policy for Electronic Commerce*, 14 BERKELEY TECH. L.J. 745 (1999).

distinct plants that are asexually reproduced, while the Plant Variety Protection Act (PVPA), 7 U.S.C.A. §§ 2321–2583, creates rights in sexually reproduced plants. The PVPA is wholly administered by the Department of Agriculture, which assists the Commissioner of Patents with administering the Plant Patent Act. These statutes differ from standard patent law by substituting for the specification requirement of § 112, a requirement that the patentee place a sample of the protected plant on deposit, where it can be studied by others. The PVPA also differs from patent law in that it contains research and farmer's crop exemptions and a compulsory license provision. After *Chakrabarty,* there was a question whether the limitations of the PVPA can be avoided by applying for utility patents instead. In 2001, the Supreme Court answered that question in the affirmative.[48]

b. *Designs.* Sections 171–173 of the Patent Act create patent rights in new, original, and ornamental designs for articles of manufacture. The terms "new" and "original" have essentially the same meaning as they have for utility patents. Applications are scrutinized for nonobviousness and also to make sure that the design is ornamental rather than primarily functional. Infringement is determined in a manner rather similar to the way that copyright infringement is analyzed. However, the term of protection is shorter (14 years).

Design patents are sometimes thought of as protecting designs that are so inseparable from function that they cannot be protected by copyright, see Assignment 8. While it is nice to think that patent law takes up exactly where copyright leaves off, this notion is true to only a limited extent. First, § 171 specifies that a design must be "ornamental." Designs that are dictated purely by functional considerations are not any more eligible for patent protection than they are for copyright protection. Thus, purely functional designs—for instance, dashboards and refrigerator panels—receive no protection under U.S. patent law *or* copyright law.[49] The

---

[48] *J.E.M. AG Supply, Inc. v. Pioneer Hi–Bred Intern., Inc.,* 534 U.S. 124 (2001).

[49] The exception is the boat hull, which since 1998 has its own statutory scheme in 17 U.S.C. §§ 1301–1332. Despite its narrow focus on boat hulls, this long and involved statute is entitled "Protection of Original Designs," and there is reason to believe that Congress is using this protection to test the waters for devising stronger protection for other functional designs. See Graeme B. Dinwoodie, *Essay: The Integration of International and Domestic Intellectual Property Lawmaking,* 23 COLUM.-VLA J.L. & ARTS 307 (2000) and Assignment 8.

tendency has been to try to acquire trademark rights in some feature of a successful design, but this is a problem too as it creates a term of protection that is far too long. In the view of many commentators, the absence of effective protection has put American designers and consumer product manufacturers in a competitively uncomfortable position.

Second, even for designs that fit within the legislative scheme, the general consensus is that the design statute does not work particularly well. The extensiveness of the examination system is a problem because a patent may not issue until after the popularity of the design has peaked. Moreover, decisions on what is nonobvious and what is an infringement tend to be very subjective. (See Note 12, Assignment 21.) Congress has from time to time considered new design legislation, but has never acted.[50]

---

[50] See William T. Fryer, *Industrial Design Protection in the United States of America—Present Situation and Plans for Revision*, 70 J. PAT. OFF. SOC. 821 (1988); J.H. Reichman, *Design Protection and the New Technologies: The United States Experience in a Transnational Perspective*, 19 U. BALT. L. REV. 6 (1991).

ASSIGNMENT 16—UTILITY

INSERT AT THE END OF NOTE 6 ON PAGE 633:

The Federal Circuit addressed the issue of the patentability of tools and materials used in scientific research in *In re Fisher*.[1] The case involved the patentability of DNA sub-sequences known as expressed sequence tags or "ESTs." ESTs correspond to portions of genes that are being expressed in particular tissues. The ESTs at issue in *Fisher* corresponded to genes being expressed in maize leaf tissue. The structure and function of these corresponding genes was unknown, as was the structure and function of any corresponding coded proteins. The patent applicant asserted a list of research uses for the ESTs. The PTO rejected the application, concluding that it failed to assert a "specific" and "substantial" utility as required by PTO Utility Examination Guidelines,[2] which were premised on the Supreme Court's opinion in *Brenner*.

A divided panel of the Federal Circuit affirmed the rejection, adopting the approach of the Utility Guidelines. The court held that the research uses proposed by the applicant did not meet the "substantial" utility requirement because the uses lacked "a significant and presently available benefit to the public." The court came to that conclusion because the ESTs corresponded to genes with unknown structure and function and because all of the alleged uses represented "hypothetical possibilities" since there was no evidence presented that the claimed ESTs had been used in the ways alleged. The listed research uses also lacked "specific utility" because all of the proposed uses were general. "Any EST transcribed from any gene in the maize genome has the potential to perform any one of the alleged uses."

While the panel majority viewed the claimed ESTs as "research intermediates in the identification of underlying protein-encoding genes of unknown function," a dissenting Judge Rader, saw the ESTs as more akin to a microscope or other research tool, which has its utility in "identifying and understanding a previously unknown and invisible structure." Emphasizing the incremental nature of scientific research, Judge Rader

---

[1] 421 F.3d 1365 (Fed. Cir. 2005).
[2] M.P.E.P. § 2107 (2001).

argued that the proper means for weeding out insubstantial advances is the nonobviousness requirement discussed in Assignment 18. The line between useful—and patentable—research tools and research intermediates lacking in "substantial" and "specific" utility is likely to continue to be hard to draw. Judge Rader's dissent raises an issue which arises repeatedly in discussions of patent policy: In seeking to promote technological progress by balancing the rights of inventors and users, patent doctrine provides various tools which can be applied. Controversy often arises as to which doctrine is best suited to addressing a particular policy issue.

ASSIGNMENT 17—NOVELTY

INSERT AT THE END OF THE FIRST PARAGRAPH ON PAGE 656:

A particularly interesting application of this rule arose in the case of *Smithkline Beecham Corp. v. Apotex Corp.*[1] The patent at issue in that case covered a particular "hemihydrate" crystalline form of paroxetine hydrochloride (the active ingredient in the antidepressant drug, Paxil®). The discovery of the hemihydrate crystalline form was made during the practice of a prior art process for producing a different, anhydrate crystalline form. Once the hemihydrate form had been produced it apparently "seeded" the environment, making it impossible to produce the prior art anhydrate form without producing at least trace amounts of the hemihydrate form at issue in the case. Thus, *Smithkline* argued, in attempting to produce a generic version of the prior art anhydrate form, *Apotex* would necessarily infringe the newer patent on the hemihydrate form. But a finding of infringement in these circumstances would certainly implicate the public's interest in being able to practice the prior art. Thus, the courts were faced with a dilemma, which the district court and the Federal Circuit addressed in different ways.

The district court opinion, authored by Judge Richard Posner of the Seventh Circuit Court of Appeals, who was sitting by designation as trial court judge in the case, found that the trace amounts of hemihydrate form produced as an inevitable by-product of the prior art process were too insignificant to constitute infringement. There is generally no *de minimis* exception to patent infringement, however, and the Federal Circuit rejected this approach.

Instead, the Federal Circuit held that the claims to the hemihydrate form were necessarily anticipated by the trace amounts of that form which must have been produced when the anhydrate form was manufactured prior to the discovery of the hemihydrate form. This ruling preserved the rule that "that which infringes, if later, would anticipate, if earlier" and prevented the removal of the prior art anhydrate form from the public

---

[1] 439 F.3d 1312 (Fed. Cir. 2006).

domain by relying on inherent anticipation, a doctrine which we address next, to invalidate the claim to the hemihydrate form. After reading the following discussion of inherent anticipation, consider whether the district court approach of *de minimis* infringement or the Federal Circuit approach of inherent anticipation is the preferable solution to the dilemma presented by this case.

INSERT AT THE END OF THE FIRST FULL PARAGRAPH ON PAGE 659:

In the case of *Bruckelmyer v. Ground Heaters, Inc.*,[2] the Federal Circuit considered whether a Canadian patent application that was available only in a patent prosecution file in a patent office in Canada was sufficiently "publicly accessible" to be deemed a "publication" under § 102. The court held that, despite the fact that the application itself was not abstracted or indexed, the Canadian patent that issued from it contained disclosure sufficient that "a person of ordinary skill in the art interested in the subject matter of the patents in suit and exercising reasonable diligence" would be able to locate the application in the prosecution file. Hence, the application qualified as a prior art publication.

---

[2] 445 F.3d 1374 (Fed. Cir. 2006).

ASSIGNMENT 18—NONOBVIOUSNESS AND ORIGINALITY

REPLACE STRATOFLEX, INC. v. AEROQUIP CORP., IN RE DILLON, IN RE BELL, AND ODDZON PRODUCTS, INC. v. JUST TOYS, INC. ON PAGES 679-701 AND THE NOTES FOLLOWING THEM ON PAGES 701-713 WITH THE FOLLOWING:

KSR International Co. v. Teleflex Inc.
Supreme Court of the United States, 2007.
127 S. Ct. 1727.

■ JUSTICE KENNEDY delivered the opinion of the Court.

Teleflex Incorporated sued KSR International Company for patent infringement. The patent at issue, United States Patent No. 6,237,565 B1, is entitled "Adjustable Pedal Assembly With Electronic Throttle Control." The patentee is Steven J. Engelgau. Teleflex holds the exclusive license to the patent.

Claim 4 of the Engelgau patent describes a mechanism for combining an electronic sensor with an adjustable automobile pedal so the pedal's position can be transmitted to a computer that controls the throttle in the vehicle's engine. When Teleflex accused KSR of infringing the Engelgau patent by adding an electronic sensor to one of KSR's previously designed pedals, KSR countered that claim 4 was invalid under the Patent Act, 35 U.S.C. § 103, because its subject matter was obvious.

In *Graham v. John Deere Co. of Kansas City,* 383 U.S. 1 (1966), the Court set out a framework for applying the statutory language of § 103, language itself based on the logic of the earlier decision in *Hotchkiss v. Greenwood,* 11 How. 248 (1851), and its progeny. The analysis is objective:

> "Under § 103, the scope and content of the prior art are to be determined; differences between the prior art and the claims at issue are to be ascertained; and the level of ordinary skill in the pertinent art resolved. Against this background the obviousness or

184

nonobviousness of the subject matter is determined. Such secondary considerations as commercial success, long felt but unsolved needs, failure of others, etc., might be utilized to give light to the circumstances surrounding the origin of the subject matter sought to be patented." [*Graham*] at 17-18.

Seeking to resolve the question of obviousness with more uniformity and consistency, the Court of Appeals for the Federal Circuit has employed an approach referred to by the parties as the "teaching, suggestion, or motivation" test (TSM test), under which a patent claim is only proved obvious if "some motivation or suggestion to combine the prior art teachings" can be found in the prior art, the nature of the problem, or the knowledge of a person having ordinary skill in the art. KSR challenges that test, or at least its application in this case. Because the Court of Appeals addressed the question of obviousness in a manner contrary to § 103 and our precedents, we granted certiorari. We now reverse.

I.

A.

In car engines without computer-controlled throttles, the accelerator pedal interacts with the throttle via cable or other mechanical link. The pedal arm acts as a lever rotating around a pivot point. In a cable-actuated throttle control the rotation caused by pushing down the pedal pulls a cable, which in turn pulls open valves in the carburetor or fuel injection unit. The wider the valves open, the more fuel and air are released, causing combustion to increase and the car to accelerate. When the driver takes his foot off the pedal, the opposite occurs as the cable is released and the valves slide closed.

In the 1990's it became more common to install computers in cars to control engine operation. Computer-controlled throttles open and close valves in response to electronic signals, not through force transferred from the pedal by a mechanical link. Constant, delicate adjustments of air and fuel mixture are possible. The computer's rapid processing of factors beyond the pedal's position improves fuel efficiency and engine performance.

For a computer-controlled throttle to respond to a driver's operation of the car, the computer must know what is happening with the pedal. A cable or mechanical link does not suffice for this purpose; at some point, an electronic sensor is necessary to translate the mechanical operation into digital data the computer can understand.

Before discussing sensors further we turn to the mechanical design of the pedal itself. In the traditional design a pedal can be pushed down or released but cannot have its position in the footwell adjusted by sliding the pedal forward or back. As a result, a driver who wishes to be closer or farther from the pedal must either reposition himself in the driver's seat or move the seat in some way. In cars with deep footwells these are imperfect solutions for drivers of smaller stature. To solve the problem, inventors, beginning in the 1970's, designed pedals that could be adjusted to change their location in the footwell. Important for this case are two adjustable pedals disclosed in U.S. Patent Nos. 5,010,782 (filed July 28, 1989) (Asano) and 5,460,061 (filed Sept. 17, 1993) (Redding). The Asano patent reveals a support structure that houses the pedal so that even when the pedal location is adjusted relative to the driver, one of the pedal's pivot points stays fixed. The pedal is also designed so that the force necessary to push the pedal down is the same regardless of adjustments to its location. The Redding patent reveals a different, sliding mechanism where both the pedal and the pivot point are adjusted.

We return to sensors. Well before Engelgau applied for his challenged patent, some inventors had obtained patents involving electronic pedal sensors for computer-controlled throttles. These inventions, such as the device disclosed in U.S. Patent No. 5,241,936 (filed Sept. 9, 1991) ('936), taught that it was preferable to detect the pedal's position in the pedal assembly, not in the engine. The '936 patent disclosed a pedal with an electronic sensor on a pivot point in the pedal assembly. U.S. Patent No. 5,063,811 (filed July 9, 1990) (Smith) taught that to prevent the wires connecting the sensor to the computer from chafing and wearing out, and to avoid grime and damage from the driver's foot, the sensor should be put on a fixed part of the pedal assembly rather than in or on the pedal's footpad.

In addition to patents for pedals with integrated sensors, inventors obtained patents for self-contained modular sensors. A modular sensor is designed independently of a given pedal so that it can be taken off the shelf and attached to mechanical pedals of various sorts, enabling the pedals to be used in automobiles with computer-controlled throttles. One such sensor was disclosed in U.S. Patent No. 5,385,068 (filed Dec. 18, 1992) ('068). In 1994, Chevrolet manufactured a line of trucks using modular sensors attached to the pedal support bracket, adjacent to the pedal and engaged with the pivot shaft about which the pedal rotates in operation.

The prior art contained patents involving the placement of sensors on adjustable pedals as well. For example, U.S. Patent No. 5,819,593 (filed Aug. 17, 1995) (Rixon) discloses an adjustable pedal assembly with an electronic sensor for detecting the pedal's position. In the Rixon pedal the sensor is located in the pedal footpad. The Rixon pedal was known to suffer from wire chafing when the pedal was depressed and released.

B.

KSR, a Canadian company, manufactures and supplies auto parts, including pedal systems. Ford Motor Company hired KSR in 1998 to supply an adjustable pedal system for various lines of automobiles with cable-actuated throttle controls. KSR developed an adjustable mechanical pedal for Ford and obtained U.S. Patent No. 6,151,976 (filed July 16, 1999) ('976) for the design. In 2000, KSR was chosen by General Motors Corporation (GMC or GM) to supply adjustable pedal systems for Chevrolet and GMC light trucks that used engines with computer-controlled throttles. To make the '976 pedal compatible with the trucks, KSR merely took that design and added a modular sensor.

Teleflex is a rival to KSR in the design and manufacture of adjustable pedals. As noted, it is the exclusive licensee of the Engelgau patent. The Engelgau patent discloses an adjustable electronic pedal described in the specification as a "simplified vehicle control pedal assembly that is less expensive, and which uses fewer parts and is easier to package within the vehicle." Claim 4 of the patent, at issue here, describes:

A vehicle control pedal apparatus comprising:
a support adapted to be mounted to a vehicle structure;
an adjustable pedal assembly having a pedal arm moveable in for[e] and aft directions with respect to said support;
a pivot for pivotally supporting said adjustable pedal assembly

187

with respect to said support and defining a pivot axis; and
an electronic control attached to said support for controlling a vehicle system;
said apparatus characterized by said electronic control being responsive to said pivot for providing a signal that corresponds to pedal arm position as said pedal arm pivots about said pivot axis between rest and applied positions wherein the position of said pivot remains constant while said pedal arm moves in fore and aft directions with respect to said pivot." col. 6, lines 17-36.

We agree with the District Court that the claim discloses "a position-adjustable pedal assembly with an electronic pedal position sensor attached to the support member of the pedal assembly. Attaching the sensor to the support member allows the sensor to remain in a fixed position while the driver adjusts the pedal."

Before issuing the Engelgau patent the U.S. Patent and Trademark Office (PTO) rejected one of the patent claims that was similar to, but broader than, the present claim 4. The claim did not include the requirement that the sensor be placed on a fixed pivot point. The PTO concluded the claim was an obvious combination of the prior art disclosed in Redding and Smith[:] Redding provided an example of an adjustable pedal and Smith explained how to mount a sensor on a pedal's support structure, and the rejected patent claim merely put these two teachings together.

Although the broader claim was rejected, claim 4 was later allowed because it included the limitation of a fixed pivot point, which distinguished the design from Redding's. Engelgau had not included Asano among the prior art references, and Asano was not mentioned in the patent's prosecution. Thus, the PTO did not have before it an adjustable pedal with a fixed pivot point. The patent issued on May 29, 2001 and was assigned to Teleflex.

Upon learning of KSR's design for GM, Teleflex sent a warning letter informing KSR that its proposal would violate the Engelgau patent. [When negotiations for a license failed, Teleflex sued for infringement of Claim 4.]

C.

The District Court granted summary judgment in KSR's favor. After reviewing the pertinent history of pedal design, the scope of the Engelgau patent, and the relevant prior art, the court considered the validity of the contested claim. By direction of 35 U.S.C. § 282, an issued patent is presumed valid. The District Court applied *Graham* to determine whether under summary-judgment standards KSR had overcome the presumption and demonstrated that claim 4 was obvious in light of the prior art in existence when the claimed subject matter was invented.

The District Court determined, in light of the expert testimony and the parties' stipulations, that the level of ordinary skill in pedal design was "an undergraduate degree in mechanical engineering (or an equivalent amount of industry experience) [and] familiarity with pedal control systems for vehicles." The court then set forth the relevant prior art, including the patents and pedal designs described above.

Following *Graham's* direction, the court compared the teachings of the prior art to the claims of Engelgau. It found "little difference." Asano taught everything contained in claim 4 except the use of a sensor to detect the pedal's position and transmit it to the computer controlling the throttle. That additional aspect was revealed in sources such as the '068 patent and the sensors used by Chevrolet.

Under the controlling cases from the Court of Appeals for the Federal Circuit, however, the District Court was not permitted to stop there. The court was required also to apply the TSM test. The District Court held KSR had satisfied the test. It reasoned (1) the state of the industry would lead inevitably to combinations of electronic sensors and adjustable pedals, (2) Rixon provided the basis for these developments, and (3) Smith taught a solution to the wire chafing problems in Rixon, namely locating the sensor on the fixed structure of the pedal. This could lead to the combination of Asano, or a pedal like it, with a pedal position sensor.

With principal reliance on the TSM test, the Court of Appeals reversed. It ruled the District Court had not been strict enough in applying the test, having failed to make "'finding[s] as to the specific understanding or principle within the knowledge of a skilled artisan that would have motivated one with no knowledge of [the] invention' ... to attach an

189

electronic control to the support bracket of the Asano assembly." The Court of Appeals held that the District Court was incorrect that the nature of the problem to be solved satisfied this requirement because unless the "prior art references address[ed] the precise problem that the patentee was trying to solve," the problem would not motivate an inventor to look at those references.

Here, the Court of Appeals found, the Asano pedal was designed to solve the "constant ratio problem"—that is, to ensure that the force required to depress the pedal is the same no matter how the pedal is adjusted-whereas Engelgau sought to provide a simpler, smaller, cheaper adjustable electronic pedal. As for Rixon, the court explained, that pedal suffered from the problem of wire chafing but was not designed to solve it. In the court's view Rixon did not teach anything helpful to Engelgau's purpose. Smith, in turn, did not relate to adjustable pedals and did not "necessarily go to the issue of motivation to attach the electronic control on the support bracket of the pedal assembly." When the patents were interpreted in this way, the Court of Appeals held, they would not have led a person of ordinary skill to put a sensor on the sort of pedal described in Asano.

That it might have been obvious to try the combination of Asano and a sensor was likewise irrelevant, in the court's view, because "'[o]bvious to try' has long been held not to constitute obviousness." ([Opinion below] quoting *In re Deuel,* 51 F.3d 1552, 1559 (C.A.Fed.1995).)

II.

A.

We begin by rejecting the rigid approach of the Court of Appeals. Throughout this Court's engagement with the question of obviousness, our cases have set forth an expansive and flexible approach inconsistent with the way the Court of Appeals applied its TSM test here. To be sure, *Graham* recognized the need for "uniformity and definiteness." 383 U.S., at 18. Yet the principles laid down in *Graham* reaffirmed the "functional approach" of *Hotchkiss*. *Graham* set forth a broad inquiry and invited courts, where appropriate, to look at any secondary considerations that would prove instructive.

Neither the enactment of § 103 nor the analysis in *Graham* disturbed this Court's earlier instructions concerning the need for caution in granting a patent based on the combination of elements found in the prior art. For over a half century, the Court has held that a "patent for a combination which only unites old elements with no change in their respective functions ... obviously withdraws what is already known into the field of its monopoly and diminishes the resources available to skillful men." *Great Atlantic & Pacific Tea Co. v. Supermarket Equipment Corp.,* 340 U.S. 147, 162 (1950). This is a principal reason for declining to allow patents for what is obvious. The combination of familiar elements according to known methods is likely to be obvious when it does no more than yield predictable results.   Three cases decided after *Graham* illustrates the application of this doctrine.

In *United States v. Adams,* 383 U.S. 39 (1966), a companion case to *Graham,* the Court considered the obviousness of a "wet battery" that varied from prior designs in two ways: It contained water, rather than the acids conventionally employed in storage batteries; and its electrodes were magnesium and cuprous chloride, rather than zinc and silver chloride. The Court recognized that when a patent claims a structure already known in the prior art that is altered by the mere substitution of one element for another known in the field, the combination must do more than yield a predictable result.   It nevertheless rejected the Government's claim that Adams's battery was obvious. The Court relied upon the corollary principle that when the prior art teaches away from combining certain known elements, discovery of a successful means of combining them is more likely to be nonobvious.   When Adams designed his battery, the prior art warned that risks were involved in using the types of electrodes he employed. The fact that the elements worked together in an unexpected and fruitful manner supported the conclusion that Adams's design was not obvious to those skilled in the art.

In *Anderson's-Black Rock, Inc. v. Pavement Salvage Co.,* 396 U.S. 57 (1969), the Court elaborated on this approach. The subject matter of the patent before the Court was a device combining two pre-existing elements: a radiant-heat burner and a paving machine. The device, the Court concluded, did not create some new synergy: The radiant-heat burner functioned just as a burner was expected to function; and the paving machine did the same. The two in combination did no more than they would in separate, sequential operation. In those circumstances, "while the

191

combination of old elements performed a useful function, it added nothing to the nature and quality of the radiant-heat burner already patented," and the patent failed under § 103.

Finally, in *Sakraida v. Ag Pro, Inc.,* 425 U.S. 273 (1976), the Court derived from the precedents the conclusion that when a patent "simply arranges old elements with each performing the same function it had been known to perform" and yields no more than one would expect from such an arrangement, the combination is obvious.

The principles underlying these cases are instructive when the question is whether a patent claiming the combination of elements of prior art is obvious. When a work is available in one field of endeavor, design incentives and other market forces can prompt variations of it, either in the same field or a different one. If a person of ordinary skill can implement a predictable variation, § 103 likely bars its patentability. For the same reason, if a technique has been used to improve one device, and a person of ordinary skill in the art would recognize that it would improve similar devices in the same way, using the technique is obvious unless its actual application is beyond his or her skill. *Sakraida* and *Anderson's-Black Rock* are illustrative-a court must ask whether the improvement is more than the predictable use of prior art elements according to their established functions.

Following these principles may be more difficult in other cases than it is here because the claimed subject matter may involve more than the simple substitution of one known element for another or the mere application of a known technique to a piece of prior art ready for the improvement. Often, it will be necessary for a court to look to interrelated teachings of multiple patents; the effects of demands known to the design community or present in the marketplace; and the background knowledge possessed by a person having ordinary skill in the art, all in order to determine whether there was an apparent reason to combine the known elements in the fashion claimed by the patent at issue. To facilitate review, this analysis should be made explicit. As our precedents make clear, however, the analysis need not seek out precise teachings directed to the specific subject matter of the challenged claim, for a court can take account of the inferences and creative steps that a person of ordinary skill in the art would employ.

B.

When it first established the requirement of demonstrating a teaching, suggestion, or motivation to combine known elements in order to show that the combination is obvious, the Court of Customs and Patent Appeals captured a helpful insight. See *Application of Bergel,* 48 C.C.P.A. 1102, 292 F.2d 955, 956-957 (1961). As is clear from cases such as *Adams,* a patent composed of several elements is not proved obvious merely by demonstrating that each of its elements was, independently, known in the prior art. Although common sense directs one to look with care at a patent application that claims as innovation the combination of two known devices according to their established functions, it can be important to identify a reason that would have prompted a person of ordinary skill in the relevant field to combine the elements in the way the claimed new invention does. This is so because inventions in most, if not all, instances rely upon building blocks long since uncovered, and claimed discoveries almost of necessity will be combinations of what, in some sense, is already known.

Helpful insights, however, need not become rigid and mandatory formulas; and when it is so applied, the TSM test is incompatible with our precedents. The obviousness analysis cannot be confined by a formalistic conception of the words teaching, suggestion, and motivation, or by overemphasis on the importance of published articles and the explicit content of issued patents. The diversity of inventive pursuits and of modern technology counsels against limiting the analysis in this way. In many fields it may be that there is little discussion of obvious techniques or combinations, and it often may be the case that market demand, rather than scientific literature, will drive design trends. Granting patent protection to advances that would occur in the ordinary course without real innovation retards progress and may, in the case of patents combining previously known elements, deprive prior inventions of their value or utility.

In the years since the Court of Customs and Patent Appeals set forth the essence of the TSM test, the Court of Appeals no doubt has applied the test in accord with these principles in many cases. There is no necessary inconsistency between the idea underlying the TSM test and the *Graham* analysis. But when a court transforms the general principle into a rigid rule that limits the obviousness inquiry, as the Court of Appeals did here, it errs.

C.

One of the ways in which a patent's subject matter can be proved obvious is by noting that there existed at the time of invention a known problem for which there was an obvious solution encompassed by the patent's claims.

The first error of the Court of Appeals in this case was to foreclose this reasoning by holding that courts and patent examiners should look only to the problem the patentee was trying to solve. The Court of Appeals failed to recognize that the problem motivating the patentee may be only one of many addressed by the patent's subject matter. The question is not whether the combination was obvious to the patentee but whether the combination was obvious to a person with ordinary skill in the art. Under the correct analysis, any need or problem known in the field of endeavor at the time of invention and addressed by the patent can provide a reason for combining the elements in the manner claimed.

The second error of the Court of Appeals lay in its assumption that a person of ordinary skill attempting to solve a problem will be led only to those elements of prior art designed to solve the same problem. The primary purpose of Asano was solving the constant ratio problem; so, the court concluded, an inventor considering how to put a sensor on an adjustable pedal would have no reason to consider putting it on the Asano pedal. Common sense teaches, however, that familiar items may have obvious uses beyond their primary purposes, and in many cases a person of ordinary skill will be able to fit the teachings of multiple patents together like pieces of a puzzle. Regardless of Asano's primary purpose, the design provided an obvious example of an adjustable pedal with a fixed pivot point; and the prior art was replete with patents indicating that a fixed pivot point was an ideal mount for a sensor. The idea that a designer hoping to make an adjustable electronic pedal would ignore Asano because Asano was designed to solve the constant ratio problem makes little sense. A person of ordinary skill is also a person of ordinary creativity, not an automaton.

The same constricted analysis led the Court of Appeals to conclude, in error, that a patent claim cannot be proved obvious merely by showing that the combination of elements was "obvious to try." When there is a design need or market pressure to solve a problem and there are a finite number of identified, predictable solutions, a person of ordinary skill has good reason to pursue the known options within his or her technical grasp. If this leads to the anticipated success, it is likely the product not of innovation but of ordinary skill and common sense. In that instance the fact that a combination was obvious to try might show that it was obvious under § 103.

The Court of Appeals, finally, drew the wrong conclusion from the risk of courts and patent examiners falling prey to hindsight bias. A factfinder should be aware, of course, of the distortion caused by hindsight bias and must be cautious of arguments reliant upon *ex post* reasoning. Rigid preventative rules that deny factfinders recourse to common sense, however, are neither necessary under our case law nor consistent with it.

III.

When we apply the standards we have explained to the instant facts, claim 4 must be found obvious. We agree with and adopt the District Court's recitation of the relevant prior art and its determination of the level of ordinary skill in the field. As did the District Court, we see little difference between the teachings of Asano and Smith and the adjustable electronic pedal disclosed in claim 4 of the Engelgau patent. A person having ordinary skill in the art could have combined Asano with a pedal position sensor in a fashion encompassed by claim 4, and would have seen the benefits of doing so.

* * * * *

B.

The District Court was correct to conclude that, as of the time Engelgau designed the subject matter in claim 4, it was obvious to a person of ordinary skill to combine Asano with a pivot-mounted pedal position sensor. There then existed a marketplace that created a strong incentive to convert mechanical pedals to electronic pedals, and the prior art taught a number of methods for achieving this advance. The Court of Appeals considered the issue too narrowly by, in effect, asking whether a pedal designer writing on a blank slate would have chosen both Asano and a modular sensor similar to the ones used in the Chevrolet truckline and disclosed in the '068 patent. The proper question to have asked was whether a pedal designer of ordinary skill, facing the wide range of needs created by developments in the field of endeavor, would have seen a benefit to upgrading Asano with a sensor.

In automotive design, as in many other fields, the interaction of multiple components means that changing one component often requires the others to be modified as well. Technological developments made it clear that engines using computer-controlled throttles would become standard. As a result, designers might have decided to design new pedals from scratch; but they also would have had reason to make pre-existing pedals work with the new engines. Indeed, upgrading its own pre-existing model led KSR to design the pedal now accused of infringing the Engelgau patent.

For a designer starting with Asano, the question was where to attach the sensor. The consequent legal question, then, is whether a pedal designer of ordinary skill starting with Asano would have found it obvious to put the sensor on a fixed pivot point. The prior art discussed above leads us to the conclusion that attaching the sensor where both KSR and Engelgau put it would have been obvious to a person of ordinary skill.

The '936 patent taught the utility of putting the sensor on the pedal device, not in the engine. Smith, in turn, explained to put the sensor not on the pedal's footpad but instead on its support structure. And from the known wire-chafing problems of Rixon, and Smith's teaching that "the pedal assemblies must not precipitate any motion in the connecting wires," Smith, col. 1, lines 35-37, Supplemental App. 274, the designer would know to place the sensor on a nonmoving part of the pedal structure. The most obvious nonmoving point on the structure from which a sensor can easily detect the pedal's position is a pivot point. The designer, accordingly, would follow Smith in mounting the sensor on a pivot, thereby designing an adjustable electronic pedal covered by claim 4.

Just as it was possible to begin with the objective to upgrade Asano to work with a computer-controlled throttle, so too was it possible to take an adjustable electronic pedal like Rixon and seek an improvement that would avoid the wire-chafing problem. Following similar steps to those just explained, a designer would learn from Smith to avoid sensor movement and would come, thereby, to Asano because Asano disclosed an adjustable pedal with a fixed pivot.

Teleflex indirectly argues that the prior art taught away from attaching a sensor to Asano because Asano in its view is bulky, complex, and expensive. The only evidence Teleflex marshals in support of this argument, however, is the [declaration of Clark J. Radcliffe, an expert presented by Teleflex], which merely indicates that Asano would not have solved Engelgau's goal of making a small, simple, and inexpensive pedal. What the declaration does not indicate is that Asano was somehow so flawed that there was no reason to upgrade it, or pedals like it, to be compatible with modern engines.

Like the District Court, finally, we conclude Teleflex has shown no secondary factors to dislodge the determination that claim 4 is obvious. Proper application of *Graham* and our other precedents to these facts therefore leads to the conclusion that claim 4 encompassed obvious subject matter. As a result, the claim fails to meet the requirement of § 103.

We need not reach the question whether the failure to disclose Asano during the prosecution of Engelgau voids the presumption of validity given to issued patents, for claim 4 is obvious despite the presumption. We nevertheless think it appropriate to note that the rationale underlying the presumption-that the PTO, in its expertise, has approved the claim-seems much diminished here.

IV.

[The Court goes on to hold that summary judgment is appropriate in § 103 cases, and that trial courts may take expert testimony into account to determine whether facts are in dispute. If they are not, the court may render a conclusion on the ultimate legal question.]

We build and create by bringing to the tangible and palpable reality around us new works based on instinct, simple logic, ordinary inferences, extraordinary ideas, and sometimes even genius. These advances, once part of our shared knowledge, define a new threshold from which innovation starts once more. And as progress beginning from higher levels of achievement is expected in the normal course, the results of ordinary innovation are not the subject of exclusive rights under the patent laws. Were it otherwise patents might stifle, rather than promote, the progress of useful arts. See U.S. Const., Art. I, § 8, cl. 8. These premises led to the bar on patents claiming obvious subject matter established in *Hotchkiss* and codified in § 103. Application of the bar must not be confined within a test or formulation too constrained to serve its purpose.

In re Kubin
Federal Circuit Court of Appeals, 2009.
561 F.3d 1351.

■ RADER, CIRCUIT JUDGE.

I.

This case presents a claim to a classic biotechnology invention – the isolation and sequencing of a human gene that encodes a particular domain of a protein. This court provided a primer on the basics of this technology in *In re O'Farrell*, 853 F.2d 894, 895-99 (Fed. Cir. 1988). Specifically, appellants claim DNA molecules ("polynucleotides") encoding a protein ("polypeptide") known as the Natural Killer Cell Activation Inducing Ligand ("NAIL").

Natural Killer ("NK") cells, thought to originate in the bone marrow, are a class of cytotoxic lymphocytes that play a major role in fighting tumors and viruses. NK cells express a number of surface molecules which, when stimulated, can activate cytotoxic mechanisms. NAIL is a specific receptor protein on the cell surface that plays a role in activating the NK cells.

The specification of the claimed invention recites an amino acid sequence of a NAIL polypeptide. The invention further isolates and sequences a polynucleotide that encodes a NAIL polypeptide. Moreover, the inventors trumpet their alleged discovery of a binding relationship between NAIL and a protein known as CD48. The NAIL-CD48 interaction has important biological consequences for NK cells, including an increase in cell cytotoxicity and in production of interferon. Representative claim 73 of appellants' application claims the DNA that encodes the CD48-binding region of NAIL proteins:

73. An isolated nucleic acid molecule comprising a polynucleotide encoding a polypeptide at least 80% identical to amino acids 22-221 of SEQ ID NO:2, wherein the polypeptide binds CD48.

In other words, appellants claim a genus of isolated polynucleotides encoding a protein that binds CD48 and is at least 80% identical to amino acids 22-221 of SEQ ID NO:2 – the disclosed amino acid sequence for the CD48-binding region of NAIL.

II.

The Board rejected appellants' claims as invalid under § 103. Regarding obviousness, the Board rejected appellants' claims over the combined teachings of U.S. Patent No. 5,688,690 ("Valiante") and 2 Joseph Sambrook et al., MOLECULAR CLONING: A LABORATORY MANUAL 43-84 (2d ed. 1989) ("Sambrook"). Valiante discloses a receptor protein called "p38" that is found on the surface of human NK cells. Valiante teaches that the p38 receptor is present on virtually all human NK cells and "can serve as an activation marker for cytotoxic NK cells." Valiante also discloses and claims a monoclonal antibody specific for p38 called "mAB C1.7." The Board found (and appellants do not dispute) that Valiante's p38 protein is the same protein as NAIL. A monoclonal antibody is an antibody that is mass produced in the laboratory from a single clone and that recognizes only one antigen. Monoclonal antibodies are useful as probes for specifically identifying and targeting a particular kind of cell. Valiante teaches that "[t]he DNA and protein sequences for the receptor p38 may be obtained by resort to conventional methodologies known to one of skill in the art." Valiante discloses neither the amino acid sequence of p38 recognized by mAb C1.7 nor the polynucleotide sequence that encodes p38. Sambrook, incorporated by reference in Valiante, describes methods for molecular cloning. Sambrook does not discuss how to clone any particular gene, but provides detailed instructions on cloning materials and techniques.

The Board found as a factual matter that appellants used conventional techniques "such as those outlined in Sambrook" to isolate and sequence the gene that codes for NAIL. The Board also found that appellants' claimed DNA sequence is "isolated from a cDNA library . . . using the commercial monoclonal antibody C1.7 . . . disclosed by Valiante." With

199

regard to the amino acid sequence referred to as SEQ ID NO:2, the Board found that:

> Valiante's disclosure of the polypeptide p38, and a detailed method of isolating its DNA, including disclosure of a specific probe to do so, i.e., mAb C1.7, established Valiante's possession of p38's amino acid sequence and provided a reasonable expectation of success in obtaining a polynucleotide encoding p38, a polynucleotide within the scope of Appellants' claim 73.

Because of NAIL's important role in the human immune response, the Board further found that "one of ordinary skill in the art would have recognized the value of isolating NAIL cDNA, and would have been motivated to apply conventional methodologies, such as those disclosed in Sambrook and utilized in Valiante, to do so."

Based on these factual findings, the Board turned to the legal question of obviousness under § 103. Invoking the Supreme Court's decision in *KSR International Co. v. Teleflex Inc.*, 550 U.S. 398 (2007), the Board concluded that appellants' claim was "'the product not of innovation but of ordinary skill and common sense,' leading us to conclude NAIL cDNA is not patentable as it would have been obvious to isolate it." Appellants appeal the Board's decisions[].

III.

Obviousness is a question of law based on underlying findings of fact. An analysis of obviousness must be based on several factual inquiries: (1) the scope and content of the prior art; (2) the differences between the prior art and the claims at issue; (3) the level of ordinary skill in the art at the time the invention was made; and (4) objective evidence of nonobviousness, if any. *See Graham v. John Deere Co.*, 383 U.S. 1, 17-18 (1966).

A.

As a factual matter, the Board concluded that appellants' methodology of isolating NAIL DNA was essentially the same as the methodologies and teachings of Valiante and Sambrook. . . . [T]his court determines that the Board had substantial evidence to conclude that appellants used conventional techniques, as taught in Valiante and Sambrook, to isolate a gene sequence for NAIL.

B.

The instant case also requires this court to consider the Board's application of this court's early assessment of obviousness in the context of classical biotechnological inventions, specifically *In re Deuel*, 51 F.3d 1552 (Fed. Cir. 1995). In *Deuel*, this court reversed the Board's conclusion that a prior art reference teaching a method of gene cloning, together with a reference disclosing a partial amino acid sequence of a protein, rendered DNA molecules encoding the protein obvious. *Id.* at 1559. In reversing the Board, this court in *Deuel* held that "knowledge of a protein does not give one a conception of a particular DNA encoding it." *Id.* Further, this court stated that "obvious to try" is an inappropriate test for obviousness.

> [T]he existence of a general method of isolating cDNA or DNA molecules is essentially irrelevant to the question whether the specific molecules themselves would have been obvious, in the absence of other prior art that suggests the claimed DNAs. . . . "Obvious to try" has long been held not to constitute obviousness. A general incentive does not make obvious a particular result, nor does the existence of techniques by which those efforts can be carried out.

Thus, this court must examine *Deuel*'s effect on the Board's conclusion that Valiante's teaching of the NAIL protein, combined with Valiante's/Sambrook's teaching of a method to isolate the gene sequence that codes for NAIL, renders claim 73 obvious.

With regard to *Deuel*, the Board observed that the Supreme Court in *KSR* cast doubts on this court's application of the "obvious to try" doctrine:

> To the extent *Deuel* is considered relevant to this case, we note the Supreme Court recently cast doubt on the viability of *Deuel* to the extent the Federal Circuit rejected an '"obvious to try" test. *See KSR Int'l Co. v. Teleflex Inc.,* 127 S. Ct. 1727, 1739, 82 U.S.P.Q.

2d 1385, 1394, 1396 (2007) (citing *Deuel*, 51, F.3d at 1559). Under *KSR*, it's now apparent "obvious to try" may be an appropriate test in more situations than we previously contemplated.

Insofar as *Deuel* implies the obviousness inquiry cannot consider that the combination of the claim's constituent elements was "obvious to try," the Supreme Court in *KSR* unambiguously discredited that holding. In fact, the Supreme Court expressly invoked *Deuel* as a source of the discredited "obvious to try" doctrine. The Supreme Court repudiated as "error" the *Deuel* restriction on the ability of a skilled artisan to combine elements within the scope of the prior art:

> The same constricted analysis led the Court of Appeals to conclude, in error, that a patent claim cannot be proved obvious merely by showing that the combination of elements was "obvious to try." When there is a design need or market pressure to solve a problem and there are a finite number of identified, predictable solutions, a person of ordinary skill has good reason to pursue the known options within his or her technical grasp. If this leads to the anticipated success, it is likely the product not of innovation but of ordinary skill and common sense. In that instance *the fact that a combination was obvious to try might show that it was obvious under § 103*.

KSR, 550 U.S. at 421 (internal citation omitted) (emphasis added).

The Supreme Court's admonition against a formalistic approach to obviousness in this context actually resurrects this court's own wisdom in *In re O'Farrell*, which predates the *Deuel* decision by some seven years. To differentiate between proper and improper applications of "obvious to try," this court outlined two classes of situations where "obvious to try" is erroneously equated with obviousness under § 103. In the first class of cases, what would have been "obvious to try" would have been to vary all parameters or try each of numerous possible choices until one possibly arrived at a successful result, where the prior art gave either no indication of which parameters were critical or no direction as to which of many possible choices is likely to be successful.

In such circumstances, where a defendant merely throws metaphorical darts at a board filled with combinatorial prior art possibilities, courts should not succumb to hindsight claims of obviousness. The inverse of this proposition is succinctly encapsulated by the Supreme Court's statement in *KSR* that where a skilled artisan merely pursues "known options" from a "finite number of identified, predictable solutions," obviousness under § 103 arises.

The second class of *O'Farrell*'s impermissible "obvious to try" situations occurs where what was "obvious to try" was to explore a new technology or general approach that seemed to be a promising field of experimentation, where the prior art gave only general guidance as to the particular form of the claimed invention or how to achieve it. Again, *KSR* affirmed the logical inverse of this statement by stating that § 103 bars patentability unless "the improvement is more than the predictable use of prior art elements according to their established functions.

This court in *O'Farrell* found the patentee's claims obvious because the Board's rejection of the patentee's claims had not presented either of the two common "obvious to try" pitfalls. Specifically, this court observed that an obviousness finding was appropriate where the prior art "contained *detailed enabling methodology for* practicing the claimed invention, a suggestion to modify the prior art to practice the claimed invention, and evidence suggesting that it would be successful." Responding to concerns about uncertainty in the prior art influencing the purported success of the claimed combination, this court stated: "[o]bviousness does not require absolute predictability of success . . . *all that is required is a reasonable expectation of success*." *Id.* at 903-04 (emphasis added). The Supreme Court in *KSR* reinvigorated this perceptive analysis.

KSR and *O'Farrell* directly implicate the instant case. The record shows that the prior art teaches a protein of interest, a motivation to isolate the gene coding for that protein, and illustrative instructions to use a monoclonal antibody specific to the protein for cloning this gene. Therefore, the claimed invention is "the product not of innovation but of ordinary skill and common sense." *KSR*, 550 U.S. at 421. Or stated in the familiar terms of this court's longstanding case law, the record shows that a skilled artisan would have had a resoundingly "reasonable expectation of success" in deriving the claimed invention in light of the teachings of the prior art. *See O'Farrell*, 853 F.2d at 904.

This court also declines to cabin *KSR* to the "predictable arts" (as opposed to the "unpredictable art" of biotechnology). In fact, this record shows that one of skill in this advanced art would find these claimed "results" profoundly "predictable." The record shows the well-known and reliable nature of the cloning and sequencing techniques in the prior art, not to mention the readily knowable and obtainable structure of an identified protein. Therefore this court cannot deem irrelevant the ease and predictability of cloning the gene that codes for that protein. This court cannot, in the face of *KSR*, cling to formalistic rules for obviousness, customize its legal tests for specific scientific fields in ways that deem entire classes of prior art teachings irrelevant, or discount the significant abilities of artisans of ordinary skill in an advanced area of art.

Thus, this court affirms the Board's conclusion as to obviousness.

NOTES

1. *The § 103(a) inquiry.* In theory, the inquiry here is quite similar to the examination for novelty. References are found and dated to determine whether effective dates precede the critical date, the adequacy of dissemination is determined, and the contents of the art are scrutinized. Although § 103 does not list the prior activities that come within its scope, it is universally assumed that the same art that is pertinent to nonobviousness is also the art that is relevant to novelty. This includes § 102(a) art—information known or used in the United States as well as both domestic and foreign patents and printed publications. It also includes § 102(e) art—information contained in patent applications, so long as the patent eventually issues. And, it also includes secret art under § 102(g)—inventions made in this country that have not been abandoned, suppressed, or concealed and under § 102(f)—information communicated to the applicant.[1] As with novelty, the critical date is the date on which the invention is reduced to practice; the effective date is the date on which the reference is considered accessible.

---

[1] See, e.g., *Hazeltine Research, Inc. v. Brenner*, 382 U.S. 252 (1965); *In re Bartfeld*, 925 F.2d 1450 (Fed. Cir. 1991) (§ 102(e)); *Oddzon Products, Inc. v. Just Toys, Inc.*, 122 F.3d 1396 (Fed. Cir. 1997) (§ 102(f)); *Hybritech, Inc. v. Monoclonal Antibodies, Inc.*, 802 F.2d 1367 (Fed. Cir. 1986) (§ 102(g)).

At this point, however, the analyses diverge, for while novelty is rigidly defined by the every-element test, the nonobviousness inquiry is far more open-ended. The flexible nature of § 103 raises difficult issues for the courts.

2. *Policy considerations.* The nonobviousness inquiry raises a pure policy question: how large a contribution should an inventor make to merit a patent? Justice Douglas thought the advance ought to be of major scientific significance; although the *Graham* Court read § 103 as adopting the less formidable *Hotchkiss* formulation, it was not willing to say that Congress had lowered the standard of patentability. This creates problems for inventions that are not deeply insightful, yet require considerable funds and efforts to make. As *Kubin* demonstrates, this is particularly a concern in chemical and biochemical cases. In both fields, theory is well enough advanced to predict the advantages of yet-unsynthesized structures. However, bringing these structures into being requires costly research. Absent a legal right—a patent right—to recapture the expense, it is not clear that the work will be done. Perhaps for this reason, the Federal Circuit, through its "teaching, suggestion, or motivation to combine" test, required district courts to take a very hard and skeptical look at claims of obviousness.

Has *KSR* raised the bar? What significance should be attributed to the Court's assertion that "[a] person of ordinary skill is also a person of ordinary creativity;" its statement that "progress …is expected in the normal course;" and its fear that "patents might stifle, rather than promote, the progress of useful arts"? In thinking through these issues, consider that in the years immediately preceding *KSR*, both the Federal Trade Commission and the National Academy of Sciences issued reports suggesting that patents were being granted and upheld too easily, and that the growing "thicket" of patent protection was raising transaction costs, impeding entry into existing markets, and making innovation harder to undertake.[2]

3. *Practical implementation of the obviousness requirement.* Even if there were agreement on the level of contribution that should be required, there

---

[2] Fed. Trade Comm'n, TO PROMOTE INNOVATION: THE PROPER BALANCE OF COMPETITION AND PATENT LAW AND POLICY (2003); Stephen A. Merrill et al., NAT'L ACAD. OF SCIS., A PATENT SYSTEM FOR THE 21ST CENTURY (2004).

would still be practical problems of implementation. Although the § 103 inquiry requires comparisons between sophisticated technologies, it is conducted by judges with no more training in technical matters than a law student, and by lay jurors, some of whom know more, but most of whom know a great deal less, than even law students know. As the major cases in this Assignment indicate, there has been much experimentation as courts have searched for ways to formulate a clear test for nonobviousness.

a. *The Graham framework.* *Graham* sets out a framework for assessing the legal question of obviousness or nonobviousness against a background of "basic factual inquiries": "the scope and content of the prior art are to be determined; differences between the prior art and the claims at issue are to be ascertained; and the level of ordinary skill in the pertinent art resolved." The Court anticipated a "case-by-case development" based on this framework. Prior to *KSR*, the Federal Circuit attempted to give more structure to the inquiry by imposing the "teaching, suggestion, or motivation to combine" ("TSM") test. Is the *Graham* framework sufficient to guide lower courts and the PTO? Does *KSR* help to structure the inquiry?

b. *The Person of Ordinary Skill in the Art.* Note the importance of the "ordinary artisan" standard to the determination of nonobviousness. It not only protects the public domain by rendering inventions that are effectively available to ordinary people in the field unpatentable, it also tailors patent law to particular fields. That is, it makes the standard for patentability turn on the depth of knowledge in each field: it is easier to patent in arts that are less advanced, and harder to patent in areas that are more sophisticated. As a result, the lure of patents is likely to attract more capital to fields where more work is required.

Given the importance of the level of skill in the art, there are surprisingly few opinions on the issue. At the Federal Circuit's inception, it set out factors to be considered in determining the level of ordinary skill in the art in *Environmental Designs, Ltd. v. Union Oil Co.*,[3] yet it has rarely discussed those factors in its opinions. One Federal Circuit case, decided while *KSR* was pending at the Supreme Court, is unusual in that the level of skill in the art was essentially determinative of the outcome of the obviousness inquiry. In *Dystar Textilfarben GmBH v. C. H. Patrick*

---

[3] 713 F.2d 693, 696 (Fed. Cir. 1983).

Co.,[4] which involved an improvement in indigo dye technology, there was a dispute as to whether the "person having ordinary skill in the art" (sometimes called the "PHOSITA") should be a "dyer" with virtually no technical education or knowledge or a "dyeing process designer" with knowledge of chemistry and systems engineering. The court reversed a jury verdict of nonobviousness, concluding that the proper PHOSITA was the "dyeing process engineer" and that such a "skilled chemist" would have found it obvious to combine prior art elements to produce the claimed dyeing technology.

The Federal Circuit's lack of attention to the level of skill in the art may have been a side effect of the TSM test, with the search for evidence of a "teaching, suggestion, or motivation to combine" largely obviating the need for a detailed inquiry into the level of skill in the art. How is the role of the person of ordinary skill in the art likely to change in view of *KSR*? If it becomes more important to understand the level of skill in the art, how will the PTO and courts gain the necessary understanding?

In the past, the Federal Circuit has seemed to consider itself bound by its prior determinations of the state of knowledge in a field. Thus, the standard in biotechnology was set by *D euel* even though the case was decided over a decade ago and the work at issue was completed long before that—and long before the advent of sequencing devices and other genomic research innovations. By the same token, some observers suggest that the level of skill the court imputes to the software industry is too high in light of the complexity of modern computer science.[5] *KSR*'s emphasis on the level of creativity of the person with ordinary skill may, however, signal a new direction in this jurisprudence as well.

    c.   *Secondary considerations.* The so-called secondary considerations (or "objective indicia of nonobviousness") are factors external to the invention itself that demonstrate its inventiveness. They include long-felt need for a solution to the problem the invention addresses, the failure of

---

[4] 464 F.3d 1356 (Fed. Cir. 2006).

[5] For discussions of these issues, see Dan L. Burk & Mark A. Lemley, *Is Patent Law Technology-Specific?*, 17 BERKELEY TECH. L.J. 1155 (2002); Lawrence M. Sung, *On Treating Past as Prologue*, 2001 J. L. TECH & POL'Y 75; Joseph P. Meara, *Just Who Is The Person Having Ordinary Skill In The Art? Patent Law's Mysterious Personage*, 77 WASH. L. REV. 267 (2002).

others to find such a solution, the commercial success of the invention in the marketplace, and acquiescence—the willingness of others to accept the patent as valid and take a license or forgo use of the invention. Their use represents another attempt to find an objective test for nonobviousness, although they too have met with considerable controversy.

On the one hand, it does seem that these are signs that the invention is a significant advance. If need for the innovation existed for a long time, it can be assumed that others would have invented it had this been easy to do. Since the need persisted until this applicant came along, he must have made the kind of breakthrough necessary to earn a patent. Similarly, if others tried to invent and failed, but the applicant tried and succeeded, her contribution must not have been obvious. By the same token, there are many entrepreneurs ready to earn an easy dollar. If the invention is a great commercial success, one of them would have brought it to market sooner if it was obvious to make. Finally, acquiescence is an indication that the people who *do* know the technology agree that the advance merits a patent.

On the other hand, these factors may be present for reasons other than the intrinsic creativity of the invention. Developments in other fields may make easy something that was formerly difficult. Suddenly, a long-felt need will be met and failure will be overcome by a commercially successful new product. Furthermore, if the inventor charges licensees less than the cost of challenging the patent, there will be acquiescence rather than litigation. The Federal Circuit's response here is to recognize both the value and the danger of relying on these factors. It requires the lower courts to look at secondary considerations in every case, but also to consider whether there is a nexus between the invention and the factor. Absent a showing that the factor is present because of inventiveness, the consideration will not be taken into account in determining nonobviousness.[6] While this resolution may not be theoretically satisfying, it does focus the lower courts on issues that can be measured without a high level of technological skill.[7]

---

[6] See, e.g., *Stratoflex, Inc. v. Aeroquip Corp.*, 713 F.2d 1530 (Fed. Cir. 1983).

[7] For further discussion, compare Rochelle C. Dreyfuss, *The Federal Circuit: A Case Study in Specialized Courts*, 64 N.Y.U. L. REV. 1 (1989) (delineating the benefits of secondary considerations), with, Robert P. Merges, *Economic Perspectives on Innovation: Patent Standards and Commercial Success*, 76 CAL. L. REV. 803 (1988) (noting their disadvantages).

d. *Objective indicia of obviousness?* The Federal Circuit has emphasized "objective indicia of *nonobviousness*," yet the Supreme Court in *Graham* referred to "indicia of obviousness or nonobviousness." Are there objective factors that might evidence obviousness, rather than nonobviousness? In this regard, *KSR* announced at least two new external factors that should be considered in the obviousness determination. These factors relate to ways in which context might render an invention obvious. Most important, the Court reminded us that patents are not the only incentive to invent: "demands known to the design community or present in the marketplace" can motivate ordinary persons with skill in the art to make advances in their fields.[8] The opinion further suggested that persons of ordinary skill can be expected to adapt collateral developments to their own problems.[9]

e. *Teaching away.* Some cases are made easy by the fact that the prior art "teaches away" from the invention in the sense that it discourages doing what the inventor has done. Indeed, on the same day that the Supreme Court invalidated the plow patent in *Graham*, it decided *United States v. Adams*,[10] which upheld the patent on a battery utilizing plain water as the electrolyte. Although wet batteries were well known and every element of the invention could be found in other batteries, the Court found that long-accepted theories in the art should have deterred anyone from trying to put together the battery at issue in the case. "[K]nown disadvantages in old devices which would naturally discourage the search for new inventions may be taken into account in determining obviousness."[11] Accordingly, the patent in Adams was upheld. One must be careful here, however. The mere fact that an experiment fails is not reason enough to discard the reference. If it provides a basis for the applicant's work, it might nonetheless be considered relevant.[12]

---

[8] The Federal Circuit has begun to implement the *KSR* approach to these issues in cases such as *Ball Aerosol & Specialty Container Inc. v. Limited Brands Inc.*, 555 F.3d 984 (Fed. Cir. 2009).

[9] *Leapfrog Enterprises Inc. v. Fisher-Price Inc.*, 485 F.3d 1157 (Fed. Cir. 2007) is an early example of the Federal Circuit's post-*KSR* approach to this issue. In *Leapfrog*, the court held that updating a mechanical advice using electronics was an obvious adaptation.

[10] 383 U.S. 39, 86 S. Ct. 708, 15 L.Ed.2d 572 (1966).

[11] Id. at 52.

[12] See *Bristol-Myers Squibb Co. v. Ben Venue Laboratories*, 246 F.3d 1368 (Fed. Cir. 2001).

Prior work may also obscure the problem the inventor needs to resolve. In *Eibel Process Co. v. Minnesota & Ontario Paper Co.*,[13] for example, the invention was in the field of paper making. At the time, paper was made by pouring wet stock onto a conveyer belt ("wire") which moved it through a drying environment. The industry had tried to speed up operations by moving the wire quickly, but if it moved too fast, the product turned out to be uneven. The inventor found a solution: he changed the pitch of the container from which the stock was poured. The Court held the invention nonobvious, stating that "[t]he invention was not the mere use of a high or substantial pitch to remedy a known source of trouble. It was the discovery of the source not before known and the application of the remedy for which Eibel was entitled to be rewarded in his patent."[14] The industry had not understood that the stock needed to be moving at a speed close to that of the wire when it hit the wire; Eibel's discovery of the problem merited a patent even though the solution was trivial once the problem was understood.

f.   *Obvious-to-try.* As fields of knowledge grow, particular approaches and experiments can become obvious. For example, once a device for sequencing genes is invented, it is obvious to use it to find interesting genomic material and information. Should the *scientific* obviousness of an experiment render its result *legally* obvious? Prior to *KSR*, the Federal Circuit has said no: "'Obvious to try' has long been held not to constitute obviousness. A general incentive does not make obvious a particular result, nor does the existence of techniques by which those efforts can be carried out."[15]   Instead, the court asked whether there was a reasonable expectation of success. If there were many approaches to choose from, if there were many pitfalls along the way, the successful outcome would be deemed nonobvious.[16]

The *KSR* Court labeled the Federal Circuit's analysis on this point as "in error." But did the Supreme Court entirely reject the approach? The Court spoke of "design need or market pressure" as incentives to pursue obvious lines of research. Nonetheless, it stressed that the invention must have been among "a finite number of identified, predictable solutions" and

---

[13] 261 U.S. 45, 43 S. Ct. 322, 67 L. Ed. 523 (1923).

[14] Id. at 68.

[15] *In re Deuel*, 51 F.3d 1552, 1559 (Fed. Cir. 1995) (citing *In re O'Farrell*, 853 F.2d 894, 903 (Fed. Cir.1988)).

[16] *In re Eli Lilly & Co.*, 902 F.2d 943, 945 (Fed. Cir. 1990).

that the research must have lead to "the anticipated success." These factors strongly resemble the ones the Federal Circuit had been using. Indeed, in *Kubin* the Federal Circuit describes its analysis as consistent with its own prior precedent.

The Federal Circuit's post-*KSR* cases in the chemical and pharmaceutical arenas seem to take a strongly fact-specific approach to determining whether a particular outcome of a known approach is predictable enough to render the result obvious.[17] In *Abbott Laboratories v. Sandoz Inc.*,[18] for example, the court explained that the determination of obviousness requires consideration of the context, including "characteristics of the science or technology, its state of advance, the nature of the known choices, the specificity or generality of prior art, and the predictability of results in the area of interest."

Consider also Judge Rader's argument, discussed in note 6 of Assignment 16, that the doctrine of nonobviousness is a more appropriate means to weed out insubstantial advances than the utility doctrine. Does *KSR*'s rejection of the Federal Circuit's "obvious to try" analysis provide support to Judge Rader's position?

4. *Combinations of prior technology.* When the analysis of nonobviousness depends, as it usually does, on more than one piece of prior art, courts have considered an array of other issues.

a. *"Combination patents."* As *Ag Pro* demonstrates, "combinations" were at one time split out for separate consideration. Because combination inventions are clearly made up of known elements, they were considered likely to be obvious. Thus, a special showing of synergy (or as the case puts it, synergistic results) was required. In theory, synergy should have been as easy to spot as teaching away. In practice, however, such was not the case.

One difficulty with the formulation was that a great deal turned on whether an invention should be classified as a combination and yet, at some

---

[17] Compare, for example, *Kubin* and *PharmaStem Therapeutics v. Viacell Inc.*, 491 F.3d 1342 (Fed. Cir. 2007), with, *Proctor and Gamble Co. v. Teva Pharm.*, 566 F.3d 989 (Fed. Cir. 2009), *Ortho-McNeil Pharma. v. Mylan Laboratories*, 520 F.3d 1358 (Fed. Cir. 2008), *Sanofi-Synthelabo v. Apotex, Inc.*, 550 F.3d 1075 (Fed. Cir. 2008), and *Takeda Chem. Indus. Ltd. v. Alphapharm Pty. Ltd.*, 492 F.3d 1350, 1359-62 (Fed. Cir 2007).
[18] 544 F.3d 1341, 1351 (Fed. Cir. 2008).

level of particularity, every advance is a combination. After all, innovation is largely a process of analogizing to earlier work, borrowing relevant bits and pieces from several sources. Indeed, an inventor's special gift may well be the ability to appreciate the benefits of combining disparate elements.[19] Moreover, close inspection of any invention will reveal how it works: two things never add up to more than the sum of their parts. For these reasons, the Federal Circuit rejected the combination-patent idea along with the search for synergy.[20]

Will *KSR* revive the combination-patent analysis? The Supreme Court cited *Ag Pro*, but managed to avoid the term synergy. However, it talked about the invention at issue in *KSR* as a combination and cited many propositions tied to notions about inventive combinations. Thus, it seems clear the Court expects the PTO and lower courts to give special consideration to combinations. The Court acknowledged that "inventions in most, if not all, instances rely upon building blocks long since uncovered," which suggests that there is little point in treating combinations as a unique category, yet stated that "[t]he combination of familiar elements according to known methods is likely to be obvious when it does no more than yield predictable results." Does *KSR* offer a more well-defined standard than lack of synergy?

b. *Motivation to combine.* Prior to *KSR*, the Federal Circuit had required, in cases involving combinations of prior technology, evidence of "a teaching, motivation, or suggestion to select and combine the references relied on as evidence of obviousness."[21] For example, in *In re Lee*, the court reversed an obviousness finding of the Board of Patent Appeals and Interferences, saying:

> The Board's findings must extend to all material facts and must be documented on the record, lest the 'haze of so-called expertise' acquire insulation from accountability. 'Common knowledge and common sense,' even if assumed to derive from the agency's

---

[19] For vivid examples of how inventions build upon each other, see HENRY PETROSKI, THE EVOLUTION OF USEFUL THINGS (Alfred A. Knopf 1992).
[20] See, e.g., *Stratoflex*, supra note 6.
[21] *In re Lee*, 277 F.3d 1338, 1343 (Fed. Cir. 2002).

expertise, do not substitute for authority when the law requires authority.[22]

This approach made the determination of obviousness less subjective and recognized that finding productive combinations is an important part of inventiveness. However, the so-called "TSM" test—especially as applied in *Lee*—was seen as a key reason why patents of rather low technological merit were proliferating.[23]

Clearly, *KSR* is meant to reject a rigid application of this approach. What role should it now play? The Court emphasized the predictability of results: how is that to be determined if not from the teachings of the prior art? The idea that examiner's can rely on "common sense" can be criticized as leaving obviousness determinations open to a "20-20 hindsight" problem. How can this concern be reconciled with KSR's admonition against "rigid preventative rules that deny factfinders recourse to common sense"?

5. *The Court of Appeals for the Federal Circuit.* Interestingly, the Federal Circuit was itself a response to the § 103 problem. In the early 1970's, Congress had created a commission to make recommendations for improving the administration of federal justice. The Hruska Commission that was formed identified patent law as one of the areas in which the delivery of justice could be improved. It suggested that Congress create a specialized court with the technical expertise and experience necessary to decide difficult technological issues expediently.[24] The Federal Circuit was established in 1982 to hear patent appeals from the district courts in all of the federal circuits. It was no surprise to the patent bar that *Stratoflex* appeared so soon after the court was established, for the judges of the new

---

[22] Id. at 1344-45. See also *In re Rouffet*, 149 F.3d 1350, 1359 (Fed. Cir. 1998) ("even when the level of skill in the art is high, the Board must identify specifically the principle, known to one of ordinary skill, which suggests the claimed combination. In other words, the Board must explain the reasons one of ordinary skill in the art would have been motivated to select the references and to combine them to render the claimed invention obvious.").

[23] For a particularly scathing review of the patent system prior to *KSR*, see Adam B. Jaffe & Josh Lerner, INNOVATION AND ITS DISCONTENTS: HOW OUR BROKEN PATENT SYSTEM IS ENDANGERING INNOVATION AND PROGRESS, AND WHAT TO DO ABOUT IT (Princeton University Press 2004).

[24] See *Commission on Revision of the Federal Court Appellate System, Structure and Internal Procedures: Recommendations for Change*, reprinted in 67 F.R.D. 195 (1975).

court took the resolution of the nonobviousness problem as their premier challenge.[25]

The Federal Circuit has two important advantages over the regional circuits that previously decided patent appeals. First, it can require all the district courts to use the same objective tests of nonobviousness. Second, because every patent appeal winds up in this court, there is no longer an incentive to shop for a forum with a higher or lower standard of nonobviousness. Cases like *Graham*, where the same patent was upheld on one circuit and invalidated on another, can no longer occur. The law on nonobviousness may not be theoretically perfect (and may, as *KSR* demonstrates, require revision by the Supreme Court), but it is at least administered even-handedly.[26]

6. *Does § 103 render the § 102 inquiry superfluous?* Since § 103 looks at the same art as § 102, but lacks its rigidity of application, it is easy to fall into the trap of thinking that § 103 renders § 102 superfluous, for anything that is not new also appears to be obvious. Close attention to the details of the nonobviousness inquiry makes the independent significance of § 102 clearer.

(i) Inherency. In Assignment 17, we saw that information inherent in a reference counts for novelty purposes, even if use of the information is not specifically indicated. Inherency is not, however, considered sufficient for nonobviousness. In order for a reference to be utilized, the element of interest must be expressly pointed out. In terms of the search model discussed in the Introduction to Assignment 17, it is clear why this is so. It would be too costly to require inventors to research all prior art with enough insight to appreciate every scrap of information inherent in it, and then combine all of this learning to produce the invention. But it is cost-effective to look for an *entirely* effectuated invention in earlier work. Accordingly, inherency is a feature of § 102(a) jurisprudence, but it is not used in the § 103 analysis.[27]

---

[25] See, e.g., Howard T. Markey, *The Phoenix Court*, 10 AIPLA Q.J. 227 (1982).

[26] See, e.g., Rochelle C. Dreyfuss, *The Federal Circuit: A Case Study in Specialized Courts*, 64 N.Y.U. L. REV. 1 (1989). For a more recent (and less sanguine) study of the court, see Arti K. Rai, *Engaging Facts and Policy: A Multi-Institutional Approach to Patent System Reform*, 103 COLUM. L. REV. 1035 (2003).

[27] See, e.g., *Cohesive Tech. v. Water Corp.*, 543 F.3d 1351 (Fed. Cir. 2008), for a recent discussion of this point.

(ii) Field of reference and "analogous arts." Note 1 in Assignment 17 discussed the fact that every field is considered fair game when novelty is the issue. But such is not the case in § 103. The information that is relevant to the nonobviousness inquiry must either be "within the field of the inventor's endeavor" or in an analogous art, that is, in a field "reasonably pertinent to the particular problem with which the inventor was involved."[28]

Under Federal Circuit law, the analysis of a case involving analogous art is highly sensitive to the way that the problem is characterized and the fields the PTO (or court) believes the inventor would consult to solve that problem. For example, in *In re Clay*,[29] the invention was a way to store liquid hydrocarbon in a partially empty tank by filling the dead space with a gel. The prior art taught the use of gel to improve oil well production by filling subterranean cavities as they were emptied of petroleum. The court rejected use of this art on the ground that it was not analogous. Although it too was in the petroleum field, Clay was trying to prevent the loss of liquid stored in a partly empty tank; the reference was about maximizing oil production.

Conceivably, *KSR* will alter this analysis. Somewhat enigmatically, the Court stated that "[o]ne of the ways in which a patent's subject matter can be proved obvious is by noting that there existed at the time of invention a known problem for which there was an obvious solution encompassed by the patent's claims." Apparently, this means that an invention can be obvious if there is *any* known problem that obviously leads to the claimed invention, even if it is not the problem the patentee was addressing. Although the Court did not limit the known problem to a particular field, it seems unlikely that it meant to drop the limitation to analogous arts entirely. Indeed, by expanding the inquiry to *problems* different from the patentee's, the need to limit the *field* of those problems to that of the patentee becomes all the more important, for otherwise, highly inventive efforts could fail to qualify for protection. At the very least, *KSR*'s rejection of the requirement of a "teaching, suggestion, or motivation to combine" is likely to revive the importance of the analogous art inquiry. Since it would be hard to find evidence of a "teaching, suggestion, or

---

[28] See, e.g., *Union Carbide Corp. v. American Can Co.*, 724 F.2d 1567 (Fed. Cir. 1984); *In re Wood*, 599 F.2d 1032 (C.C.P.A.1979).
[29] 966 F.2d 656 (Fed. Cir. 1992).

motivation to combine" far-flung references, the now-defunct TSM requirement made it less important to identify the appropriate set of references at the outset of the analysis.

In at least one post-*KSR* case, the Federal Circuit has taken an expansive view of what prior art is cognizable for obviousness purposes. In *In re Icon Health & Fitness, Inc.*, 496 F.3d 1374 (Fed. Cir. 2007), the court held a folding mechanism for a Murphy bed relevant to a patent relating to treadmills:

> Nothing about Icon's folding mechanism requires any particular focus on treadmills; it generally addresses problems of supporting the weight of such a mechanism and providing a stable resting position. Analogous art to Icon's application, when considering the folding mechanism and gas spring limitation, may come from any area describing hinges, springs, latches, counterweights, or other similar mechanisms—such as the folding bed in Teague.

The court rejected the argument that the Murphy bed art was not analogous. Though it did not revise the two-prong test it used in *Clay*, the test's application in *Icon Health* seems more expansive than its application in pre-*KSR* Federal Circuit case law.

7. *Process patents.* The inventiveness of new processes has also been the subject of considerable litigation. A strong argument can be made that a lower standard of nonobviousness is appropriate in process cases. After all, § 100(b) of the Patent Act defines processes to include a new method for using a known process, machine, manufacture, compositions of matter, or material. It appears to be aimed at giving inventors who fail to qualify for product protection some means of recouping the cost of development (but without removing anything from the public domain).

Until 1985, the law was administered in this way. However, in that year, the Federal Circuit decided *In re Durden*,[30] which raised the standard for patenting processes. *Durden* rejected a patent on a method claim whose only inventive feature was that a starting material (i.e. one of the ingredients) was new. The court reasoned that since the method itself was known in the prior art, the invention was obvious.

---

[30] 763 F.2d 1406 (Fed. Cir. 1985).

Durden was greeted with much criticism in the patent bar,[31] especially in that part of the bar concerned with biotechnology patents. Process patents are sometimes important to this industry for the reason suggested above: they create a financial return on researching new uses for known materials. However, the industry also needs process protection for another reason. Some of the commercially significant research in biotechnology involves the isolation and characterization of naturally occurring genes and the use of these genes to manufacture known proteins. Although the genes themselves are often patented, competitors can take them out of the country, where their use will not infringe the patent. The proteins produced are then re-imported into this country. Since the proteins were known and were not patentable, there is still no infringement. However, importation into the United States of a product manufactured by a process patented in the United States *is* an infringement, § 271(g). Hence, the special need for process patents. If the genetic researcher can get a patent on the *process* for using the gene, she is protected. She can sue the importer of the protein under § 271(g) for importing a product (the protein) that is manufactured by a process patented in the United States.

At the behest of the biochemistry industry, Congress amended § 103 to add § 103(b).[32] This subsection creates a special rule for any biotechnological process on which a patent application is filed simultaneously with an application for a patent on a composition of matter that is either a starting material in the process or the end product of the process. Section 103(b) provides that if this composition of matter is found to be novel and nonobvious, then the process will also be considered nonobvious.

Section 103(b) has not proved as valuable as Congress hoped. First, it applies only to biotechnology processes. Second, the process and product claims must be made at the same time (indeed, both must, at the time they were invented, have been owned by the same person or subject to an obligation of assignment to the same person) and the validity of the claims rise and fall together. In any event, the Federal Circuit has since retreated

---

[31] See, e.g., Harold C. Wegner, *Much Ado About Durden*, 71 J. PAT. OFF..SOC., 785 (1985); Harold C. Wegner, *Biotechnology Process Patents: Judicial or Legislative Remedy*, 73 J. PAT. OFF. SOC. 24 (1991).

[32] The paragraphs of § 103 were also, for the first time, separately designated with letters.

from *Durden*. For example, in *In re Ochiai*,[33] the court was again faced with a question about the nonobviousness of a known process using and resulting in new compounds. The applicant had claimed a method for reacting a newly discovered (and patented) acid with other chemicals to produce a new member of the "cephem" family of compounds having antibiotic properties. The examiner and the Board rejected the process claim, claim 6, on *Durden* grounds. The Federal Circuit reversed, stating:

> The process invention Ochiai recites in claim 6 specifically requires use of none other than its new, nonobvious acid as one of the starting materials. One having no knowledge of this acid could hardly find it obvious to make any cephem using this acid as an acylating agent, much less the particular cephem recited in claim 6.
> * * *
> In addition, although the prior art references the examiner discussed do indeed teach the use of various acids to make various cephems, they do not define a class of acids the knowledge of which would render obvious the use of Ochiai's specifically claimed acid. The Board noted that Ochiai's specifically claimed acid is 'similar' to the acids used in the prior art. Likewise, the examiner asserted that the claimed acid was 'slightly different' from those taught in the cited references. Neither characterization, however, can establish the obviousness of the use of a starting material that is new and nonobvious, both in general and in the claimed process. The mere chemical possibility that one of those prior art acids could be modified such that its use would lead to the particular cephem recited in claim 6 does not make the process recited in claim 6 obvious 'unless the prior art suggested the desirability of [such a] modification.' *In re Gordon*, 733 F.2d 900, 902, 221 U.S.P.Q. 1125, 1127 (Fed. Cir.1984).

It remains to be seen how *KSR* will influence decisions in process-patent cases.

8. *Presumption of validity.* Section 282 of the Act creates a presumption that a patent is valid. As we have seen, similar presumptions exist in both copyright and trademark law. In both systems, the presumption has the effect of requiring the challenger to disprove validity, cf. Assignments 3 and

---

[33] 71 F.3d 1565 (Fed. Cir. 1995).

The application of this principle to patent law is not, however, straightforward. Since patents are issued only after rigorous examination, a strong argument can be made that they should be presumed valid only as to art that was placed before the examiner. Excluding other art from the presumption would offer better protection to the public domain (because courts could judge patentability under the preponderance-of-the-evidence standard that the PTO would have utilized had it seen the prior art, rather than under the clear-and-convincing evidence standard that often accompanies presumptions). Furthermore, removing the presumption from unexamined prior art would motivate applicants to find and present all relevant prior art at the time of examination.

Weakening the presumption does, however, have at least two negative effects. First, it could lead to "information dumps" at the PTO—that is, applicants would have an incentive to give the PTO so much information, examination would become inefficient. Second, it increases the risk undertaken by those who invest in commercializing inventions. The higher profits needed to attract financing to riskier propositions could, in turn, increase the price of patented inventions.

The Federal Circuit has, nearly from its inception, taken the view that the presumption of validity applies even with respect to unexamined prior art:

> Introduction of more pertinent prior art than that considered by the examiner does not ... 'weaken' or 'destroy' the presumption. Nor does such introduction 'shift' the burden of persuasion. The presumption continues its procedural burden-assigning role throughout the trial.[34]

Does *KSR* change this result? At the end of Part III, the Court said it need not reach the issue. However, it also said that, given the failure to disclose Asano during examination, the "rationale underlying the presumption-that the PTO, in its expertise, has approved the claim-seems much diminished."

Issues concerning the presumption of validity generally arise in the course of litigating patentability in proceedings between private parties. A related question concerns the degree of deference that should be given to

---

[34] *Stratoflex*, 713 F.2d at 1534.

PTO fact finding.[35] The Federal Circuit had been using the "clearly erroneous" test, a stricter standard than the "arbitrary and capricious" and "unsupported by substantial evidence" tests set out in the Administrative Procedure Act, which governs the review of agency action generally.[36] In part, the court reasoned that the stricter standard was consonant with historical practice. And, since the PTO's decisions can be challenged in two ways: by direct review to the Federal Circuit or by filing an original action in the district court, the Federal Circuit also considered it necessary to examine PTO fact finding on the same standard used for reviewing lower court decisions.[37]

However, the Supreme Court disagreed. *Dickinson v. Zurko*[38] was a challenge to the PTO's denial of a patent on a method for increasing computer security. The Federal Circuit used the "clearly erroneous" test to set aside the factual findings underlying the determination of obviousness. The Supreme Court reversed, holding that the APA standard applied. After brushing aside the historical argument, the Court suggested that the anomaly created by reviewing district court decisions and PTO decisions on different standards could be handled by allowing the Federal Circuit to "adjust related review standards where necessary." Since the Supreme Court has not allowed the Federal Circuit to adjust reviewing standards in the past, this language is something of a surprise.[39] Moreover, the deference that will now be accorded to the PTO contrasts rather starkly with the way that the Court treated PTO decisions in the cases in this Assignment. Could it be that the Court was influenced by the fact that the PTO *denied* Zurko's patent, whereas the patents in *Graham* and *Sakraida* had both been *granted*? Will the Court come to regret its decision in *Zurko*? Or, will *Zurko* encourage the PTO to bring its practice in line with that of other administrative agencies?

9. *Originality (derivation).* As in copyright, patent protection is available only to the original creator of the work. The clearest statement of this requirement is found in § 102(f), which bars a patent if the subject

---

[35] See 35 U.S.C. § 141.

[36] 5 U.S.C. § 706(2)(A) and (E).

[37] *In re Zurko*, 142 F.3d 1447 (Fed. Cir. 1998).

[38] 527 U.S. 150, 119 S. Ct. 1816, 144 L.Ed.2d 143 (1999).

[39] See *Dennison Mfg. Co. v. Panduit Corp.*, 475 U.S. 809, 106 S. Ct. 1578, 89 L.Ed.2d 817 (1986) (per curiam).

matter was not invented by the applicant. See also § 111, which requires that the application be made by the inventor, and §§ 115–116, requiring applicants to swear that they believe themselves to be the original and first inventors of the subject matter of the application. Because the applicant who runs afoul of these provisions can be said to have "derived" the invention from another, patent attorneys usually speak of "derivation" rather than "originality." Traditionally, derivation requires evidence of conception by another and evidence from which it can be inferred that there was a communication to the inventor that was complete enough to enable one with ordinary skill to practice the invention.

Despite the clear bar on inventions derived from others, there are rather few cases decided on pure originality grounds. Proof of communication can be hard to come by. Moreover, it is often much easier to simply consider the first inventor's work as part of the prior art, and then reject the second inventor's application on the ground that the invention is obvious or not novel in light of the earlier work. For example, consider the case in which A invents a widget in the United States and shows it to B, who then applies for a patent. Derivation requires a showing that the invention was conceived by the first inventor (here, A) and the complete conception was communicated in an enabling way to the applicant (B).[40] It is often easier to simply show that the invention was used by another (namely, A) in the United States (§ 102(a)) or invented in this country by another who did not abandon, suppress, or conceal it (§ 102(g)(2)). If B did not brazenly apply for a patent on A's precise invention but instead made some minor changes, the application could be rejected on § 103 grounds.

Why, then, is § 102(f) broken out as a separate section? One answer is evident from *Oddzon Products, Inc. v. Just Toy, Inc.*[41] That case involved the "Vortex" tossing ball, Oddzon's commercial embodiment of one of its design patents, and a competing alleged knock-off made by Just Toys, Inc. Just Toys defended itself against an infringement charge by arguing that the patent claims were obvious in light of two confidential ball designs, which had "inspired" the Oddzon inventor. Such confidential designs would not defeat a patent under § 102(a), which is limited to inventions that are somewhat public, or under § 102(g)(2), where the "not abandoned,

---

[40] See, e.g., *Johnson & Johnson v. W.L. Gore Assoc.*, 436 F.Supp. 704, 711 (D.Del.1977).
[41] 122 F.3d 1396 (1997).

suppressed, or concealed" language means that the art must be in use or in the process of being patented or commercialized. Another possible reason for a separate derivation provision is that under § 102(f), foreign knowledge can defeat a patent. That is not possible under § 102(a) or § 102(g)(2) because these provisions are limited to material known, used, or made "in this country." Thus, an invention known only to, let us say, one other American or to a foreigner may not be effective anticipation. However, the applicant will nonetheless be unable to receive a patent if, instead of inventing the invention herself, this other American—or the foreigner—told her about it.[42]

Oddzon is most well known for its holding that § 102(f) art may be combined with other types of prior art to find a patent claim obvious under § 103. Do you agree with the court's decision to combine § 102(f) with § 103 and to reject the patent on the ground that the secret information, when added to publicly available information, rendered the Vortex ball obvious? These §§ 102(f)/103 rejections blur the distinction between provisions that maintain the integrity of the public domain and provisions that insure that the patent is awarded to a true inventor. They also raise litigation costs. The distinction is blurred because information told only to an applicant is not really available to the world. As a result, the applicant accomplished something that no ordinary artisan could have done. Costs increase because the possibility of such a rejection creates incentives to investigate everything the applicant ever heard or saw, and requires a court or the PTO to indulge in complicated determinations about the interaction between public material and information whose exact scope is uncertain. Significantly, other patent systems consider secret art that is fully enabling to be patent defeating, but generally do not use secret art in combination with other references for nonobviousness purposes. Some of the Federal Circuit judges have urged their colleagues to take a similar approach here.[43] Assignment 20 takes up other issues involving secret art.

10. *The last sentence of § 103(c): common ownership.* Prior to 1984, the combination of § 103 with §§ 102(f) or (g) sometimes worked considerable mischief in large research organizations. Imagine, for

---

[42] Section 102(f) is also not affected by § 104's bar on using foreign inventive activities.

[43] See, e.g., *Lamb–Weston, Inc. v. McCain Foods, Ltd.,* 78 F.3d 540, 546 (Fed. Cir. 1996) (Newman, J., dissenting); *Gambro Lundia AB v. Baxter Healthcare Corp.,* 110 F.3d 1573 (Fed. Cir. 1997).

example, that a scientist is assigned to develop a new product. After working on the project for a while, he comes up with a key insight. However, before he can bring the invention to the point where it can be practiced, priorities within the firm change, and the scientist is assigned to another task. Some years later, interest is rekindled. But since the first scientist is busy, a second scientist takes over the project. The second scientist combines the earlier insight with her own findings and completes the project. What happens when the firm tries to get a patent? The first researcher's work may be deemed to render the invention obvious on the basis of §§ 102(f)/103, or possibly §§ 102(g)/103.[44]

This state of affairs was highly inefficient as it led firms to institute procedures to prohibit their employees from sharing information. Finding this practice a waste of expensive talent, Congress enacted the second paragraph of § 103(c), which prevents the work of one inventor from being considered in reviewing the patent application of another when both did the work that is the subject of the application for the same company or when their work was subject to an obligation of assignment to the same entity.[45] Some claim that Congress has not gone far enough, and that other joint research efforts, such as collaborative academic work, also need special treatment.[46] Would a better approach be to overrule *Oddzon*?

---

[44] See, e.g., *Kimberly–Clark Corp. v. Johnson & Johnson*, 745 F.2d 1437 (Fed.Cir.1984). Section 102(g) is in the picture because it too permits invalidation based on secret art. That is, in the hypothetical, the work of the first researcher could be considered an invention invented by another in the United States. Even if not communicated to the second researcher, it could be disqualifying.

[45] At the same time, § 116, was modified so that successive researchers will sometimes be considered joint inventors.

[46] See, e.g., The Cooperative Research and Technology Enhancement (CREATE) Act of 2003, H.R. 2391, 18th Cong., 1st Sess. (2003).

ASSIGNMENT 21—INFRINGEMENT AND CONTRIBUTORY INFRINGEMENT

INSERT IN PLACE OF NOTE 1a. ON PAGE 800:

a. *Claim interpretation.* As *Fromson* demonstrates, the claims, no matter how carefully drawn, can turn out to be ambiguous. After all, the patentee drafted the application when the discovery was in its infancy: she may not have completely understood what she was observing, and may not have had a literature from which to draw a vocabulary. By the time an infringement action is brought, her wording may not resonate with current understandings in the field, making the claims difficult to interpret. Moreover, as Justice Kennedy makes clear in *Festo*, language does not always fully capture innovation. Once an infringement suit is brought, the patentee may have incentives to advocate a broad interpretation of the claim language, which may or may not accord with her original interpretation or with the interpretation that a person having ordinary skill in the art would have assigned to the language at the time the discovery was made. The patent claims serve an important notice function because they determine the legal rights of members of the public. Questions of balancing adequate notice to the public with adequate recognition of the scope of a patentee's invention thus arise in construing the literal scope of the claims as they do in the debate over the doctrine of equivalents.

There are several sources of information that a court might consider in construing the language of patent claims:

(i) First, there is the ordinary meaning of the claim term in general usage.

(ii) Supplementing the ordinary meaning that a judge may have "in her head" are dictionary definitions, which might come from general dictionaries or from technical dictionaries relevant to the technical field of the invention.

(iii) The specification of the patent may define terms explicitly or may provide context, which can inform the interpretation of claim terms. Where claim terms appear in more than one claim, the relationship between those claims may also provide context for claim interpretation.

(iv) The prosecution history of the patent (the publicly available record of proceedings in the PTO) reflects the arguments the patentee made in order to obtain the patent. It can be examined, first to see whether words in claims that were cancelled reflect on the meaning of the claims that were allowed, and second, to determine whether the applicant said anything to the examiner that revealed her meaning. Furthermore, if the prosecution history reveals that the examiner regarded some aspect of the claims in the application as unpatentable, and the applicant, in response, relinquished claims to that aspect, the patentee will be estopped from later arguing for an interpretation of the allowed claims that will give her rights over the relinquished technology.

(v) Treatises and scientific publications may also provide evidence of the meaning of particular claim terms in a technical field.

(vi) Finally, courts considering ambiguous claims will often rely on expert testimony. Experts in the field of the invention can testify as what the wording means to the person with ordinary skill in the art; experts in drafting patents can describe the usage of similar wording in other applications. Expert testimony is very valuable to district court judges, who must interpret claim language in many technical fields in which they have little or no background. On the other hand, expert testimony may be suspect because it is prepared in the context of litigation and there will frequently be expert testimony on both sides of a claim construction dispute.

Because all of these potential sources of information about how to construe claim language may not agree, the Federal Circuit has sought to structure the claim construction process in a way that will serve the public notice function. In *Phillips v. AWH Corp.*,[1] the en banc Federal Circuit reviewed and attempted to clarify its claim construction jurisprudence. In that case, the court reiterated the principle that claim construction begins with the ordinary meaning of a claim term to a person having ordinary skill in the art, emphasizing that "the person of ordinary skill in the art is deemed to read the claim term not only in the context of the particular claim in which the disputed term appears, but in the context of the entire patent, including the specification." The court stressed the importance of the specification in construing claim language: "As we stated in *Vitronics*,

---

[1] 415 F.3d 1303 (Fed. Cir. 2005) (en banc).

the specification 'is always highly relevant to the claim construction analysis. Usually, it is dispositive; it is the single best guide to the meaning of a disputed term.' 90 F.3d at 1582." The court also reiterated a longstanding distinction between "intrinsic evidence," which includes the claim language, the specification, and the prosecution history and "extrinsic evidence," which includes expert testimony, dictionaries, treatises, and so forth. Extrinsic evidence is deemed less reliable than intrinsic evidence in claim interpretation.

A primary issue in *Phillips* was the role of dictionaries in claim construction. Some of the court's earlier cases had indicated that dictionaries should play a primary role in claim construction, prior even to the role of the specification and other intrinsic evidence. The intention behind reliance on dictionary definitions was to solve a problem that can arise in reading claims in the context of the specification. A patent specification often contains descriptions of specific "embodiments" of the claimed invention. These embodiments are examples of the claimed invention, but the courts have long warned against "reading limitations into the claims" from these specific embodiments. In *Phillips*, the Federal Circuit reiterated the warning against reading limitations into the claims, but rejected any presumption in favor of dictionary definitions. The court endorsed the primacy of intrinsic evidence—especially the specification—while leaving judges free to consult other sources in attempting to discern the meaning that a claim would have had to a person of ordinary skill in the art.

Another claim interpretation issue is the role, if any, that the product or process accused of infringement should play. In order to fulfill their public notice function, claims should have the same meaning regardless of the accused product or process at issue in a particular suit. In *Wilson Sporting Goods Co. v. Hillerich & Bradsby Co.*, the Federal Circuit reiterated its "rule that claims may not be construed with reference to the accused device."[2] Nonetheless, in *Wilson Sporting Goods*, the court declined to rule on a claim construction issue because it lacked information about the accused product. The court explained that:

> [A] court may not use the accused product or process as a
> form of extrinsic evidence to supply limitations for patent claim

---

[2] 442 F.3d 1322, 1330 (Fed. Cir. 2006).

language. Thus, the rule forbids a court from tailoring a claim construction to fit the dimensions of the accused product or process and to reach a preconceived judgment of infringement or noninfringement. In other words, it forbids biasing the claim construction process to exclude or include specific features of the accused product or process. The rule, however, does not forbid awareness of the accused product or process to supply the parameters and scope of the infringement analysis, including its claim construction component.[3]

Does this distinction make sense? Should it be possible to interpret patent claims without reference to any accused product or process? What are the benefits of "awareness of the accused product or process" in interpreting claims in infringement litigation? Are the benefits sufficient to offset the danger of bias?

INSERT AT THE END OF THE CARRY-OVER PARAGRAPH AT THE TOP OF PAGE 805:

On remand, the Federal Circuit reasoned that only the foreseeability exception arguably applied to the case. It then held that question to be one of law, and sent the case back to the district court to decide it, based on the factual questions (1) "whether an ordinarily skilled artisan would have thought an aluminum sleeve to be an unforeseeable equivalent of a magnetizable sleeve in the context of the invention;" and (2) "whether a person of ordinary skill in the art would have considered the accused two-way sealing ring to be an unforeseeable equivalent of the recited pair of sealing rings."[4]

The district court then decided that the equivalents were foreseeable at the time of the amendment.[5] In affirming, the Federal Circuit added that: "An equivalent is foreseeable if one skilled in the art would have known that the alternative existed in the field of art as defined by the original claim scope, even if the suitability of the alternative for the

---

[3] Id. at 1331.

[4] 344 F.3d 1359, 1371-72 (Fed. Cir. 2003) (en banc).

[5] *Festo Corp. v. Shoketsu Kinzoku Kogyo Kabushiki Co.*, 2005 U.S. Dist. LEXIS 11621 (D. Mass. June 13, 2005); *Festo Corp. v. Shoketsu Kinzoku Kogyo Kabushiki Co., Ltd.*, 2006 U.S. Dist. LEXIS 542 (D. Mass. Jan. 10, 2006) (order denying motion to amend judgment).

particular purposes defined by the amended claim scope were unknown."[6] This opinion came down after the Supreme Court's decision in *KSR*, see this Supplement, Assignment 18. Do you think this formulation of the foreseeability test was influenced by *KSR*? Should it be?

INSERT AT THE END OF NOTE 9 ON PAGE 811:

The increasing globalization of commerce, along with the rise of the "information economy," has raised significant questions about the interpretation of §§ 271(f) and 271(g) and the extent to which the current statutory treatment of extraterritoriality is sufficient to deal with infringement issues posed by the global economy. In 2004, the Federal Circuit held in *Pellegrini v. Analog Devices, Inc.*[7] that the § 271(f) prohibition of the export of "components" of a patented invention to be combined offshore did not encompass the export of plans or instructions for a patented item to be manufactured abroad. In a similar approach to intangible information, the court held in *Bayer AG v. Housey Pharmaceuticals, Inc.*,[8] that § 271(g) did not forbid the importation of *data* produced as a result of the practice abroad of a process patented in the United States. Such "intangible information" did not constitute a "product made by a process patented in the United States."

The interpretation of § 271(f) has raised similar questions, leading to Supreme Court review. In *Union Carbide Chemicals & Plastics Technology Corp. v. Shell Oil Co.*,[9] the Federal Circuit held that the prohibition on supplying "any component of a patented invention that is especially made or especially adapted for use in the invention and not a stable article or commodity of commerce" applied to the supply of a catalyst used in a process, performed entirely abroad, which was patented in the United States. In *Eolas Technologies Inc. v. Microsoft Corp.*[10] and *AT&T Corp. v. Microsoft Corp.*,[11] the Federal Circuit went even further, holding first, that intangible information could also be considered a "component" for purposes of § 271(f), and second, that every reproduction

---

[6] 493 F.3d 1368, 1382 (Fed. Cir. 2007).
[7] 375 F.3d 1113 (Fed. Cir. 2004).
[8] 340 F.3d 1367 (Fed. Cir. 2003).
[9] 425 F.3d 1366 (Fed. Cir. 2005).
[10] 399 F.3d 1325 (Fed. Cir. 2005).
[11] 414 F.3d 1366 (Fed. Cir. 2005).

of the information could be considered "supplied" from the United States, even if the reproduction occurred abroad.

The Supreme Court stemmed this expansion by reversing the decision in *Microsoft v. AT&T.*[12] That case concerned a patent on a computer used to digitally encode and compress recorded speech. Microsoft infringed the patent because its Windows operating system incorporates software code that, when installed, enables a computer to process speech in the manner claimed by the patent. Microsoft sent foreign manufacturers discs (or, in some cases, electronic transmissions) of the software so that they could install Windows on their computers and sell them. The question before the Court was whether infringement liability under U.S. patent law extended to the reproductions made and distributed outside the United States. The Supreme Court held that U.S. law could not be applied extraterritorially to cover this activity:

> Section 271(f) prohibits the supply of components "from the United States ... in such manner as to actively induce the combination of *such components*." § 271(f)(1) (emphasis added). Under this formulation, the very components supplied from the United States, and not copies thereof, trigger § 271(f) liability when combined abroad to form the patented invention at issue. Here, the copies of Windows actually installed on the foreign computers were not themselves supplied from the United States. Indeed, those copies did not exist until they were generated by third parties outside the United States.[13]

Following the Supreme Court's ruling, the en banc Federal Circuit, in *Cardiac Pacemakers, Inc. v. St. Jude Med., Inc.,* 576 F.3d 1348, 1365 (Fed. Cir. 2009), overruled *Union Carbide* and held that § 271(f) does not apply to method claims.

Another issue raised by modern technology is what one might call "divided claims" or "cross-territorial" infringement, in which components of a patented system are spread across more than one country. In this situation, a patentee might conceivably obtain patent protection in all relevant countries, yet be able to prove infringement in none. The Federal

---

[12] 550 U.S. 437 (2007).
[13] Id., at 453.

Circuit confronted this issue in the case of *NTP, Inc. v. Research in Motion, Ltd.*[14] The case involved the popular Blackberry handheld devices used as part of a system for wireless electronic mail. Research in Motion argued that its system did not infringe under § 271(a) because a key relay was located in Canada. Accordingly, the invention was not used "within the United States" as required. The Federal Circuit opined that the location of "use" of the system was "the place where control of the system is exercised and beneficial use of the system obtained." The court then held that the Blackberry system was used in the place where the handheld devices were manipulated to send and receive messages—and thus in the United States. The court took a different view of the asserted method claims, however, holding that a method claim is not infringed unless all of the steps of the method are performed in the United States.

Consider the policy ramifications of expansive interpretations of the extraterritorial reach of United States patent laws. Clearly, the expansive interpretation of these provisions assists patentees in coping with a global marketplace. However, extraterritorial application of U.S. law ignores the interests of other countries. In *AT&T*, the Supreme Court stressed comity goals by noting the importance of legislators taking "account of the legitimate sovereign interests of other nations when they write American laws."[15] This case is a good example of why such care is needed. Many countries do not recognize patents in software as such. It would be anomalous for activity considered lawful where it occurs to give rise to infringement liability in a foreign location.

A related question is whether worldwide infringement litigation can be made more efficient by allowing patentees to present all of their claims in a single action. In *Voda v. Cordis Corp.*,[16] a litigant took exactly this approach, invoking supplemental jurisdiction to try claims of infringement of foreign patents that were related to claims involving a U.S. patent. The advantage of such consolidated adjudication is that it reduces the transaction costs associated with litigation against an accused infringer who sells a single product throughout the global marketplace. While the coverage of various national patents may differ, many of the factual issues regarding the activities of the accused infringer and the nature of the

---

[14] 418 F.3d 1282 (Fed. Cir. 2005).
[15] 127 S. Ct. at 1758.
[16] 476 F.3d 887 (Fed. Cir. 2007).

accused product will be common to the claims. Nonetheless, the Federal Circuit held that a district court would abuse its discretion if it permitted such a case to go forward. It reasoned, among other things, that such a case would be too complex, particularly for jurors, and that it would violate the "act of state" doctrine, the Paris Convention, and the TRIPS Agreement. Should courts as a matter of comity agree to hear such consolidated cases? United States courts do adjudicate matters governed by foreign law in some contexts. Does the adjudication of patent claims raise particular concerns? The American Law Institute has approved the Project on Intellectual Property: Principles Governing Jurisdiction, Choice of Law, and Judgments in Transnational Disputes. It creates a framework for consolidating multijurisdictional infringement actions in patent, copyright, and trademark cases and also sets out choice of law rules that protect sovereignty interests.

INSERT THE FOLLOWING AFTER NOTE 10 ON PAGE 811:

11. *Infringement claims involving more than one actor.* A different type of issue of "divided infringement"[17] was considered in the case of *BMC Resources, Inc. v. Paymentech*, 498 F.3d 1373 (Fed. Cir. 2007). There, the patentee alleged infringement of a method claim in a situation in which the alleged infringer did not itself perform all of the steps of the patented method. The claims involved payment processing services. Some of the steps in the patented method were performed by third parties, such as ATM networks and credit-card-issuing financial institutions. The Federal Circuit reaffirmed the longstanding rule that direct infringement requires that all of the steps of a method claim be performed by a single actor. While a party "cannot avoid infringement . . . simply by contracting out steps of a patented process to another entity," there is no direct infringement "where one party did not control or direct each step of the patented process." Because indirect infringement liability must be predicated on direct infringement by someone, there was no secondary liability in the case. The court acknowledged that this strict rule for process claims might allow some gaming of the system to avoid infringement. Nonetheless the court opined that these concerns did not outweigh the need to differentiate between indirect infringement, which

---

[17] For an analysis of these issues see Mark A. Lemley, David W. O'Brien, Ryan M. Kent, Ashok Ramani, and Robert Van Nest, *Divided Infringement Claims*, 33 AIPLA Q.J. 255 (2005).

requires some level of knowledge or intent, and direct infringement, which is a strict-liability offense. Moreover, the court argued, most of the time the multiple actor issue can be avoided by careful claim drafting.

Do you agree with the Federal Circuit's approach to this issue? Why wasn't this question definitively resolved long ago? Do new technologies change the analysis? Can you think of situations in which it would be difficult to draft claims to avoid this problem?

12. *Infringement of Design Patents.* Our discussion in this casebook focuses on utility patents. Design patents are quite different, since the determination of infringement requires the comparison of a visual depiction of a patented design to the accused product's design. The basic test for design patent infringement asks "if, in the eye of an ordinary observer, giving such attention as a purchaser usually gives, two designs are substantially the same, if the resemblance is such as to deceive such an observer, inducing him to purchase one supposing it to be the other, the first one patented is infringed by the other." *Gorham Co. v. White,* 81 U.S. 511, 528 (1871). The Federal Circuit had added an interpretive gloss to this test, requiring that "the accused device must appropriate the novelty in the patented device which distinguishes it from the prior art. That is, even though the court compares two items through the eyes of the ordinary observer, it must nevertheless, to find infringement, attribute their similarity to the novelty which distinguishes the patented device from the prior art." *Litton Systems, Inc. v. Whirlpool Corp.,* 728 F.2d 1423, 1444 (Fed. Cir. 1984). The Federal Circuit essentially repudiated this "points of novelty" test in *Egyptian Goddess, Inc. v. Swisa et al.,* 543 F.3d 665 (Fed. Cir. 2008). There the court held that the ordinary observer test should be the sole test for determining whether a design patent has been infringed. The court sharpened the ordinary observer test, however, by requiring that the ordinary observer be presumed to be familiar with the prior art.

ASSIGNMENT 22—THE INTEREST IN PUBLIC ACCESS

INSERT ON PAGE 826 AFTER JUDGE NEWMAN'S DISSENT IN INTEGRA:

As you saw, Judge Newman's dissent in *Integra* was mainly a discussion of the outcome in *Madey*—which is to say, the wisdom of interpreting the *common law* research exemption narrowly. However, the *statutory exemption*, § 271(e)(1), which was, in fact, the only issue in the *Integra* case, drew the Supreme Court's attention. Note two things about the following opinion: first, its broad sweep, permitting a wide range of preclinical drug research. Second, consider footnote c (which is footnote 7 in the unedited version of the opinion). Like Judge Newman, the Court distinguishes between *experimenting on* a patented invention to learn more about it, and *experimenting with* patented inventions that function as research tools.

Merck KGaA v. Integra Lifesciences I, Ltd.
Supreme Court of the United States, 2005.
545 U.S. 193, 125 S. Ct. 2372, 162 L.Ed.2d 160.

■ JUSTICE SCALIA delivered the opinion of the Court.

This case presents the question whether uses of patented inventions in preclinical research, the results of which are not ultimately included in a submission to the Food and Drug Administration (FDA), are exempted from infringement by 35 U.S.C. § 271(e)(1).

I

It is generally an act of patent infringement to "mak[e], us[e], offe[r] to sell, or sel[l] any patented invention ... during the term of the patent therefore." § 271(a). In 1984, Congress enacted an exemption to this general rule, see Drug Price Competition and Patent Term Restoration Act of 1984, § 202, 98 Stat. 1585, as amended, 35 U.S.C. § 271(e)(1), which provides:

"It shall not be an act of infringement to make, use, offer to sell, or sell within the United States or import into the United States a patented invention (other than a new animal drug or veterinary biological product) solely for uses reasonably related to the development and submission of information under a Federal law which regulates the manufacture, use, or sale of drugs ...."

The Federal Food, Drug, and Cosmetic Act (FDCA), 21 U.S.C. § 301 *et seq.*, is "a Federal law which regulates the manufacture, use, or sale of drugs." Under the FDCA, a drugmaker must submit research data to the FDA at two general stages of new-drug development.[a] First, a drugmaker must gain authorization to conduct clinical trials (tests on humans) by submitting an investigational new drug application (IND). The IND must describe "preclinical tests (including tests on animals) of [the] drug adequate to justify the proposed clinical testing." Second, to obtain authorization to market a new drug, a drugmaker must submit a new drug application (NDA), containing "full reports of investigations which have been made to show whether or not [the] drug is safe for use and whether [the] drug is effective in use." Pursuant to FDA regulations, the NDA must include all clinical studies, as well as preclinical studies related to a drug's efficacy, toxicity, and pharmacological properties.

II.

A.

Respondents Integra Lifesciences I, Ltd., and the Burnham Institute, own five patents related to the tripeptide sequence Arg-Gly-Asp, known in single-letter notation as the "RGD peptide." The RGD peptide promotes cell adhesion by attaching to [specific] integrins, receptors commonly located on the outer surface of certain endothelial cells.

Beginning in 1988, petitioner Merck KGAA provided funding for

---

[a] Drugmakers that desire to market a generic drug (a drug containing the same active ingredients as a drug already approved for the market) may file an abbreviated new drug application (ANDA) with the FDA. See 21 U.S.C. § 355(j). The sponsor of a generic drug does not have to make an independent showing that the drug is safe and effective, either in preclinical or clinical studies. See § 355(j)(2)(A). It need only show that the drug includes the same active ingredients as, and is bioequivalent to, the drug that it is mimicking.

angiogenesis research conducted by Dr. David Cheresh at the Scripps Research Institute (Scripps). Angiogenesis is the process by which new blood vessels sprout from existing vessels; it plays a critical role in many diseases, including solid tumor cancers, diabetic retinopathy, and rheumatoid arthritis. In the course of his research, Dr. Cheresh discovered that it was possible to inhibit angiogenesis by blocking the integrins on proliferating endothelial cells. In 1994, Dr. Cheresh succeeded in reversing tumor growth in chicken embryos, first using a monoclonal antibody (LM609) he developed himself and later using a cyclic RGD peptide (EMD 66203) provided by petitioner [and covered by respondent's patents]. Dr. Cheresh's discoveries were announced in leading medical journals and received attention in the general media.

With petitioner's agreement to fund research at Scripps due to expire in July 1995, Dr. Cheresh submitted a detailed proposal for expanded collaboration between Scripps and petitioner on February 1, 1995. The proposal set forth a 3-year timetable in which to develop "integrin antagonists as angiogenesis inhibitors," beginning with *in vitro* and *in vivo* testing of RGD peptides at Scripps in year one and culminating with the submission of an IND to the FDA in year three. Scripps and petitioner concluded an agreement of continued collaboration in September 1995.

Pursuant to the agreement, Dr. Cheresh directed *in vitro* and *in vivo* experiments on RGD peptides provided by petitioner from 1995 to 1998. These experiments focused on EMD 66203 and two closely related derivatives, EMD 85189 and EMD 121974, and were designed to evaluate the suitability of each of the peptides as potential drug candidates. Accordingly, the tests measured the efficacy, specificity, and toxicity of the particular peptides as angiogenesis inhibitors, and evaluated their mechanism of action and pharmacokinetics in animals. Based on the test results, Scripps decided in 1997 that EMD 121974 was the most promising candidate for testing in humans. Over the same period, Scripps performed similar tests on LM609, a monoclonal antibody developed by Dr. Cheresh[b]

---

[b] Scripps licensed the patent for the monoclonal antibody to Ixsys, a California biotechnology company. Based on research conducted at Scripps and at Ixsys in consultation with Dr. Cheresh, an IND application for a humanized version of the antibody called Vitaxin was filed with the FDA on December 30, 1996. In addition to toxicology tests, the application included information from Dr. Cheresh's *in vitro* and *in vivo* experiments related to the antibody's mechanism of action and efficacy as an inhibitor of angiogenesis. Ixsys began clinical testing of the antibody as an angiogenesis

Scripps also conducted more basic research on organic mimetics designed to block [the relevant] integrins in a manner similar to the RGD peptides; it appears that Scripps used the RGD peptides in these tests as "positive controls" against which to measure the efficacy of the mimetics.

In November 1996, petitioner initiated a formal project to guide one of its RGD peptides through the regulatory approval process in the United States and Europe. Petitioner originally directed its efforts at EMD 85189, but switched focus in April 1997 to EMD 121974. Petitioner subsequently discussed EMD 121974 with officials at the FDA. In October 1998, petitioner shared its research on RGD peptides with the National Cancer Institute (NCI), which agreed to sponsor clinical trials. NCI filed an IND for EMD 121974 in 1998.

B.

On July 18, 1996, respondents filed a patent-infringement suit against petitioner, Scripps, and Dr. Cheresh in the District Court for the Southern District of California. Respondents' complaint alleged that petitioner willfully infringed and induced others to infringe respondents' patents by supplying the RGD peptide to Scripps, and that Dr. Cheresh and Scripps infringed the same patents by using the RGD peptide in experiments related to angiogenesis. Respondents sought damages from petitioner and a declaratory judgment against Dr. Cheresh and Scripps. Petitioner answered that its actions involving the RGD peptides did not infringe respondents' patents, and that in any event they were protected by the common-law research exemption and 35 U.S.C. § 271(e)(1).

At the conclusion of trial, the District Court held that, with one exception, petitioner's pre-1995 actions related to the RGD peptides were protected by the common-law research exemption, but that a question of fact remained as to whether petitioner's use of the RGD peptides after 1995 fell within the § 271(e)(1) safe harbor. With the consent of the parties, the District Court gave the following instruction regarding the § 271(e)(1) exemption:

> "To prevail on this defense, [petitioner] must prove by a preponderance of the evidence that it would be objectively

---

inhibitor in February 1997.

reasonable for a party in [petitioner's] and Scripps' situation to believe that there was a decent prospect that the accused activities would contribute, relatively directly, to the generation of the kinds of information that are likely to be relevant in the processes by which the FDA would decide whether to approve the product in question.

"Each of the accused activities must be evaluated separately to determine whether the exemption applies. "

"[Petitioner] does not need to show that the information gathered from a particular activity was actually submitted to the FDA."

The jury found that petitioner, Dr. Cheresh, and Scripps infringed respondents' patents and that petitioner had failed to show that its activities were protected by § 271(e)(1). It awarded damages of $15 million.

In response to post-trial motions, the District Court dismissed respondents' suit against Dr. Cheresh and Scripps, but affirmed the jury's damage award as supported by substantial evidence, and denied petitioner's motion for judgment as a matter of law. With respect to the last, the District Court explained that the evidence was sufficient to show that "any connection between the infringing Scripps experiments and FDA review was insufficiently direct to qualify for the [§ 271(e)(1) exemption]."

A divided panel of the Court of Appeals for the Federal Circuit affirmed in part, and reversed in part. The panel majority affirmed the denial of judgment as a matter of law to petitioner, on the ground that § 271(e)(1)'s safe harbor did not apply because "the Scripps work sponsored by [petitioner] was not clinical testing to supply information to the FDA, but only general biomedical research to identify new pharmaceutical compound." Judge Newman dissented. We granted certiorari to review the Court of Appeals' construction of § 271(e)(1).

III.

Though the contours of this provision are not exact in every respect, the statutory text makes clear that it provides a wide berth for the use of patented drugs in activities related to the federal regulatory process.

As an initial matter, we think it apparent from the statutory text that § 271(e)(1)'s exemption from infringement extends to all uses of patented inventions that are reasonably related to the development and submission of *any* information under the FDCA. This necessarily includes preclinical studies of patented compounds that are appropriate for submission to the FDA in the regulatory process. There is simply no room in the statute for excluding certain information from the exemption on the basis of the phase of research in which it is developed or the particular submission in which it could be included.

Respondents concede the breadth of § 271(e)(1) in this regard, but argue that the only preclinical data of interest to the FDA is that which pertains to the safety of the drug in humans. In respondents' view, preclinical studies related to a drug's efficacy, mechanism of action, pharmacokinetics, and pharmacology are not reasonably included in an IND or an NDA, and are therefore outside the scope of the exemption. We do not understand the FDA's interest in information gathered in preclinical studies to be so constrained. To be sure, its regulations provide that the agency's "primary objectives in reviewing an IND are ... to assure the safety and rights of subjects," 21 CFR 312.22(a) (2005), but it does not follow that the FDA is not interested in reviewing information related to other characteristics of a drug. To the contrary, the FDA requires that applicants include in an IND summaries of the pharmacological, toxicological, pharmacokinetic, and biological qualities of the drug in animals. The primary (and, in some cases, only) way in which a drugmaker may obtain such information is through preclinical *in vitro* and *in vivo* studies.

Moreover, the FDA does not evaluate the safety of proposed clinical experiments in a vacuum; rather, as the statute and regulations reflect, it asks whether the proposed clinical trial poses an "unreasonable risk." This assessment involves a comparison of the risks and the benefits associated with the proposed clinical trials. Accordingly, the FDA directs that an IND must provide sufficient information for the investigator to "make his/her

238

own unbiased risk-benefit assessment of the appropriateness of the proposed trial."

The Court of Appeals' conclusion that § 271(e)(1) did not protect petitioner's provision of the patented RGD peptides for research at Scripps appeared to rest on two somewhat related propositions. First, the court credited the fact that the "Scripps-Merck experiments did not supply information for submission to the [FDA], but instead identified the best drug candidate to subject to future clinical testing under the FDA processes." The court explained:

> "The FDA has no interest in the hunt for drugs that may or may not later undergo clinical testing for FDA approval. For instance, the FDA does not require information about drugs other than the compound featured in an [IND] application. Thus, the Scripps work sponsored by [petitioner] was not 'solely for uses reasonably related to' clinical testing for FDA."

Second, the court concluded that the exemption "does not globally embrace all experimental activity that at some point, however attenuated, may lead to an FDA approval process."[c]

We do not quibble with the latter statement. Basic scientific research on a particular compound, performed without the intent to develop a particular drug or a reasonable belief that the compound will cause the sort of physiological effect the researcher intends to induce, is surely not "reasonably related to the development and submission of information" to the FDA. It does not follow from this, however, that § 271(e)(1)'s exemption from infringement categorically excludes either (1) experimentation on drugs that are not ultimately the subject of an FDA submission or (2) use of patented compounds in experiments that are not ultimately submitted to the FDA. Under certain conditions, we think the

---

[c] The Court of Appeals also suggested that a limited construction of § 271(e)(1) is necessary to avoid depriving so-called "research tools" of the complete value of their patents. Respondents have never argued the RGD peptides were used at Scripps as research tools, and it is apparent from the record that they were not. See 331 F.3d. at 878 (NEWMAN, J., dissenting) ("Use of an existing tool in one's research is quite different from study of the tool itself"). We therefore need not—and do not—express a view about whether, or to what extent, § 271(e)(1) exempts from infringement the use of "research tools" in the development of information for the regulatory process.

exemption is sufficiently broad to protect the use of patented compounds in both situations.

As to the first proposition, it disregards the reality that, even at late stages in the development of a new drug, scientific testing is a process of trial and error. In the vast majority of cases, neither the drugmaker nor its scientists have any way of knowing whether an initially promising candidate will prove successful over a battery of experiments. That is the reason they conduct the experiments. Thus, to construe § 271(e)(1), as the Court of Appeals did, not to protect research conducted on patented compounds for which an IND is not ultimately filed is effectively to limit assurance of exemption to the activities necessary to seek approval of a generic drug: One can know at the outset that a particular compound will be the subject of an eventual application to the FDA only if the active ingredient in the drug being tested is identical to that in a drug that has already been approved.

The statutory text does not require such a result. Congress did not limit § 271(e)(1)'s safe harbor to the development of information for inclusion in a submission to the FDA; nor did it create an exemption applicable only to the research relevant to filing an ANDA [an application] for approval of a generic drug. Rather, it exempted from infringement *all* uses of patented compounds "reasonably related" to the process of developing information for submission under *any* federal law regulating the manufacture, use, or distribution of drugs. We decline to read the "reasonable relation" requirement so narrowly as to render § 271(e)(1)'s stated protection of activities leading to FDA approval for all drugs illusory. Properly construed, § 271(e)(1) leaves adequate space for experimentation and failure on the road to regulatory approval: At least where a drugmaker has a reasonable basis for believing that a patented compound may work, through a particular biological process, to produce a particular physiological effect, and uses the compound in research that, if successful, would be appropriate to include in a submission to the FDA, that use is "reasonably related" to the "development and submission of information under . . . Federal law." § 271(e)(1).

For similar reasons, the use of a patented compound in experiments that are not themselves included in a "submission of information" to the FDA does not, standing alone, render the use infringing. The relationship of the use of a patented compound in a particular experiment to the

240

"development and submission of information" to the FDA does not become more attenuated (or less reasonable) simply because the data from that experiment are left out of the submission that is ultimately passed along to the FDA. Moreover, many of the uncertainties that exist with respect to the selection of a specific drug exist as well with respect to the decision of what research to include in an IND or NDA. As a District Court has observed, "[I]t will not always be clear to parties setting out to seek FDA approval for their new product exactly which kinds of information, and in what quantities, it will take to win that agency's approval." *Intermedics, Inc. v. Ventritex, Inc.,* 775 F. Supp. 1269, 1280 (N.D.Cal.1991), aff'd, 991 F.2d 808 (C.A.Fed.1993). This is especially true at the preclinical stage of drug approval. We thus agree with the Government that the use of patented compounds in preclinical studies is protected under § 271(e)(1) as long as there is a reasonable basis for believing that the experiments will produce "the types of information that are relevant to an IND or NDA."

* * *

Before the Court of Appeals, petitioner challenged the sufficiency of the evidence supporting the jury's finding that it failed to show that "all of the accused activities are covered by [§ 271(e)(1)]." That court rejected the challenge on the basis of a construction of § 271(e)(1) that was not consistent with the text of that provision or the relevant jury instruction.[d] Thus, the evidence presented at trial has yet to be reviewed under the standards set forth in the jury instruction, which we believe to be consistent with, if less detailed than, the construction of § 271(e)(1) that we adopt today. We decline to undertake a review of the sufficiency of the evidence under a proper construction of § 271(e)(1) for the first time here. Accordingly, we vacate the judgment of the Court of Appeals and remand the case for proceedings consistent with this opinion.

---

[d] The relevant jury instruction provided only that there must be a "decent prospect that the accused activities would contribute, relatively directly, to the generation of the kinds of information that are likely to be relevant in the processes by which the FDA would decide whether to approve the product in question." It did not say that, to fall within § 271(e)(1)'s exemption from infringement, the patented compound used in experimentation must be the subject of an eventual application to the FDA. And it expressly rejected the notion that the exemption only included experiments that produced information included in an IND or NDA.

INSERT AT THE END OF THE FIRST FULL PARAGRAPH ON PAGE 835:

In *Illinois Tool Works, Inc. v. Independent Ink, Inc.,*[1] the Supreme Court held definitively that there is no presumption that a patentee possesses market power in the context of an antitrust case. The Court noted that the types of tying arrangements involved in the dispute had been eliminated as a basis for a finding of patent misuse when Congress enacted § 271(d) of the patent statute. Noting that "Congress, the antitrust enforcement agencies, and most economists have all reached the conclusion that a patent does not necessarily confer market power upon the patentee," the Court saw no reason to continue to employ such a presumption in the antitrust context.

REPLACE NOTE 5 ON PAGE 838 WITH THE FOLLOWING:

5. *Essential medicines: exhaustion, parallel importation, price discrimination, and compulsory licensing.* One problem that all countries must grapple with is the clash between relying on patents to encourage pharmaceutical research and putting the cost of medicines out of the reach of most patients. In some countries, including Canada, price controls or government purchase programs keep retail costs reasonable. Should Americans be permitted to buy their medication in Canada? Should they be allowed to order medicine abroad via the Internet? Should third parties be allowed to buy product in Canada and import it for resale in the United States?

Adams creates patent law's analogue to the first sale doctrine of copyright law, holding that a patent holder's interest in a particular embodiment (e.g. a bottle of pills) is exhausted once it is sold under his authority. The Supreme Court has recently reaffirmed a broad reading of the first sale doctrine in *Quanta Computer, Inc. v. LG Elecs.*, 128 S.Ct. 2109 (2008). But *Adams* and *Quanta* involved wholly domestic sales: should exhaustion apply internationally? That is, is the U.S. patent holder's interest exhausted by a sale made in Canada? Federal Circuit case prior to *Quanta* held that international sales do not exhaust patent rights within the

---

[1] 547 U.S. 28 (2006).

United States.[2] The Federal Circuit has reaffirmed that conclusion in *Quanta*'s wake.[3] However, the question may well return to the Federal Circuit soon. The Supreme Court has granted certiorari in *Costco Wholesale Corp. v. Omega, S.A.,* Supreme Court No. 08-1423, *opinion below, Omega S.A. v. Costco Wholesale Corp.,* 541 F.3d 982 (9th Cir. 2008). *Costco* raises the issue of international exhaustion in the copyright context.

Arguably, exhaustion should not apply internationally because of factors affecting the international sale price such as the fact that in Canada pharmaceuticals are sold at prices set by the Canadian government. Thus, importation of (cheap) Canadian medicine should not be permitted. On the other hand, radically different prices within North America (or even within the developed world) strike many as grossly unfair. As of this writing, Congress has considered legislation that would permit Americans to purchase prescription drugs abroad.[4] At the same time, however, pharmaceutical companies strongly oppose such legislation, citing safety concerns with non-FDA-approved drugs.

The problem raised by this activity is not, however, merely about the technicalities of the first sale doctrine or even about the prices U.S. patients pay for drugs. Pharmaceutical companies claim to earn half their revenue and most of their profits in the United States. Thus, the real issue is whether reduced prices will diminish incentives to undertake the substantial expense to bring new drugs to market. In other words, the question is whether Americans are willing to utilize their higher purchasing power to subsidize research that improves their own lives, but which the entire world then utilizes at significantly lower cost. Is there a way for countries to agree to share in the cost of health research? The TRIPS Agreement does not prevent members from controlling prices or barring parallel importation,[5] thus it does not currently deal with this issue.

---

[2] See *Jazz Photo Corp. v. International Trade Comm'n,* 264 F.3d 1094, 1105 (Fed. Cir. 2001) (stating that international sales do not exhaust U.S. rights).

[3] *Fujifilm Corp. v. Benun,* 605 F.3d 1366, (Fed. Cir. 2010).

[4] Pharmaceutical Market Access and Drug Safety Act of 2009, H.R. 1298 and S. 525. As its name implies, safety issues stemming from the lack of FDA supervision are also considered in the proposed legislation.

[5] TRIPS Agreement, art. 6.

How is your view of parallel importation affected by the problem of supplying essential medicines to less developed countries? For example, many African countries are struggling with HIV/AIDS and cannot afford to pay either the U.S. or the Canadian price for medication. The TRIPS Agreement's compulsory licensing provisions clearly permit African governments to authorize local manufacturers to make the medicines their citizens need.[6] Pharmaceuticals are, however, difficult to manufacture at the purity required and African countries lack the necessary infrastructure. There are nations (India and Brazil are examples) that are excellent generic drug manufacturers. Could they sell to Africa without the patent holder's authorization? Prior to the Doha Declaration, the answer was clearly no: unauthorized manufacture is permissible for health crises, but only to meet "predominantly" domestic needs. Thus, Indian generic producers could supply India, but not Botswana.

The Doha Declaration recognized this problem, and in ¶ 6, promised to find a solution. In 2003, the WTO members agreed on a framework that would allow export of generic drugs to countries without the capacity to manufacture essential medications for themselves. In 2005, this agreement was translated into an amendment to TRIPS (the first and only so far, in fact.) However, the amendment still lacks the number of formally adopting countries to put it into effect.

Patent owners are not so much worried about supplying product to Africa at prices that citizens there can afford; they are mainly worried that without clear rules against international exhaustion, the medicines they supply to Africa will be reimported into developed countries, undercutting their prices. Are there any good solutions to this problem that would ensure that essential medicines get to those who need them but cannot afford to pay the going rate?[7]

---

[6] TRIPS Agreement, art. 31(b) has a special provision for cases of "national emergency." Indeed, art. 27(2) permits members to exclude from patentability inventions necessary to protect human health. Moreover, developing countries enjoy certain transition privileges that allow them to avoid patenting.

[7] For more on these issues, see Jean O. Lanjouw, *A New Global Patent Regime For Diseases: U.S. and International Legal Issues*, 16 HARV. J.L. & TECH. 85 (2002); Susan K. Sell, *TRIPS and the Access to Medicines Campaign*, 20 WIS. INT'L L.J. 481 (2002); Keith E. Maskus, *Ensuring Access to Essential Medicines: Some Economic Considerations*, 20 WIS. INT'L L.J. 563 (2002).

REPLACE NOTE 8 ON PAGE 841 WITH THE FOLLOWING:

8. *The statutory experimental use defense.* The § 271(e)(1) exemption from infringement liability for "uses reasonably related to the development and submission of information under a Federal law which regulates drugs" was enacted in response to the *Roche* decision discussed in *Madey*. It was enacted concurrently with patent term extensions to compensate for delays in obtaining FDA approval. § 271(e)(1) has generally been interpreted broadly by the Supreme Court. The *Merck* opinion excerpted above adopts a broad reading of the statute with respect to what uses are "reasonably related" to FDA approval. The earlier *Eli Lilly & Co. v. Medtronic, Inc.* case reads the statute broadly to cover medical devices as well as drugs.[8]

Is this broad reading of the statutory exemption inconsistent with the extremely narrow reading of the common law exemption adopted by the Federal Circuit in *Madey*? The Federal Circuit also seems to have adopted a narrow reading of 271(e)(1) with regard to a question explicitly left open in *Merck*. The Supreme Court declined to decide whether the exemption applied to patents on inventions being used as research tools to develop information related to other drugs or devices needing FDA approval (see footnote c in the excerpted opinion). The Federal Circuit, however, answered this question in the negative in *Proveris Scientific Corp. v. Innovasystems, Inc.*, 536 F.3d 1256, 1258 (Fed. Cir. 2008), holding that the 271(e)(1) exemption did not apply to the manufacturer of a device for measuring the physical parameters of aerosol sprays used in nasal spray drug delivery devices even if the device was used to develop information for submission to the FDA.

---

[8] 496 U.S. 661 (1990).

ASSIGNMENT 23—REMEDIES

REPLACE NTP, INC. v. RESEARCH IN MOTION, LTD. AND ROCHE PRODUCTS, INC. v. BOLAR PHARMACEUTICAL CO., INC. ON PAGES 862-874 WITH THE FOLLOWING:

In re Seagate Technology, LLC
United States Court of Appeals for the Federal Circuit, 2007 (en banc).
497 F.3d 1360 .

■ MAYER, CIRCUIT JUDGE.

Seagate Technology, LLC ("Seagate") petitions for a writ of mandamus directing the United States District Court for the Southern District of New York to vacate its orders compelling disclosure of materials and testimony that Seagate claims is covered by the attorney-client privilege and work product protection. We ordered en banc review, and now grant the petition. We overrule *Underwater Devices Inc. v. Morrison-Knudsen Co.*, 717 F.2d 1380 (1983), and we clarify the scope of the waiver of attorney-client privilege

Background

Convolve, Inc. and the Massachusetts Institute of Technology (collectively "Convolve") sued Seagate [] alleging infringement of [three US patents]. Convolve also alleged that Seagate willfully infringed the patents. Prior to the lawsuit, Seagate retained Gerald Sekimura to provide an opinion concerning Convolve's patents, and he ultimately prepared three written opinions [regarding lack of infringement, invalidity, and potential unenforceability of Convolve's patents]. There is no dispute that Seagate's opinion counsel operated separately and independently of trial counsel at all times. In early 2003, pursuant to the trial court's scheduling order, Seagate notified Convolve of its intent to rely on Sekimura's three opinion letters in defending against willful infringement, and it disclosed all of his work product and made him available for deposition. Convolve then moved to compel discovery of any communications and work product of Seagate's other counsel, including its trial counsel. [The district court granted the motions.]

Seagate petitioned for a writ of mandamus. We stayed the discovery orders and, recognizing the functional relationship between our willfulness jurisprudence and the practical dilemmas faced in the areas of attorney-client privilege and work product protection, sua sponte ordered en banc review of the petition. The en banc order set out the following questions:

1. Should a party's assertion of the advice of counsel defense to willful infringement extend waiver of the attorney-client privilege to communications with that party's trial counsel?
2. What is the effect of any such waiver on work-product immunity?
3. Given the impact of the statutory duty of care standard announced in *Underwater Devices, Inc. v. Morrison-Knudsen Co.*, 717 F.2d 1380 (Fed. Cir. 1983), on the issue of waiver of attorney-client privilege, should this court reconsider the decision in Underwater Devices and the duty of care standard itself?

Discussion

Because patent infringement is a strict liability offense, the nature of the offense is only relevant in determining whether enhanced damages are warranted. Although a trial court's discretion in awarding enhanced damages has a long lineage in patent law, the current statute, similar to its predecessors, is devoid of any standard for awarding them. Absent a statutory guide, we have held that an award of enhanced damages requires a showing of willful infringement. But, a finding of willfulness does not require an award of enhanced damages; it merely permits it.

This court fashioned a standard for evaluating willful infringement in *Underwater Devices Inc. v. Morrison-Knudsen Co.*, 717 F.2d 1380, 1389-90 (Fed. Cir. 1983):

> "Where . . . a potential infringer has actual notice of another's patent rights, he has an affirmative duty to exercise due care to determine whether or not he is infringing. Such an affirmative duty includes, inter alia, the duty to seek and obtain competent legal advice from counsel before the initiation of any possible infringing activity."

247

This standard was announced shortly after the creation of the court, and at a time "when widespread disregard of patent rights was undermining the national innovation incentive." *Knorr-Bremse Systeme Fuer Nutzfahreuge GmbH v. Dana Corp.*, 383 F.3d 1337, 1343 (Fed. Cir. 2004) (en banc). Indeed, in *Underwater Devices*, an attorney had advised the infringer that "[c]ourts, in recent years, have—in patent infringement cases—found [asserted patents] invalid in approximately 80% of the cases," and on that basis the attorney concluded that the patentee would not likely sue for infringement.

Over time, our cases evolved to evaluate willfulness and its duty of due care under the totality of the circumstances, and we enumerated factors informing the inquiry. In light of the duty of due care, accused willful infringers commonly assert an advice of counsel defense. Under this defense, an accused willful infringer aims to establish that due to reasonable reliance on advice from counsel, its continued accused activities were done in good faith. Typically, counsel's opinion concludes that the patent is invalid, unenforceable, and/or not infringed. Although an infringer's reliance on favorable advice of counsel, or conversely his failure to proffer any favorable advice, is not dispositive of the willfulness inquiry, it is crucial to the analysis. Since Underwater Devices, we have recognized the practical concerns stemming from our willfulness doctrine, particularly as related to the attorney-client privilege and work product doctrine.

We cautioned [in *Quantum Corp. v. Plus Development Corp.*, 940 F.2d 642, 643 (Fed. Cir. 1991)] that an accused infringer "should not, without the trial court's careful consideration, be forced to choose between waiving the privilege in order to protect itself from a willfulness finding, in which case it may risk prejudicing itself on the question of liability, and maintaining the privilege, in which case it may risk being found to be a willful infringer if liability is found."

In this case, we confront the willfulness scheme and its functional relationship to the attorney-client privilege and work product protection. In light of Supreme Court opinions since Underwater Devices and the practical concerns facing litigants under the current regime, we take this opportunity to revisit our willfulness doctrine and to address whether waiver resulting from advice of counsel and work product defenses extend to trial counsel.

248

I. Willful Infringement

The term willful is not unique to patent law, and it has a well-established meaning in the civil context. For instance, our sister circuits have employed a recklessness standard for enhancing statutory damages for copyright infringement. Under the Copyright Act, a copyright owner can elect to receive statutory damages, and trial courts have discretion to enhance the damages, up to a statutory maximum, for willful infringement. 17 U.S.C. § 504(c). Although the statute does not define willful, it has consistently been defined as including reckless behavior. Just recently, the Supreme Court addressed the meaning of willfulness as a statutory condition of civil liability for punitive damages. *Safeco Ins. Co. of Am. v. Burr*, 549 U.S. 1104, Nos. 06-84, -100, slip op. (June 4, 2007). Safeco involved the Fair Credit Reporting Act ("FCRA"), which imposes civil liability for failure to comply with its requirements. Whereas an affected consumer can recover actual damages for negligent violations of the FCRA, 15 U.S.C. § 1681o(a), he can also recover punitive damages for willful ones, 15 U.S.C. § 1681n(a). Addressing the willfulness requirement in this context, the Court concluded that the "standard civil usage" of "willful" includes reckless behavior. Significantly, the Court said that this definition comports with the common law usage, "which treated actions in 'reckless disregard' of the law as 'willful' violations."

In contrast, the duty of care announced in Underwater Devices sets a lower threshold for willful infringement that is more akin to negligence. This standard fails to comport with the general understanding of willfulness in the civil context, Richland Shoe Co., 486 U.S. at 133 ("The word 'willful' . . . is generally understood to refer to conduct that is not merely negligent."), and it allows for punitive damages in a manner inconsistent with Supreme Court precedent. Accordingly, we overrule the standard set out in Underwater Devices and hold that proof of willful infringement permitting enhanced damages requires at least a showing of objective recklessness. Because we abandon the affirmative duty of due care, we also reemphasize that there is no affirmative obligation to obtain opinion of counsel. We fully recognize that "the term [reckless] is not self-defining." *Farmer v. Brennan*, 511 U.S. 825, 836 (1994). However, "[t]he civil law generally calls a person reckless who acts . . . in the face of an unjustifiably high risk of harm that is either known or so obvious that it should be known." *Id.*

Accordingly, to establish willful infringement, a patentee must show by clear and convincing evidence that the infringer acted despite an objectively high likelihood that its actions constituted infringement of a valid patent. The state of mind of the accused infringer is not relevant to this objective inquiry. If this threshold objective standard is satisfied, the patentee must also demonstrate that this objectively-defined risk (determined by the record developed in the infringement proceeding) was either known or so obvious that it should have been known to the accused infringer. We leave it to future cases to further develop the application of this standard.

[In omitted sections of the opinion, the court holds that the decision to waive the attorney-client and work product privileges with respect to pre-litigation attorney opinions concerning validity or infringement does not imply waiver of those privileges with respect to trial counsel.]

■ GAJARSA CIRCUIT JUDGE, concurring, with whom CIRCUIT JUDGE NEWMAN joins.

I agree with the court's decision to grant the writ of mandamus; however, I write separately to express my belief that the court should take the opportunity to eliminate the grafting of willfulness onto section 284. As the court's opinion points out, although the enhanced damages clause of that section "is devoid of any standard for awarding [such damages]," this court has nevertheless read a willfulness standard into the statute. Because the language of the statute unambiguously omits any such requirement, see 35 U.S.C. § 284 ("[T]he court may increase the damages up to three times the amount found or assessed."), and because there is no principled reason for continuing to engraft a willfulness requirement onto section 284, I believe we should adhere to the plain meaning of the statute and leave the discretion to enhance damages in the capable hands of the district courts.

(Separate concurring opinion of Judge Newman omitted.)

NTP, Inc. v. Research In Motion, Ltd.
United States District Court, E.D. Virginia, 2003.
270 F.Supp.2d 751.

[Plaintiff NTP, Inc. ("NTP") alleged that certain technology manufactured by Defendant Research In Motion, Ltd. ("RIM") directly and indirectly infringes upon thirty-one claims in seven patents (the "Campana patents"). The Campana patents sought to integrate electronic mail with wireless transmission. Prior to the Campana patents, the transfer of electronic mail was landline based. The Campana patents sought to increase the ability for individuals to gain access to their incoming and pending email, without requiring them to access a telephone line. The accused devices were the BlackBerry Pager, the BlackBerry Enterprise Server ("BES"), and the BlackBerry "wireless email solution." After the court denied defendant's motion for summary judgment, 261 F.Supp.2d 423 (E.D. Virginia, 2002), a jury trial was held.]

■ SPENCER, DISTRICT JUDGE

At the conclusion of the trial, the jury returned a verdict in favor of NTP, finding that various RIM products and services infringed the Campana Patents. In addition, the jury made an express finding that RIM willfully infringed the Campana Patents. NTP has filed a series of post-trial motions seeking enhanced damages and attorney fees, as well as prejudgment and postjudgment interest.

II.

A. Enhanced Damages

Upon a finding of infringement by the jury, "the court may increase the damages up to three times the amount found" if the jury also finds that the defendant willfully infringed the patents-in-suit. 35 U.S.C. § 284. Enhanced damages not only operate as a punitive measure against individual infringing defendants, but they also serve an overarching purpose as a deterrence of patent infringement. However, these damages are not meant to compensate the plaintiff. In assessing enhanced damages, it is first necessary that the fact-finder determine that the defendant is liable for willful infringement. Such a finding, however, does not mandate that the court award enhanced damages. Indeed, the court must engage in a separate analysis to determine whether the egregiousness of the defendant warrants enhanced damages, and if so, the extent of those damages. The decision whether to award enhanced damages is within the sound discretion of the court.

When addressing the issue of enhanced damages, courts "must consider factors that render defendant's conduct more culpable, as well as factors that are mitigating or ameliorating." *Read Corp. v. Portec, Inc.,* 970 F.2d 816, 826 (Fed.Cir.1992). A court is obliged to consider all relevant circumstances in reaching this determination. In *Read,* the Federal Circuit established that courts should consider the following factors together in determining the degree of the infringer's culpability: (1) whether the infringer deliberately copied the ideas or design of another; (2) whether the infringer, upon notice of the other's patent protection, investigated the scope of the patent and formed a good-faith belief that it was invalid or that it was not infringed; (3) the infringer's behavior as a party to the litigation; (4) the infringer's size and financial condition; (5) the closeness of the case; (6) the duration of the infringer's misconduct; (7) any remedial action by the infringer; (8) the infringer's motivation for harm; and (9) whether the infringer attempted to conceal its misconduct. After taking all of the *Read* factors into consideration, it is clear that enhanced damages are warranted. However, RIM's behavior does not warrant treble damages.

1. Whether RIM Deliberately Copied

RIM asserts that this factor should mitigate enhanced damages. There is no evidence that RIM copied any of the Campana Patents. Indeed, NTP concedes this much. It is apparent that RIM developed and conceived its BlackBerry products entirely independent of the Campana patents. Therefore, the absence of copying by RIM is a mitigating factor.

2. Sufficiency of Investigation

Possibly the most controverted issue with regards to enhanced damages is the sufficiency of RIM's investigation of the Campana Patents and whether its reliance on the oral opinion of Charles Meyer, RIM's lead in-house counsel, regarding infringement of those patents was in good faith and met RIM's duty of care. NTP is adamant that RIM's investigation was far from adequate, and as a result, RIM failed to satisfy its affirmative duty of care. RIM argues that, based on the totality of the circumstances, its investigation into the Campana Patents met its duty of care. However, RIM's argument as to the "totality of the circumstances"—namely, RIM's investigation *after* NTP filed suit—discounts the fact that NTP only asserted willfulness from the date of NTP's notice letter on January 27, 2000, to the day RIM received its oral opinion from Larry Nixon. Under these circumstances, it is more probative to evaluate RIM's actions immediately after it received the January 2000 notice letter from NTP.

Upon receiving actual notice of another's patent, a potential infringer "has an affirmative duty of care that normally requires the potential infringer to obtain competent legal advice before infringing or continuing to infringe." However, even if a potential infringer obtains legal advice, liability for willful infringement may still attach if that advice is not competent. Thus, the probative question is, whether "under all the circumstances, a reasonable person would prudently conduct himself with any confidence that a court might hold the patent invalid or not infringed." Whether an opinion is incompetent depends on an objective evaluation of the evidence. In order for an opinion to be effective and indicative of the defendant's good faith intent, it "must be premised upon the best information known to the defendant." Furthermore, the Federal Circuit has also noted that oral opinions, especially those that are not objective, carry little weight. However, even if an opinion incorrectly concludes that an infringer would not be liable for infringement, such opinion will mitigate enhanced damages if it is found to be competent.

The January 27, 2000 letter sent by NTP to RIM (the "Notice Letter") listed six patents owned by NTP and referred to a "distinct commercial advantage" available to RIM if it entered into a licensing agreement with NTP. The letter also included the following statement: "As you are aware, the patent laws cover direct infringement, contributory infringement, and inducement to infringe." Finally, the letter included documentation regarding the BlackBerry Desktop Software Installation Guide, the Getting Started Guide, and the BlackBerry solution. RIM adduced evidence that, upon receipt of the Notice Letter sometime during the first week of February 2000, some investigation was done by Charles Meyer with the assistance of in-house patent attorney Krishna Pathiyal, Director of Wireless Innovation Gary Mousseau, and Chief Executive Officer Mike Lazaridis. Both Lazaridis and Mousseau provided "technical assistance" to Meyer and Pathiyal as to how RIM's products worked. As part of his investigation, Meyer performed research to find out who NTP was, read the patent specifications, and reviewed all independent claims of each patent to see if RIM was somehow violating the patent. During the course of his investigation, Meyer met with Lazaridis three or four times and gave Lazaridis two oral reports that were not reduced to writing, because, as he surmised, "there was no need" to reduce them to writing. As a result of this investigation, Meyer concluded that, because one element of all the independent claims was missing, none of RIM's products infringed the six patents identified by NTP in the Notice Letter. On February 27, 2000, Meyer then sent a response to NTP (the "Response Letter") where he asked for more time to complete RIM's "due diligence," and he requested that NTP send a copy of the claims of the pending patent application as well as other documentation that led NTP to believe that RIM should take a license with respect to the Campana Patents. Meyer testified that, from the time he received the Notice Letter to the time he sent the Response Letter, he spent approximately 40 hours researching the patents. Meyer further testified that he spent an additional 10–20 hours with Lazaridis and Pathiyal discussing the patents.

Based on the evidence advanced at trial, it is difficult to determine whether RIM actually conducted any investigation at all. There were inconsistencies in the testimony of Charles Meyer, Krishna Pathiyal, Mike Lazaridis, and Gary Mousseau as to the amount of time spent investigating the Campana Patents, and who was involved in the investigation. Other circumstances that contributed to the doubt that any investigation was conducted include the demeanor of the witnesses, and the lack of any documentation of any aspect of the investigation whatsoever. For example, Charles Meyer's explanation concerning the failure to write notes on the face of the patents was implausible. Meyer's explanation was further undermined when he testified that, instead of writing on the patents, he took notes regarding the patents on separate sheets of paper, but later testified that he failed to locate any of those notes. Moreover, RIM could not locate its copy of the Notice Letter.

In any event, assuming that RIM conducted an investigation, it was not sufficient to meet its required duty of care because Meyer's oral opinion was not competent. A reasonably prudent person under these circumstances would not have confidence that a court would render a finding of non-infringement or invalidity. First, neither Meyer nor Pathiyal were outside counsel. Therefore, it was more likely that any opinion issued by them would not be objective. Second, Meyer did not conduct a study of invalidity, order a copy of the prosecution history of the patents, or conduct a search of prior art. In addition, Meyer used both Lazaridis and Mousseau, interested parties, as technical resources.

3. RIM's Litigation Behavior

RIM consistently engaged in a variety of questionable litigation tactics throughout the course of this action. RIM's method of conducting discovery including its trickling of the delivery of documents, its failure to work with NTP to streamline document production, and its last-minute cancellation of a deposition scheduled to be taken in Waterloo, Ontario, made discovery unnecessarily arduous. Furthermore, RIM's decision to file premature motions for summary judgment before claim construction, and numerous summary judgment motions after construction, which essentially challenged the claim construction, was both wasteful of judicial resources and unduly burdensome to NTP. Along the same lines, RIM continued to improperly challenge the claim construction with the attempted proffering of Larry Nixon as an expert witness. The primary purpose of this testimony was to adduce evidence as to the perceived incorrect claim construction. Finally, RIM attempted to confuse and mislead the jury by conducting a demonstration of the TekNow! system which RIM asserted as prior art, by using updated software that did not exist at the time the system was used.

Accordingly, taking all these circumstances into consideration, RIM's litigation behavior was sufficiently egregious to be considered an enhancing factor.

4. RIM's Size and Financial Condition

As RIM repeatedly acknowledged throughout its pleadings and its closing argument, NTP is a very small corporation, while RIM, in comparison, is a much larger entity. Thus, the primary consideration of this Court is the amount of enhanced damages that RIM can withstand. Such damages should not be awarded if it would severely affect the defendant's financial condition or unduly prejudice the defendant's non-infringing business. NTP argues that RIM received three billion dollars from investors, and according to co-CEO Jim Balsillie, the damages awarded by the jury represents a "small percentage" of RIM's cash reserves. RIM does not dispute that this statement was made, but instead focuses on other aspects of its financial condition. For example, RIM asserts that, on December 19, 2002, it reported a net loss of $92.3 million dollars for that quarter. RIM also asserts that $23.1 million represents a third of RIM's total revenue for its most recent fiscal quarter. RIM asserts that, as a result of its losses, it has had to announce employee layoffs. RIM surmises that, if damages are enhanced, it will result in larger losses and more layoffs.

The evidence established that the BlackBerry line of products is the core of RIM's business. Consequently, there will be little prejudice to RIM's non-infringing business. RIM will not be allowed to focus solely on its revenue and net loss on one hand, while discounting its considerable investment pool on the other. RIM is large enough to withstand enhanced damages in this case.

5. Closeness of the Case

Enhanced damages should not be awarded if the defendant puts forth a "meritorious good faith defense and a substantial challenge to infringement." A case is close if it was "hard-fought" or the jury could have found for the defendant on the issues of infringement, validity, and willfulness, and could have awarded substantially less damages.

RIM argues that it raised substantial arguments with respect to claim construction. However, in light of the fact that many of RIM's failed motions for summary judgment were aimed at challenging claim construction, RIM's argument here carries little weight. Moreover, RIM was not successful on any of its eight motions for summary judgment. RIM's infringement was clear. Indeed, it offered no real defense to NTP's infringement case at trial. RIM's evidence at trial further demonstrated that RIM's anticipation and obviousness defenses were not substantial. For example, Dr. Jeffrey Reed, RIM's own expert, was not able to correlate any piece of prior art to the specific elements and limitations of the asserted claims. Therefore, because RIM did not put forth a "meritorious good faith defense," or a "substantial challenge to infringement," this was not a close case.

6. Duration of RIM's Misconduct

NTP asserts that enhanced damages are appropriate due to RIM's infringement for well over three years, including two in which RIM willfully infringed the Campana Patents. RIM argues that the relevant period of any misconduct should be from the time this lawsuit was initiated until May 12, 2002, when it received its first oral opinion from Larry Nixon. NTP also notes that RIM continues to infringe the Campana Patents as evidenced by Chief Financial Officer Dennis Kavelman's statement during a post-verdict telephone conference that RIM's "products are unchanged." (NTP App. A, at 6.)

Under these circumstances, the duration of RIM's infringing activities was not so egregious to constitute an enhancing factor. However, the duration was too long to be mitigating. Therefore, this factor is neutral.

7. Remedial Action Taken by the Defendant

NTP asserts that, in light of Kavelman's assertion that RIM's products are "unchanged," that it has not undertaken any remedial action whatsoever. RIM counters this by stating that it is working on designing around the Campana Patents. (Lazaridis Decl. & 7.) However, RIM noted that such efforts have not been successful thus far. RIM's failed effort to design around the Campana Patents is not sufficient to constitute remedial action because it does not benefit NTP, the owner of the infringed patents, in any way. It is undisputed that, as of the conclusion of the trial, RIM has not engaged in any remedial action designed to benefit NTP by reducing RIM's infringing activities. Accordingly, RIM's failure to engage in such remedial action constitutes an enhancing factor.

8. Motivation for Harm

RIM had no motivation to harm NTP, and NTP concedes this point. Therefore, this is a basis for mitigating enhanced damages.

9. Concealment of Misconduct

Again, there is no evidence that RIM attempted to conceal any misconduct, and NTP concedes this. Therefore, this is also a basis for mitigating enhanced damages.

Based on the preceding discussion of the *Read* factors, enhanced damages are warranted in this case. However, RIM's conduct is not so egregious to warrant treble damages. Accordingly, the qualifying compensatory damages, as awarded by the jury, will be enhanced by a factor of 0.5. NTP has also asked this Court to enhance post-verdict compensatory damages. As discussed earlier, RIM has not taken any remedial measures to decrease its infringing activities. In fact, shortly after receiving an unfavorable jury verdict, it publicly announced that its products will remain "unchanged." Furthermore, it has stipulated to the infringement of four new models of BlackBerry handheld devices which it fully intends to market and sell. Therefore, there is a sufficient basis to enhance post-verdict damages. Accordingly, the post-verdict compensatory damages will also be enhanced by a factor of 0.5.

B. Attorney's Fees

As a general rule, absent statutory authority, a "prevailing litigant is ordinarily not entitled to collect a reasonable attorneys' fee from the loser." *Alyeska Pipeline Service Co. v. Wilderness Society,* 421 U.S. 240, 247, 95 S.Ct. 1612, 44 L.Ed.2d 141 (1975). In patent infringement suits, district courts "in exceptional cases may award reasonable attorney fees to the prevailing party." 35 U.S.C. § 285 (2000). The purpose of this section is to award attorney fees in extraordinary cases where there is:

> [A] finding of unfairness or bad faith in the conduct of the losing party, or some other equitable consideration of similar force, which makes it grossly unjust that the winner of the particular law suit be left to bear the burden of his counsel fees which prevailing litigants normally bear.

Machinery Corp. of America v. Gullfiber AB, 774 F.2d 467, 471 (Fed.Cir.1985).

When considering a request for attorney fees under § 285, "the trial judge undertakes a two-step inquiry: he or she must determine whether there is clear and convincing evidence that the case is 'exceptional,' and if so, whether an award of attorney fees to the prevailing party is warranted." *Interspiro USA, Inc. v. Figgie Int'l Inc.* 18 F.3d 927, 933 (Fed.Cir.1994). The first step is a question of fact reviewed for clear error. The second is within the discretion of the trial judge and is reviewed for abuse of discretion. The two steps are interrelated, as "the amount of the attorney fees depends on the extent to which the case is exceptional. In other words, the exceptionality determination highly influences the award setting."

An express finding of willfulness provides a sufficient basis for the award of attorney fees. As a general rule, attorney's fees under section 285 may be justified by any valid basis for awarding increased damages under section 284. Additional factors which may make a case exceptional include: actual wrongful intent or gross negligence, the closeness of the case and the parties' conduct, including evidence of bad faith, misconduct during litigation, fraud, and vexatious or frivolous litigation, inequitable conduct, and whether it would be grossly unfair for the prevailing party to bear the cost of litigation, or where the conduct of the losing party is marked by bad-faith or unfairness.

If this Court decides that this is an exceptional case, it must be determined "whether an award of attorney fees to the prevailing party is warranted." Courts may consider the litigation behavior of both the infringer and the patentee. To that end, "the trial judge is in the best position to weigh considerations such as the closeness of the case, the tactics of counsel, the conduct of the parties, and any other factors that may contribute to a fair allocation of the burdens of litigation as between winner and loser." In any event, an award for attorney's fees must be reasonable. *Gentry Gallery, Inc. v. Berkline Corp.,* 134 F.3d 1473, 1480 (Fed.Cir.1998).

Although the moving party must show that attorney fees are warranted, in the face of the jury's express finding of willful infringement, which, standing alone, is a sufficient basis to award attorney's fees, RIM must put forth a showing as to why attorney fees are not warranted in this case. RIM argues that this is not an exceptional case by asserting the closeness of the case, its own good faith defenses, and NTP's litigation conduct. However, based on the discussion of the *Read* factors, it is clear that this is an exceptional case. Again, there is substantial doubt as to whether any investigation of the Campana Patents occurred upon receipt of the Notice Letter. Even if an investigation was conducted, it was not sufficient to meet its duty of care. RIM's litigation behavior, including its discovery tactics, post-trial motions which rehashed issues previously

259

dealt with on summary judgment, its attempt to advance evidence through an expert that the claim construction is erroneous, and its fraudulent demonstration of the TekNow! system with updated software installed by Gary Mousseau, also adds to the exceptionality of this case. Moreover, as discussed earlier, this was not a close case. Therefore, there is clear and convincing evidence that this case is sufficiently exceptional to warrant an award of attorney fees.

RIM advances a compelling argument regarding the difference between the number of patents and claims that NTP asserted in the beginning of the litigation, and the number asserted at trial. RIM notes that when NTP filed suit, it claimed infringement of eight patents having a combined total of over 2,400 claims. RIM further notes that NTP initially refused to limit the number of claims, first filing a "conditional" reduction of the asserted claims to 1,300, then to 500 shortly before the *Markman* hearing. Upon motion by RIM to compel NTP to further reduce its claims, the number of asserted claims was reduced to thirty-one. That number was finally reduced to sixteen claims on the eve of trial.

[I]n light of the fact that NTP slowly whittled down many of the asserted claims throughout the course of the case up until the eve of trial, it is appropriate to reduce the amount of this award. This Court, however, cannot determine to a mathematical certainty the portion of NTP's fees that was devoted to litigating claims that were not asserted. In any event, because NTP accumulated a majority of its fees with respect to other aspects of litigating the case, this Court will reduce NTP's award of attorney fees by 20%.

EBay Inc. v. Mercexchange, L. L. C.
Supreme Court of the United States, 2006.
126 S. Ct. 1837, 164 L. Ed. 2d 641.

■ JUSTICE THOMAS delivered the opinion of the Court.

Ordinarily, a federal court considering whether to award permanent injunctive relief to a prevailing plaintiff applies the four-factor test historically employed by courts of equity. Petitioners eBay Inc. and Half.com, Inc., argue that this traditional test applies to disputes arising under the Patent Act. We agree and, accordingly, vacate the judgment of the Court of Appeals.

I

Petitioner eBay operates a popular Internet Web site that allows private sellers to list goods they wish to sell, either through an auction or at a fixed price. Petitioner Half.com, now a wholly owned subsidiary of eBay, operates a similar Web site. Respondent MercExchange, L. L. C., holds a number of patents, including a business method patent for an electronic market designed to facilitate the sale of goods between private individuals by establishing a central authority to promote trust among participants. MercExchange sought to license its patent to eBay and Half.com, as it had previously done with other companies, but the parties failed to reach an agreement. MercExchange subsequently filed a patent infringement suit against eBay and Half.com in the United States District Court for the Eastern District of Virginia. A jury found that MercExchange's patent was valid, that eBay and Half.com had infringed that patent, and that an award of damages was appropriate.[a] Following the jury verdict, the District Court denied MercExchange's motion for permanent injunctive relief. The Court of Appeals for the Federal Circuit reversed, applying its "general rule that courts will issue permanent injunctions against patent infringement absent exceptional circumstances." 401 F.3d 1323, 1339 (2005). We granted certiorari to determine the appropriateness of this general rule.

II

According to well-established principles of equity, a plaintiff seeking a permanent injunction must satisfy a four-factor test before a court may grant such relief. A plaintiff must demonstrate: (1) that it has suffered an irreparable injury; (2) that remedies available at law, such as monetary damages, are inadequate to compensate for that injury; (3) that, considering the balance of hardships between the plaintiff and defendant, a remedy in equity is warranted; and (4) that the public interest would not be disserved by a permanent injunction. *See, e.g., Weinberger v. Romero-Barcelo*, 456 U.S. 305, 311–313 (1982); *Amoco Production Co. v. Gambell*, 480 U.S. 531, 542 (1987). The decision to grant or deny permanent injunctive relief is an act of equitable discretion by the district

---

[a] Ebay and Half.com continue to challenge the validity of MercExchange's patent in proceedings pending before the United States Patent and Trademark Office.

court, reviewable on appeal for abuse of discretion. *See, e.g., Romero-Barcelo*, 456 U.S., at 320. These familiar principles apply with equal force to disputes arising under the Patent Act. As this Court has long recognized, "a major departure from the long tradition of equity practice should not be lightly implied." Ibid.; *see also Amoco*, supra, at 542. Nothing in the Patent Act indicates that Congress intended such a departure. To the contrary, the Patent Act expressly provides that injunctions "may" issue "in accordance with the principles of equity." 35 U.S.C. § 283.[b]

To be sure, the Patent Act also declares that "patents shall have the attributes of personal property," § 261, including "the right to exclude others from making, using, offering for sale, or selling the invention," §154(a)(1). According to the Court of Appeals, this statutory right to exclude alone justifies its general rule in favor of permanent injunctive relief. 401 F.3d, at 1338. But the creation of a right is distinct from the provision of remedies for violations of that right. Indeed, the Patent Act itself indicates that patents shall have the attributes of personal property "[s]ubject to the provisions of this title," 35 U.S.C. § 261, including, presumably, the provision that injunctive relief "may" issue only "in accordance with the principles of equity," § 283.

This approach is consistent with our treatment of injunctions under the Copyright Act. Like a patent owner, a copyright holder possesses "the right to exclude others from using his property." *Fox Film Corp. v. Doyal*, 286 U.S. 123, 127 (1932); *see also id.*, at 127–128 ("A copyright, like a patent, is at once the equivalent given by the public for benefits bestowed by the genius and meditations and skill of individuals, and the incentive to further efforts for the same important objects" (internal quotation marks omitted)). Like the Patent Act, the Copyright Act provides that courts "may" grant injunctive relief "on such terms as it may deem reasonable to prevent or restrain infringement of a copyright." 17 U.S.C. § 502(a). And as in our decision today, this Court has consistently rejected invitations to replace traditional equitable considerations with a rule that an injunction automatically follows a determination that a copyright has been infringed. *See, e.g., New York Times Co. v. Tasini*, 533 U.S. 483, 505 (2001) (citing

---

[b] Section 283 provides that "[t]he several courts having jurisdiction of cases under this title may grant injunctions in accordance with the principles of equity to prevent the violation of any right secured by patent, on such terms as the court deems reasonable."

Campbell v. Acuff-Rose Music, Inc., 510 U.S. 569, 578, n. 10 (1994)); *Dun v. Lumbermen's Credit Assn.*, 209 U.S. 20, 23–24 (1908).

Neither the District Court nor the Court of Appeals below fairly applied these traditional equitable principles in deciding respondent's motion for a permanent injunction. Although the District Court recited the traditional four-factor test, 275 F. Supp. 2d, at 711, it appeared to adopt certain expansive principles suggesting that injunctive relief could not issue in a broad swath of cases. Most notably, it concluded that a "plaintiff's willingness to license its patents" and "its lack of commercial activity in practicing the patents" would be sufficient to establish that the patent holder would not suffer irreparable harm if an injunction did not issue. *Id.*, at 712. But traditional equitable principles do not permit such broad classifications. For example, some patent holders, such as university researchers or self-made inventors, might reasonably prefer to license their patents, rather than undertake efforts to secure the financing necessary to bring their works to market themselves. Such patent holders may be able to satisfy the traditional four-factor test, and we see no basis for categorically denying them the opportunity to do so. To the extent that the District Court adopted such a categorical rule, then, its analysis cannot be squared with the principles of equity adopted by Congress. The court's categorical rule is also in tension with *Continental Paper Bag Co. v. Eastern Paper Bag Co.*, 210 U.S. 405, 422–430 (1908), which rejected the contention that a court of equity has no jurisdiction to grant injunctive relief to a patent holder who has unreasonably declined to use the patent.

In reversing the District Court, the Court of Appeals departed in the opposite direction from the four-factor test. The court articulated a "general rule," unique to patent disputes, "that a permanent injunction will issue once infringement and validity have been adjudged." 401 F.3d at 1338. The court further indicated that injunctions should be denied only in the "unusual" case, under "exceptional circumstances" and "'in rare instances . . . to protect the public interest.'" *Id.*, at 1338–1339. Just as the District Court erred in its categorical denial of injunctive relief, the Court of Appeals erred in its categorical grant of such relief. Cf. *Roche Products v. Bolar Pharmaceutical Co.*, 733 F.2d 858, 865 (CAFed 1984) (recognizing the "considerable discretion" district courts have "in determining whether the facts of a situation require it to issue an injunction").

* * *

263

Accordingly, we vacate the judgment of the Court of Appeals, and remand for further proceedings consistent with this opinion.

■ CHIEF JUSTICE ROBERTS, with whom JUSTICE SCALIA and JUSTICE GINSBURG join, concurring.

* * *

From at least the early 19th century, courts have granted injunctive relief upon a finding of infringement in the vast majority of patent cases. This "long tradition of equity practice" is not surprising, given the difficulty of protecting a right to exclude through monetary remedies that allow an infringer to use an invention against the patentee's wishes—a difficulty that often implicates the first two factors of the traditional four-factor test. This historical practice, as the Court holds, does not entitle a patentee to a permanent injunction or justify a general rule that such injunctions should issue. The Federal Circuit itself so recognized in *Roche Products, Inc. v. Bolar Pharmaceutical Co.*, 733 F.2d 858, 865–867 (1984). At the same time, there is a difference between exercising equitable discretion pursuant to the established four-factor test and writing on an entirely clean slate. "Discretion is not whim, and limiting discretion according to legal standards helps promote the basic principle of justice that like cases should be decided alike." *Martin v. Franklin Capital Corp.*, 546 U. S. 132, 139 (2005) (slip op., at 6). When it comes to discerning and applying those standards, in this area as others, "a page of history is worth a volume of logic." *New York Trust Co. v. Eisner*, 256 U.S. 345, 349 (1921) (opinion for the Court by HOLMES, J.)

■ JUSTICE KENNEDY, with whom JUSTICE STEVENS, JUSTICE SOUTER, and JUSTICE BREYER join, concurring.

* * *

To the extent earlier cases establish a pattern of granting an injunction against patent infringers almost as a matter of course, this pattern simply illustrates the result of the four-factor test in the contexts then prevalent. The lesson of the historical practice, therefore, is most helpful and instructive when the circumstances of a case bear substantial parallels to litigation the courts have confronted before.

In cases now arising trial courts should bear in mind that in many instances the nature of the patent being enforced and the economic function of the patent holder present considerations quite unlike earlier cases. An industry has developed in which firms use patents not as a basis for producing and selling goods but, instead, primarily for obtaining licensing fees. *See* FTC, TO PROMOTE INNOVATION: THE PROPER BALANCE OF COMPETITION AND PATENT LAW AND POLICY, ch. 3, pp. 38–39 (Oct. 2003), available at http://www.ftc.gov/os/2003/10/innovationrpt.pdf (as visited May 11, 2006, and available in Clerk of Court's case file). For these firms, an injunction, and the potentially serious sanctions arising from its violation, can be employed as a bargaining tool to charge exorbitant fees to companies that seek to buy licenses to practice the patent. *See ibid.* When the patented invention is but a small component of the product the companies seek to produce and the threat of an injunction is employed simply for undue leverage in negotiations, legal damages may well be sufficient to compensate for the infringement and an injunction may not serve the public interest. In addition injunctive relief may have different consequences for the burgeoning number of patents over business methods, which were not of much economic and legal significance in earlier times. The potential vagueness and suspect validity of some of these patents may affect the calculus under the four-factor test.

The equitable discretion over injunctions, granted by the Patent Act, is well suited to allow courts to adapt to the rapid technological and legal developments in the patent system. For these reasons it should be recognized that district courts must determine whether past practice fits the circumstances of the cases before them. With these observations, I join the opinion of the Court.

REPLACE NOTES 2 THROUGH 4 ON PAGES 878–880 WITH THE FOLLOWING:

2. *Willful infringement.* As *Seagate* and *RIM* explain, there are two provisions that permit district courts to enhance damage awards. 35 U.S.C. §§ 284-85. Section 284 has been interpreted by the courts to require a finding of "willful infringement" before damages can be enhanced. As discussed in *Seagate*, the Federal Circuit had held in *Underwater Devices* that infringers could avoid a finding of willful infringement only by meeting a "duty of care" not to infringe. *Seagate* revises that standard to require a showing of recklessness on the part of the infringer. What is the purpose of enhancing damages for willful infringement? What consequences would you expect from a duty of care standard for willfulness? The *Seagate* recklessness standard? Which

265

approach is preferable?

One reason for enhanced damages remedies was suggested in the Introduction: unless the infringer faces the possibility of being put into a worse position by reason of the infringement than it would have been with a license, it would have a strong incentive to infringe. In effect, the infringer would be enjoying a compulsory license. Is there nonetheless reason to be concerned about enhanced royalties in cases where the defendant is providing the market with a popular (and, in *RIM,* an award-winning) product, and the plaintiff holds patents that it has never exploited? As the relief associated with patent infringement increases, so-called "patent trolls" are lured into the game.[1] These are companies whose business is to look for patents that are arguably being infringed, and then to file suits, mainly with the idea of securing settlements. Companies like RIM have little choice but to play hardball and refuse such settlements, otherwise large portions of their resources go to paying royalties as opposed to paying for research, development, and distribution of new products. When a court considers whether to award punitive damages against a company like RIM, which guessed wrong about whether it was infringing, should the court take into account the dynamics of trolling and the effect of its decision on the cost of doing business?

Omitted portions of *Seagate* deal with questions of the waiver of attorney-client privilege in order to present evidence of non-willfulness. The duty of care standard spawned an industry of attorney opinion letters, intended to demonstrate compliance with the standard. Case law had evolved to suggest that failing to produce an attorney opinion justified an adverse inference of willful infringement. The en banc Federal Circuit held that no such inference was appropriate.[2] After *Knorr-Bremse* and *Seagate*, should attorneys still recommend that their clients obtain opinions of outside counsel when they are aware of potential infringement?

---

[1] See Brenda Sandburg, *Battling the Patent Trolls*, THE RECORDER, July 30, 2001, available at http://www.law.com/jsp/statearchive.jsp? type=Article & oldid=ZZZ4DX7MSPC (noting that in 1999, patent claims against Intel totaled over $15 billion); Michael J. Meurer, *Controlling Opportunistic and Anti–Competitive Intellectual Property Litigation*, 44 B.C. L. REV. 509 (2003).
[2] *Knorr-Bremse Systeme Fuer Nutzfahrzeuge GmbH v. Dana Corp.*, 383 F.3d 1337 (Fed. Cir. 2004).

2.a. *The NTP v. RIM saga.* The *NTP v. RIM* district court opinion excerpted above is a small portion of a complex saga. In an order issued August 5, 2003, the District Court awarded compensatory damages of $33,446,172.90; attorney's fees in the amount of $4,203,160.79; prejudgment interest of $2,022,838; and enhanced damages of $14,032,161. RIM was permanently enjoined from making, using, offering to sell, selling, or importing in or into the United States the Blackberry products found to infringe NTP's patents. That injunctive order was stayed pending appeal. On appeal, the Federal Circuit overturned some of the jury's findings of infringement, based on a legal analysis of § 271's applicability to divided infringement (see discussion of the case in the supplement to Assignment 21), but upheld substantial infringement liability. After remand, the case was settled in March 2006, with RIM agreeing to pay $612.5 million to NTP. The NTP patents-in-suit were simultaneously the subject of reexamination proceedings in the USPTO. Those proceedings resulted in the invalidation of the NTP patents in early 2006. The reexamination was appealed to the BPAI, which affirmed most of the rejections, but found several claims to be valid. NTP is appealing the rejections to the Federal Circuit. Meanwhile, NTP has recently brought suit against Apple, Google, HTC, LG Electronics, Microsoft, and Motorola, alleging that their cell phone technology infringes its patents.[3] To make matters in the RIM case even more complicated, NTP alleged that the PTO engaged in improper communications with RIM during the reexamination. Those allegations led to FOIA requests by NTP, which in turn led to litigation. The saga has been reported by many media outlets including, for example, BNA's Patent, Trademark & Copyright Law Daily.[4] For our purposes, however, the district court opinion provides a good example of the analysis courts engage in to determine whether to enhance damage awards. Should this analysis change as a result of

---

[3] See, e.g., Steve Lohr, *Smartphone Patent Suits Challenge Big Makers*, NY TIMES (July 9, 2010) at B1.

[4] See, e.g., for a sample, 4th Circuit Largely Affirms Decision on PTO, Commerce Replies to NTP FOIA Inquiries (Feb. 2, 2009); PTO Leaves Gaps in Responding to Panel's Probes on Blackberry Case, Productivity (Jun. 17, 2008); NTP Lawyer Files Action Seeking to Compel PTO to Respond to FOIA Disclosure Requests (Jun. 14, 2006); NTP Charges Misconduct in PTO's Review Of Patents in BlackBerry Dispute (May 17, 2006); Judge Weighs Final Order in Blackberry Case; NTP Urges Shutdown Threat; RIM Sees Chaos (Feb. 27, 2006); PTO Voids Patent in BlackBerry Case; Patentee Claims Illegality, Undue Influence (Feb. 24, 2006); Mixed Rulings Delivered in Rehearing Of BlackBerry Manufacturer Infringement Suit (August 3, 2005).

3. *Injunctive relief.* While the Supreme Court issued a unanimous opinion in the *eBay* case, the concurrences by Justices Roberts and Kennedy suggest important differences in perspective as to the frequency with which the traditional equitable test for injunctive relief should be used to deny a permanent injunction to a patentee after a finding of infringement. Which concurrence has the better argument? Have modern trends—most notably the increase in non-practicing patent owners and the increasing prevalence of products incorporating many separate patented inventions—changed the equities such that fewer injunctions should issue in patent cases? Since the *eBay* case was decided, district courts have applied the four-factor test to deny injunction after a finding of patent infringement in numerous cases. Most, like the first such case, *z4 Technologies, Inc. v. Microsoft Corp,*[5] involve non-practicing patentees. In *z4 Technologies* the patented invention was a "small component" of Microsoft's Windows XP and Office software.

4. *Declaratory relief.* One way for a party starting a new venture to avoid patent infringement is to bring a suit for a declaration of patent invalidity, unenforceability, or noninfringement. Under the terms of the Declaratory Judgment Act, there must be a genuine case or controversy,[6] language that the Federal Circuit interpreted as imposing a two-pronged requirement: "First, the defendant's conduct must have created on the part of the plaintiff a reasonable apprehension that the defendant will initiate suit if the plaintiff continues the allegedly infringing activity. Second, the plaintiff must actually have either produced the device [that is arguably infringing] or have prepared to produce that device."[7] The Supreme Court rejected the first prong of the test in *MedImmune, Inc. v. Genentech, Inc.*[8] *MedImmune* considered the ability of a licensee to challenge the validity of a patent under the *Declaratory Judgment Act.*[9] In that case, the Court ruled that a licensee need not "refuse to pay royalties and commit material breach of the license agreement before suing to declare the patent invalid, unenforceable or not infringed." Importantly, the Court also rejected the Federal Circuit's "reasonable apprehension of suit" test for declaratory

---

[5] 434 F. Supp. 2d 437 (E.D. Tex. 2006).
[6] 28 U.S.C. §§ 2201–02.
[7] *Goodyear Tire & Rubber Co. v. Releasomers, Inc.,* 824 F.2d 953 (Fed. Cir. 1987).
[8] 546 U.S. 1169 (2006).
[9] 28 U. S. C. § 2201(a).

judgment jurisdiction. The Federal Circuit responded to *MedImmune* by employing a much lower standard for declaratory judgment jurisdiction in *SanDisk Corp. v. STMicroelectronics, Inc.*,[10] where it opined that jurisdiction is available "where a patentee asserts rights under a patent based on certain identified ongoing or planned activity of another party."

The Federal Circuit continues to consider whether there has been "meaningful preparation" to infringe, however, as part of a totality of the circumstances approach to whether there is a sufficiently immediate controversy between the parties, *Cat Tech LLC v. TubeMaster, Inc.*, 528 F.3d 871 (Fed. Cir. 2008), and to require "a controversy of such 'immediacy and reality' as to require the district court to accept declaratory jurisdiction." *Innovative Therapies, Inc. v. Kinetic Concepts, Inc.*, 599 F.3d 1377, 1382 (Fed. Cir. 2010) (citing *Sandisk* at 1378).

---

[10] 480 F.3d 1372 (Fed. Cir. 2007).